A CRITICAL BIBLIOGRAPHY
OF THE
PUBLISHED WRITINGS
OF
ROMAIN ROLLAND

By

WILLIAM THOMAS STARR
NORTHWESTERN UNIVERSITY

NORTHWESTERN UNIVERSITY PRESS
EVANSTON, ILLINOIS
1950

NORTHWESTERN UNIVERSITY STUDIES

Virgil B. Heltzel, *editor*

Humanities Series Twenty-one

Open access edition funded by the National Endowment for the Humanities/Andrew W. Mellon Foundation Humanities Open Book Program.

William Thomas Starr. A Critical Bibliography of the Published Writings of Romain Rolland. Evanston, Ill.: Northwestern University Press, 1950.

ISBN 978-0-8101-3870-4 (paper)
ISBN 978-0-8101-3871-1 (ebook)

CONTENTS

INTRODUCTION

> Au seuil d'une nouvelle série de l'histoire de *Jean-Christophe,* dont le caractère de critique un peu vive risquera de blesser tour à tour les lecteurs de tous les partis, je prie mes amis et ceux de Jean-Christophe de ne jamais prendre nos jugements comme définitifs.
>
> Chacune de nos pensées n'est qu'un moment de notre vie. . . . Nous savons que nous nous trompons. Quand nous reconnaîtrons nos erreurs, nous les condamnerons plus durement que vous. Chaque jour nous nous efforçons d'atteindre un peu de vérité. Lorsque nous serons au terme, vous jugerez ce que valait notre effort.[1]

The time has come to assess this writer, whose whole life was so completely dominated by his unquenchable thirst for truth, and by an equally unquenchable need for liberty. Rolland himself suggests the need for a bibliography of his writings and of the writings about him. Continually seeking for truth, he was never immobilized by one idea or system. However, some of his critics have studied only part of his work, only the better-known writings, and have emphasized wrongly certain ideas at the expense of others. Other critics have stopped at a certain period of Rolland's life and refused to go further, while Rolland himself marched ahead. Because of the many, varied, and conflicting estimates of the man and his work, because of his undeniable importance, a real need exists for a critical bibliography of Romain Rolland's published writings and of works about him.

Some aspects of his activities and thinking have remained relatively little known and still await adequate studies. Others have been the object of repeated articles and monographs, some of which appear to have spoken the last word on their subjects. Other articles and books, because of the biased stands of the writers, or because of the lack of perspective, leave much to be desired. Emotions aroused by the two World Wars and the many conflicts of the intervening period, especially those aroused by communism, fascism, Russia, Germany, pacifism, violence and non-violence, colonialism, and the foreign policies of various European nations, too often obscured the view and warped the judgments of those who wrote about Romain Rolland.

A musician at heart, M. Rolland was trained for an academic career in history, and combined the two fields of interest in his lectures on the history of musical forms and of the arts, and in his critical articles on contemporary art and music. To the present little has been written concerning his not very numerous historical writings, except about those which deal with music. What was the part played in his development, in his later ideas, in his

[1] *Jean-Christophe. Sables mouvants. Cahiers de la Quinzaine,* 8e série, 4e cahier (4 novembre 1905), p. 15.

biographies, novels, and dramas, by his training as a professional historian? What was his attitude towards history and historians? We know in some degree what he thought of Renan, and even partially how he was influenced by Renan. As his correspondence and journals are published there will undoubtedly be available more material on these subjects. Rolland's conception of history is fairly well known in its broad outlines, especially as expressed in his opening lecture at the Ecole des Hautes Etudes; "La musique et l'histoire générale", but there are other, and numerous remarks and observations about history scattered throughout his writings, and noticeably in his correspondence with Malwida von Meysenbug. All of these references to history could certainly be studied profitably in relation to his creative writings. There are some references to Rolland's training in history, to his teachers, to his ideas about history in Wilson's work on the pre-war biographies, in Knorrenschild's work on the historical bases of the "Théâtre de la Révolution." Beckwith studies these problems to some extent in his dissertation on the formation of Rolland's aesthetics. However, as yet, no systematic investigation of Rolland the historian has been undertaken.

With reference to Rolland and music, there are two aspects which should be treated, and they cannot always be separated: Rolland the critic and musician, and Rolland the historian of music. Some of his writings on the history of music may be called, without undue exaggeration, epoch-making; others are, at least, enduring contributions in this field. Very few critical articles seem to have been written about his thesis on the history of the opera before Lully and Scarlatti, and there has been little more than enthusiastic recognition of his work in musicology. His influence in the development of this field yet remains to be studied. Who were the students who have studied under him and followed in this field? What was the impact of some of his writings, such as his thesis, in the fields of music and the history of music?

On the other hand, Rolland the musician, the critic of music, has been more frequently and more thoroughly studied. Several articles have appeared on the various volumes dealing with musicians, *Musiciens d'au-jourd' hui*, *Musiciens d'autrefois*, *Voyage musical aux pays du passé*, and the volumes on Beethoven. These works are criticized, favorably and otherwise, in more or less detail; some additions and corrections are suggested. Two or three articles study Rolland the musical critic, and attempt a general survey of his activities in this field. None of these articles covers the subject completely and adequately. One of the favorite subjects is the relation of music and his musical criticism to the novels, especially of course to *Jean-Christophe*. A study of his critical judgments on music expressed in his novels and other non-musical writings should be undertaken by one versed in music and musical criticism. One thesis has already been reported on this subject: "La musique dans le roman littéraire de *Jean-Christophe*" (see Lessinnes, no. 940). Similar investigations of his other works would add welcome information to any study of his musical criticism. Music has played such an important part in Rolland's life, development, and works that it surely deserves more study than has yet been accorded to it. No writer has given us a critical study of its importance and influence on Rolland; various writers have done little more than to mention its importance and to repeat the same statements about the effect of music on his childhood and youth, about its importance in his understanding of Germany. The subject has still not been adequately explored, mainly because of lack of material. Now that his correspondence is beginning to appear, more and more material is available. A simple perusal of the first of the "Cahiers Romain Rolland", his correspondence with Malwida von Meysenbug clearly indicates that some of these judgments about the influence of music will have to be modified.

Rolland did not limit his critical writings to musical criticism and the history of music. His articles about contemporary art ("Salons de 1901", "Salons de 1903," in the *Revue de Paris*), of contemporary art and literature ("Chronique parisienne," in the *Bibliothèque universelle et Revue suisse*, 1912, 1913) and his *Millet* contain some very interesting judgments about the art and literature of those years. Moreover, they are even more interesting for what they reveal about Rolland himself, and could profitably be studied in connection with his creative writings, to determine what ideas were uppermost in his mind at those times, and how they developed and evolved later. The whole germ of *L'Ame enchantée* can be found in the "Chronique parisienne" in the *Bibliothèque universelle et Revue suisse*, 1912, 1913.

In connection with his views on art and society, Tolstoy's influence, which has generally been either denied or affirmed, without perhaps an adequate investigation, would furnish a profitable field for study, and should be done in a thorough manner as a sound basis for more general works on Romain Rolland. The last volume of *Jean-Christophe*, for instance, is called Tolstoyan by one critic, Goethean by another. A better knowledge of Tolstoy's influence on Rolland could settle such questions. In his *Voyage intérieur*, Rolland says that Tolstoy's influence on him was aesthetic and moral, but not at all intellectual. Many of the existing studies now indulge in generalities that leave the core of the problems untouched. The influence of Renan, of Michelet, of Shakespeare has also been touched upon. Schickelé, for example, emphasizes the importance for Rolland of Rossi's troupe of Shakespeare players, in Rome. Beckwith and others suggest the probable influence of Renan's *Prêtre de Némi* and of his *Drames philosophiques*. Descotes in his biography also points out the importance of Michelet in

Rolland's "Théâtre de la Révolution," but does not study it further than to point out a parallelism between the essential idea of *Le Quatorze juillet* and Michelet's account of the capture of the Bastille. None of these influences appears to have been studied in detail.

None of his writings in history or music seems to have satisfied Rolland completely. As one of his critics has pointed out, Rolland's temperament and ideas led him, in his search for truth, for strength, for courageous examples, to write biographies of men of gigantic stature; but in these he found definite limitations. Consequently he turned to imaginative writing in an effort to create his own hero, a hero who would satisfy all Rolland's desires, a hero who would free himself from hampering bonds and who would thereby bring hope and courage to his readers, a hero who would portray the development of strength and joy in spite of obstacles and suffering. In imaginative writing, both his training as a historian and his interest in the arts could be employed in works destined to bring a more personal message than the other fields of expression.

The most important of these works are the novels *Jean-Christophe* and *L'Ame enchantée*, although *Colas Breugnon* and *Clerambault* cannot be disregarded, and the tender love idyl, *Pierre et Luce*, has much in common with the volume *Antoinette* of *Jean-Christophe*. In the realm of the "roman fleuve" or "roman cycle," his importance is uncontested. Albert Thibaudet in his history of French literature after 1870 assigns to Rolland an important place in the development of this form. However, the reception of *Jean-Christophe* by the critics and by the public has varied greatly at different times and in different places. Indeed, some of the most hotly debated questions are whether *Jean-Christophe* is a novel, whether it is a work of art, whether it is "French." Such a stylist as André Gide has accused Rolland of being so little French in style that the novel gains by translation,[2] and Rémy de Gourmont says that if Rolland wrote "plus proprement," he would put him among the passable writers.[3] Vogt (who is Swiss) considers some of Rolland's writing as being more Swiss than French, and compares him, without any detailed discussion, to Protestant and Swiss writers, to Jean-Jacques Rousseau. There have been several good studies on his style, one of *Colas Breugnon* (Schüler, no. 826), one of *Jean-Christophe* (Kraucher, no. 871), and one of *Pierre et Luce* (Fest, no. 889). Richter (no. 760) studies various points of style in *Colas Breugnon, Le Temps viendra, Le Théâtre du peuple*, and *Beethoven*. Fest studies *Pierre et Luce* from the point of view of its musical composition and attempts to explain its artistic effect on the basis of its musical form. There are also some good

[2] *Nouvelle Revue Française* (juin, juillet 1919), pp. 35–36; 278–286. *Oeuvres complètes*, VIII, 298; IX, 115.

[3] "Un de viris", *La France* (30 novembre 1914).

remarks on Rolland's style in *Jean-Christophe* by Seippel and Zweig in their biographies. The last two chapters in Beckwith's work on the development of Rolland's aesthetics are devoted to a study of his style. Those who propose to study the subject further, and there is still room for such studies, would do well to see what Rolland himself has to say about literary style. Such remarks as the following, written in 1903, merit reflection:

> La raison, représentée ici par le poète [Vincent d'Indy, who wrote both the music and the libretto], veut une action simple, réaliste, logique. . . .Le sentiment, repésenté par le musicien, est bien plus romantique. . . .Pour moi, je suis avec le sentiment et je trouve qu'il a raison contre la raison même.[4]

In a conversation with Lucien Price in 1935, Rolland, according to Mr. Price, said:

> In every artist there is a conflict between expressing exactly what he means in pure classic line and the desire to utter the vastness of subconscious thought. Artists of the second rank express only the second. . .yet, after all, art is a feeble instrument to express life and especially the subconscious.[5]

Rolland's style is undoubtedly quite unlike classic French style and differs markedly from that of most nineteenth century French writers. He endeavored to express the vastness of subconscious thought more frequently than he tried to express in classic lines exactly what he meant. However, his style, or lack of style, differs materially from the artistic style of symbolists, impressionists, or surrealists. In his article in the *Frankfurter Zeitung* Lerch finds Rolland a precursor of the expressionists. Rolland is not satisfied with the mere reproduction of outer impressions, but expresses, or tries to express, his inner experience of these outer impressions. Lerch's article is rather short, and although the material reappears more extensively in his volume *Romain Rolland und die Erneuerung der Gesinnung*, more could be written on this subject.

There are various characteristic devices in Rolland's style: inversions, interpolations, repetitions, contradictions within the sentence, that should be studied further in his works. There occur certain expressions and constructions that more than one French critic has labeled germanisms. Yet Rolland was not familiar enough with German to have received such an influence. Fite (no. 890) points out the symbolism of names; and various critics have pointed out the symbolism of certain characters, especially in *L'Ame enchantée*, in which Rolland seems to have yielded to this tendency more than elsewhere. Further investigations of these questions might lead to some interesting discoveries regarding Rolland's art. His style is strongly

---

[4] "Vincent d'Indy," *Revue de Paris*, I (1903), 401–420.

[5] Price, Lucien, "Romain Rolland Converses," *Atlantic*, CLVI (December, 1935), 718–726.

colored, or discolored, by his reaction to "artistic" writing, to the doctrine prevailing in his youth of art for art's sake; he tends to avoid such writing the greater part of the time. Not infrequently, however, the subject carries him away, and at such times the style becomes lyrical, metaphorical, highly colored. Such passages have to be counted in many cases among the very best pages that have come from his pen; in other cases, they are considerably less satisfying. French writers have criticized his style, generally adversely, but none has studied it in detail. Such studies as have been made are by Germans.

One study of Rolland's narrative technique in *Jean-Christophe* (Jäger, no. 879) has already appeared; it does not, however, exhaust the subject, and is only fair. Studies in his technique as illustrated in his other novels, which have frequently been criticized on rather general grounds, have not appeared.[6] Many of the French writers, especially those of an older generation, criticized the lack of unity, of harmony and proportions among the various parts of the novel, the inadequate action of some parts, the "chest of drawers" technique in *Dans la maison*, where, on one floor after another, we are introduced to various kinds of French people, the inhabitants of the apartment building in which Christophe lived. Rolland repeated this technique in *L'Ame enchantée* also. These and other criticisms are generally scattered and are more or less inconclusive. In general, younger critics, who have perhaps penetrated more deeply into the novel, find a different sort of unity than the older writers sought. The changing attitude of the critics towards Rolland's novels seems especially interesting in the history of his influence in a world of changing ideas and ideals.

The one aspect of Rolland the novelist which, with very few exceptions, the critics praise, is his creation of living, vivid characters in his novels. (This is much less true in his dramas.) The characters in *Jean-Christophe* are particularly vivid. Who can forget Christophe himself, whose development from childhood through adolescence to young manhood and maturity is presented in unforgettable pages of analysis, portrayal in action, and description? The volumes of Christophe's childhood and adolescence are scarcely to be equalled in French literature for their intuitive grasp and delicate portrayal of those important formative years. It is perhaps interesting to note in this connection that Rolland, strongly influenced by the idea of becoming (*devenir, das Werden*), has portrayed these formative, changing years better than the mature years of Christophe. In the later volumes, Olivier, Grazia, Antoinette, all are vividly drawn and portrayed in action in the various circumstances of their lives. The secondary characters, especially the feminine ones, are equally well, if more briefly drawn. In much the same way that Christophe is brought before our eyes, such

[6] Except that on *Pierre et Luce*, by Otto Fest.

characters as Rosa, Sabine, Ada, Minna, Otto, Uncle Gottfried live vigorous lives of their own. Even *La Foire sur la place*, which has so often been denounced as merely a series of bitter criticisms of certain aspects of "art" in the French capital, contains some well drawn characters: Sylvian Kohn, Ben Hecht, and Moche among others. At least one critic, Albert Guérard, finds the secondary characters to be so living and vivid that they will probably live on in world literature. Christophe himself, this critic finds, is occasionally a symbol rather than a flesh and blood character. (I have suggested the probable reason for this above.) Another critic studies briefly the secondary characters as functions of Christophe. They are part of his destiny, but are not on the same plane as the central character, as were the characters in the novels of Balzac, Stendhal, Flaubert, and even Proust, whose works, he seems to feel, are closer to Rolland's than to those of any other novelist.[7]

If the critics generally acclaim the portrayal of character in Rolland's novels, they are far from unanimity in their judgments about the moral worth, the esthetic and ethical value of the novels and of the characters. To some, Christophe is completely amoral; to others he is the glorification of a complete break with the past. Studies have appeared on Rolland's portrayal of Jews (Ziegler, no. 728), of Jews and Germans (Krakowski, no. 860), on his ability to portray German character. One completely inadequate thesis has appeared on his feminine characters (Kämpffer, no. 859), and at least one on this subject is now in preparation. The characters in *L'Ame enchantée* seem occasionally to be less vividly and powerfully drawn than those of *Jean-Christophe*. Annette herself and Sylvie are well done, especially in the first volumes. In the later ones there is a distinct tendency for them to become the oracles of their creator, symbols of his ideals. There have appeared various articles treating, among other subjects, the character construction in this novel. None has treated the subject fully and satisfactorily. Further investigations concerning the judgments made about the characters by critics and writers of various nations might go far towards answering the question of why the novels have so frequently been judged to be neither works of art nor French.

The delineation of character in *Clerambault* is much less effective than in the two longer novels. Altamira (no. 772) has perhaps pointed out the basic flaw in the novel: the artistic incompatibility of a novel depicting the atmosphere in Paris during the first World War and of a treatise discussing war, pacifism, and militarism. The presentation of character, he feels, suffers greatly in the novel as the result of this duality. Colas Breugnon, on the other hand, is another of Rolland's well presented characters; there

[7] Buraud, G., "Romain Rolland créateur de valeurs", in *Hommages à Romain Rolland*. Editions du Mont-Blanc, pp. 36–48.

is little description as such; we see Colas rather through his diary, in his actions and reflections. French critics have rather uniformly criticized the style of this short novel; the numerous alexandrines, the repetitions, the frequent alliterations, and the rabelaisian style are generally offensive to the French ear. German critics, however, are much more favorably impressed. One very thorough stylistic study of the novel (Schüler, no. 826) makes clear the reasons for its popularity in Germany. It is noteworthy that it was early translated into Russian, where it seems to have remained a favorite, and has inspired one opera, *The Master of Clamecy* by Dmitri Kabalevski. It is probable that there have appeared studies on Colas in Russian. In any event a study of the reception of this and other of Rolland's works in Russia would be a fertile field for one who is properly equipped with a knowledge of Russian. Rolland had much correspondence with Lunacharskii, Gorky, and other Russians, who admired greatly some or all of his works, especially *Beethoven, Colas Breugnon,* and *Jean-Christophe.* One book has appeared on Rolland and Russia (Relgis, no. 958). Since I have not had access to this work, I cannot say whether it is about Rolland's ideas concerning Russia, his relationship with the Communist party, or his reception there.

Most of the writing about *Jean-Christophe* and *L'Ame enchantée* has been concerned with the intentions and philosophy of the author, the purpose of the novels, and judgments concerning the validity of the ideas expressed in them, or embodied in the characters and events. Beaunier, for example, in a very good article, analyzes Christophe in relation to Rolland's ideas of art and the people. Van Tricht, Lerch, Götzfried, and Dvořak (the latter three in more general works on Rolland) have well discussed the philosophy of *Jean-Christophe* and *L'Ame enchantée.* Ostermann compares the portrayal of persons and society in Goethe's *Wilhelm Meister,* Keller's *Grüne Heinrich,* and Rolland's *Jean-Christophe.* Such studies shed further light on the questions of why this novel has been received in some countries more favorably than in others, why one part is so much more popular in one country than in another. Other studies of the essential ideas in the novels and in other works might be very fruitful in clarifying this aspect of Rolland's work and influence.

One of Rolland's great desires was to write for the theater, a vehicle of expression which can, and should be, one of the most vivid means readily accessible to the greatest number of people. Rolland's earliest imaginative writings were plays, some of which were published, while others remained as sketches or in manuscript form. One of his last works, along with *Beethoven, Les Grandes époques créatrices* and *Péguy,* was the play *Robespierre.* How is Rolland to be judged as a dramatist? Much has been written about his plays. Some of the articles are little more than brief notices. Many of the more penetrating and thorough articles are not so much analyses of the plays themselves as discussions of, and praise or blame for, the social and political ideas which the writers find expressed in the plays. Such articles are frequently so clearly biased that they are of little value save perhaps to study Rolland's influence, its nature, and where it was felt. Faguet pointed out various faults in the dramatic construction of *Aërt*, *Danton*, and *Les Loups*; Hutchens makes similar criticisms of *Le Jeu de l'amour et de la mort*, whereas Marti, in the *Bund* of Bern, calls Rolland's plays the "Iliad of the French revolution." Lehner points out the dramatic flaws in *Les Léonides*; Gsell studies briefly the relationship between Rolland's *Quatorze juillet* and his *Théâtre du peuple*. Régnier studies the cycle of the French revolution in this respect. Descotes in his biography of Rolland studies the plays especially in relation to the *Théâtre du peuple*, after a rather good discussion of the latter. He situates the plays in Rolland's works and ideas in a very illuminating way, and his criticisms of the whole cycle of the Revolution are sound and show a real insight into their dramatic qualities and defects. Detailed studies of Rolland's style in the dramas, of his portrayal of character, of their action and construction are rather few. Gerber (no. 878) studies Rolland the dramatist, but his study is more concerned with the historical sources than with a detailed analysis of each play. Knorrenschild, in his very fine work (no. 888A) on the historical sources, investigates the background thoroughly and studies the way in which it is incorporated by Rolland. A "mise au point" of the construction, character portrayal, style, artistic and dramatic worth of all Rolland's plays would be a welcome addition to the literature about Rolland.

A study of which of the plays have been given in various countries at various times would make an interesting chapter in the history of the fate of Rolland's ideas and influence. There has been a definite tendency, for example, for left wing groups and for workers' organizations to present certain of his plays (*Le Quatorze juillet* especially), and there are one or two very interesting accounts now of the timeliness of some of his plays, of *Danton* in Berlin during the revolution and in Bielorussia in 1918.

The question of the historical accuracy of his plays is frequently discussed. Knorrenschild and Gerber attempt to answer the question. The insistence on the question of historical accuracy, however, reveals a certain lack of comprehension of Rolland's purposes and ideas. As both the above writers remark, it is necessary first to read what Rolland himself said in his prefaces to *Le Jeu de l'amour et de la mort* and *Pâques fleuries*. It would be even more necessary to read his preface to *La Montespan* where he very clearly states his ideas concerning historical accuracy in the theater. As more material is published further information comes to light. In an undated letter to Louis Gillet, written around or shortly before the turn of the century, recently published in *Le Littéraire*, Rolland wrote:

> Dans le poème de dix ou douze drames sur la Révolution, croyez-vous que ce soit la Liberté ou la révolution que je chante? — Non, mais une tempête de l'humanité; je ne sers pas un parti; je vis, et je vois et je chante la Vie. La Vie et la Mort. La Force éternelle. . . .Mon héros n'est pas Danton, ni Robespierre, ni le peuple, ni l'Elite; il est la Vie.[8]

The question therefore of historical accuracy in his plays is slightly beside the point. The real question is: What was his purpose in making the particular event the subject or the background of the play, and does he attain his goal? How has his conception of history, of the treatment of history in plays, helped him to reach that goal?

Occupying a place in his work between the novels and the dramas on the one hand and his work as a historian and musicologist on the other, are Rolland's biographies, the lives of Tolstoy, Michael-Angelo, Beethoven, and Millet. The first three were originally written with the idea of bringing fresh air (as Rolland himself said in the preface to his *Vie de Beethoven*) into a Europe stifling in an atmosphere of materialism, naturalism, and cynicism. His purpose was to bring to his readers the heroic examples of great men, men to whom he himself owed much, men who faced and conquered suffering. He hoped to bring examples which would be inspiring to those who were disheartened and without moral or spiritual leadership or ideals in an epoch almost devoid of ideals. In his work, *Romain Rolland und die Erneuerung der Gesinnung*, Lerch accords an important place to the biographies in the spiritual awakening and renewal that became so important in France in the years before the first World War. One long study has appeared on his pre-war biographies and on their place in his work and in the period (Wilson, no. 922). Wilson discusses the principal purposes of these biographies, their development, and the main characteristics of Rolland's heroes. His study is good, but it should take more into account Rolland's lesser known articles of the period. Wilson's lack of insight into the relationship between the biographies and the dramas, and between the biographies and *Jean-Christophe*, is somewhat disappointing. He does some valuable spade work in rectifying certain rather frequent errors about Rolland, but there still seems to be room for a more complete work on the biographies. Now that the correspondence is being published, all that Rolland revealed in his letters must be studied in this connection.

The general ideas of Rolland, his philosophy and ideals, have been rather well discussed: Lerch in his *Die Erneuerung der Gesinnung*, Götzfried in *Das*

[8] *Le Littéraire* (8 juin 1946).

Weltbild im Spiegel seiner Werke, Torrens, and Mühlestein in their works on his social and political ideas, Starr in *Romain Rolland's Internationalism*, Levy in *L'Idéalisme de Romain Rolland*, Colin in his work on Romain Rolland and the cult of the hero, articles and monographs by various writers on Rolland the European, Beckwith and Dvořak in their works on the aesthetics and ethics of Rolland, Luisi in her study of the sense of the mystic in Rolland's life and works. There is still some need for more work on certain of these questions. For instance, some further ideas about Rolland's aesthetics might be added to Beckwith's thesis, which was completed in February 1936. A few months later, *Commune* published some very interesting pages from Rolland's diary, entitled "Du rôle de l'écrivain dans la société." These pages contain some very important ideas for the study of Rolland's aesthetics and ethics. Rolland's ideas of art in society and the rôle of the artist in society as revealed in published pages of his diaries, in his correspondence, in the various prefaces, in *Le Théâtre du peuple*, and in some of the pages of *Jean-Christophe* that appeared only in the *Cahiers de la Quinzaine* edition still furnish an important field for investigation. For instance, one whole chapter in *La Révolte*, which appeared only in the *Cahiers de la Quinzaine* is devoted to criticisms of German literature, much as similar pages in *La Foire sur la place* are devoted to criticisms of French literature; and it reveals as much about Romain Rolland as about German literature. Further study of his dramas and novels in relation to these ideas would undoubtedly increase our insight into his creative activity and the measure of success or failure of various parts of his works. Any further study of the biographies should also take these ideas into account. How far were such theories formed when he wrote *Beethoven*, *Michel-ange*, and *Tolstoï*? How far did these biographies serve and fulfill these ideals? Perhaps the answer to these questions would throw further light on why Rolland abandoned the other biographies projected (and even announced) earlier.

Another side of Rolland that has not yet received its adequate and final study is his attitude towards religion and the church—his own religion. Levy and the others mentioned above have discussed the religious nature of Rolland's thought. They have not, however, studied specifically his attitude toward organized religion, toward the Catholic church, toward Christianity. After his death there appeared two articles on this subject (Beirnaert and Paul Claudel). Neither of the articles does justice to the subject. Rolland discussed religion, the church, his own faith, in his correspondence with Malwida von Meysenbug, of which only Claudel makes use. Furthermore, Rolland's remarks about religion, the Catholic church, his own faith, are scattered throughout all his works, and would entail much more diligent study than has yet been accorded to this question. The two writers mentioned above neglect completely the "anti-clerical" side of

Rolland, who condemned the Catholic church as a political, lay organization. In 1917, for example, he wrote:

> Pour le christianisme, son abdication ne date pas d'hier. Depuis la grande compromission des temps de Constantin, au quatrième siècle, qui fit de l'Eglise du Christ une Eglise d'Etat, la pensée essentielle du Christ a été trahie par ses représentants officiels et livrée à César. Ce n'est que chez les libres personnalités religieuses, dont la plupart furent taxées d'hérésie, qu'elle se conserva (relativement) jusqu à nous.[9]

Descotes in his *Romain Rolland* presents a much better discussion of these questions, and insists somewhat on Rolland's anti-clericalism.

Rolland's writings reflect many of the ideas and currents, political, literary, social, and philosophic, of the past seventy-five years. They are directly expressed in his polemical works, articles and pamphlets, and even in his novels and plays. Indirectly they are expressed by his revolt against many of the ideals and attitudes of his time. Throughout his writings there runs on the one hand a deep current of fatalism and materialism, especially in some of his early letters to Malwida von Meysenbug. On the other hand, his idealism became more and more important, without ever dominating completely his fatalism and materialism. He eventually arrived at a sort of a synthesis of the conflict, especially when, under the impact of communism he worked out a new conception of the individual and society. Many of his pre-war (1914–1918) plays and certain critical articles on music and art of that time give expression to a deep revolt against the pessimism of the last half of the nineteenth century, against naturalism in art, and against materialistic determinism. There are echoes of other philosophies in his works: those of Hegel, Marx, Bergson are especially noticeable among later philosophers. Spinoza was his "livre de chevet," and the pre-Socratic philosophers were very important in his earlier years. Many and sometimes conflicting philosophers have left their traces in the works of this man for whom only the static was dead. The importance of the pre-Socratic philosophers has been studied by various writers. Rolland's early works appeared before the *Evolution créatrice*, 1907, and about the same time as the *Essai sur les données immédiates de la conscience*, 1889. Further investigation into his reading, into the influences of these various philosophies on his thinking and in his works, would be a welcome contribution to Rolland research.

For Rolland the static was dead, the living was that which was in continual motion and evolution. He strove always, for example, to find a comprehensive synthesis for conflicting forces: the individual and the state, national history and the development of civilization, the forces of the past and the necessity of social changes, revolution and peace, non-violence and

[9] "La Biologie de la Guerre par G.-F. Nicolai," *Les Précurseurs*, p. 167.

change. But when he found the synthesis, it was generally only to go on from that point to attack the new conflicts that inevitably arise. Rolland's thinking on these problems is essentially that of a moralist. Starting from firm convictions and philosophic bases, he vigorously attacked the problems facing him, facing Europe and the world.

Because of his deeply serious character and possibly because of Tolstoy's influence,[10] and partly no doubt because of his reaction to the currents of thought, of emotions of the time, Rolland had long desired ardently to serve society, to serve through creative writing. His struggle with his family and friends, with an indifferent social order, to break away from the academic career to devote himself solely to writing that would serve others, that would serve mankind at large, is strikingly revealed in his correspondence with Malwida von Meysenbug. The desire to help, to serve, the desire to teach, his judgments of men and society, all these are of the moralist and reformer. He always felt the need to see lucidly, to miss nothing of the society and the world around him, to judge them, to continue to love them, but to criticize when necessary, to seek to teach, to reform, to lead men towards a better life and a better social order. Investigations of the influence of Tolstoy, of Shakespeare, of his early education, of the various influences which affected him, should be undertaken in more detail, systematically, in order to write adequately of Rolland the moralist, the idealist, and the reformer. Much has been written on these subjects, but a large part is inadequate, the writers either having started with pre-conceived ideas, or, under the emotions of the time, having seen only partially the whole figure of Rolland. Even such a very good work as A. R. Levy, *L'Idéalisme de Romain Rolland*, sins somewhat in this respect, the writer starting from a postulate that absolute adherence to non-violence is the only true path to salvation. Götzfried and Lerch both treat these questions as part of larger topics.

Since Rolland was deeply emotional, extremely sensitive, and completely sincere, he soon became aware of the injustice, selfishness, and cruelty of contemporary society. The historian, musician, critic, and creator, who early had manifested a desire to act, to translate his thoughts into action, became a crusader in the struggle for justice, for a new and better society. In its manifold aspects this struggle has dominated all his work since before the first World War and became the very axis about which his life and his works revolved after the war of 1914–1918.

It is against this background that Rolland the crusader against war must be considered. Much has been written about this subject, both because of his stand during the first World War, and, afterwards, because of his attitude towards Russia and the many problems that this new phenomenon, rightly or wrongly, aroused in the rest of the world. Much that was written

[10] As we have already said, this point needs to be clarified. *Supra*, p. vii.

during those years about his stand during the war was too much colored by the passions of the moment to be of any lasting value. Many of Rolland's utterances, which seemed so radical (so traitorous to some of his contemporaries), now seem like comparatively mild, almost commonplace ideas. His stand as a crusader against war has been more or less thoroughly explored in several studies of his social and political ideals, his idealism, his internationalism.

His attitude towards the first war, towards the questions of the national state's rights, towards the question of militarism and pacifism and of the guilt of the various nations, an attitude that seemed so controversial at that time, although now generally regarded as a relatively sane and moderate position, nevertheless represented almost a complete break with the past and with the social order of the day. Most of his critics of that day have arrived now at the same position he held then. But Rolland is no longer at that point; he has gone ahead, again leaving many of his contemporaries far behind.

His break with society at that time eventually led him to extend an enthusiastic greeting to the Russian revolution. He later became an ardent defender of the U.S.S.R., in whose efforts towards a new society he saw the sole hope for the future—given the conditions prevalent at the time he was writing. However, it is important to note that he continued throughout his career to criticize adversely whatever he thought merited correction in Soviet Russia. Just as his articles during the first World War aroused bitter criticism from both sides of the battlefield, from militarists and pacifists, neutrals and belligerents, so too his writings about Russia have aroused criticism from both the opponents and the adherents of Soviet Russia. It is perhaps one of the most debated and least understood of Rolland's positions. To many non-communist critics, Rolland became a "fellow traveler" between 1927 and 1931, and remained an unqualified follower and supporter of the U.S.S.R. But Rolland, as he wrote to Gillet (that Liberty was more important to him than family, friends, or position), refused to entangle himself with any party, coterie, or group. He has rigidly maintained as complete an independence of mind and judgment as a man can keep. He never ceased criticizing the Soviet Union, not in a carping way, but for her own good, for the good of an experiment which he felt was of vital importance to the world. When he called for an alliance between Great Britain, France, and Russia in 1935 and 1936, it was for the purpose of fighting a common enemy, an enemy of the Democracies and of Soviet Russia—Fascism and Hitlerism. His visit to Russia in the early part of the summer of 1935 renewed his faith in Russia, but, as he repeatedly stated, he was not, nor did he ever become, a member of the Communist party.

Communist writers frequently criticized his stand "au-dessus de la mêlée." Several of them call him a "bourgeois," who obviously cannot overcome his "point de vue de Sirius" sufficiently to understand the necessity for action. However, it is well to note that despite these criticisms Rolland's works enjoy considerable popularity in Russia, where they have all been translated, and where Rolland himself was highly esteemed.

The question of his attitude towards Russia has been treated in relation to other topics: his internationalism (Starr, no. 923), his political and social ideas (Torrens, no. 931), his idealism and belief in non-violence (Levy, no. 934), and his heroic conception of the world (Götzfried, no. 846), among others. However, most of these studies were made in the thirties and do not make use of some of the later writings. Levy is the best in this respect. More documents, letters, and journals will shed additional light on this question. His dispute with Barbusse on the question of violence and the revolution is well known; less well known is an exchange of letters with Albert Mathiez concerning the Terror of the French Revolution, published in *L'Art dramatique*, which may add some details and information. Rolland's correspondance with Henri Guilbeaux, unpublished as yet, should be especially fertile in material for a study of this question. Such articles as that by Mr. W. H. McLain on Romain Rolland and Russia are typical of the errors and faulty judgments that are so easily committed in the absence of last-minute information.[11]

Another of the controversial questions has been his knowledge of Germany and his portrayals of that nation in his biographies and novels. Almost all the German critics who have written about Rolland and music agree that he has an exceptionally deep and sympathetic understanding of German music and German musicians. But disagreement has been complete about his knowledge and portrayal of other aspects of Germany. Indeed one critic accuses him of making grave or ridiculous errors in his portrayal of Vienna in his work on Beethoven. The same writer speculates that this may possibly be because of Rolland's intense admiration for Wagner, who so disliked Vienna. Such a speculation would need to be rather carefully verified by a close scrutiny of Rolland's attitude towards Wagner. It is true that he was one of the early enthusiasts of Wagner, but his attitude changed later. The arguments have raged most hotly in regard to his portrayal of Germany and German character in *Jean-Christophe*. Lately there have appeared at least two rather good studies, one concerning Goethe and Rolland, and the other about his knowledge of Germany through different media (visits, the influence of Malwida von Meysenbug, music) as gleaned from his correspondence and journals.

Rolland also admired Nietzsche's writings and ideas (in some of his

[11] *Romanic Review*, XXXIX (April, 1948), 126–133. For a reply, see Starr, *ibid.*, XL (April, 1949), 106–113.

letters to Malwida his remarks about Nietzsche are extremely interesting). Lerch has discussed the probable influence of the German philosopher on Rolland, and has insisted on the importance of this influence. As more of Rolland's writings are published, more information concerning this influence will undoubtedly come to light. Since Lerch and others touch upon it only as part of larger works on Rolland, it seems likely that further research into the question of Nietzsche and Rolland, in connection with the latter's knowledge of Germany, would be desirable. Such delicate factors as similarities in temperament play an undoubtedly important part, and any future investigator will have to proceed with a goodly supply of intuition as well as documentation.

A study of Rolland's knowledge of German literature has not yet been attempted. A start can be made in his *Théâtre du peuple*, where there are some interesting judgments about the Classic German theater and some of the nineteenth century German plays. This can be supplemented with his judgments in *Jean-Christophe*, and especially some pages of the novel that appeared only in the edition published in the *Cahiers de la Quinzaine*.

Rolland's interests were not limited to Europe, to Germany, Italy, and France; early in his career the voice of Asia, especially of India, had attracted him. He wrote in his "Paroles de Renan à un adolescent:" "J'ai, depuis, regretté de n'avoir pas suivi cet appel vers l'Asie, mère des arts et des religions; j'en ai été détourné par les voix de deux sirènes: Musique et Italie."[12] There are references to Hindu literature in *Jean-Christophe*.[13] In 1919 Rolland wrote in a letter to Vaillant-Couturier: ". . .nous ne pouvons plus oublier l'Asie dans nos rêves futurs. Elle ne se laissera pas oublier. Et l'intelligence ne peut se passer de ces deux forces complémentaires (i.e., Europe and Asia)."[14] His interest and contacts led him to write in 1923–1924 his *Mahatma Gandhi*, and some five years later the *Vie de Ramakrishna*, and the *Vie de Vivekananda et l'Evangile universel*. Further study of these biographies and of their reflection in Rolland's novel of that period, *L'Ame enchantée*, would further clarify his technique as a novelist, as well as his ideas about such questions as non-violence, the unity of mankind, the nature of faith and religion. Much of this has already been done, notably by Götzfried, Lerch, Levy, and Starr, as part of larger questions.

Rolland's influence, through his correspondence as well as through his novels, plays, and pamphleteering, was world wide. As a start for what is likely to be a very interesting and fruitful study—Rolland and the Orient—

[12] *Europe*, IV (janvier–avril 1924), 257-266.

[13] *Dans la maison*, pp. 127, 299.

[14] *Le Populaire*, 21 avril 1919.

the article by Kin-Yn-Yu[15] reveals the extent and importance of Rolland in China. One or two European writers refer to the frequence of the phrase, in the Orient, "L'Europe de Romain Rolland," to distinguish the good from the bad (much as Rolland himself referred to the Germany of Goethe, Schiller, and Beethoven to distinguish the best in Germany, the Germany of Weimar as opposed to the Germany of Potsdam). Rolland's contacts in various oriental countries were wide, his interest always keen and broad; many of his works have been translated into various oriental languages, and have always aroused great interest. A study of the dissemination of his works in the Orient and their reception there, would, I am sure, be richly rewarding.

In a study of Rolland's ideal of pan-humanism, of universal human unity, his ideas on history will be found quite important. As suggested above,[16] his ideas of the place of music and the arts in history reveal a broad and fertile conception of history and its place in education. Rolland the moralist, the man of action (in spite of some attempts to picture him as a dreamer and to shut him up in an ivory tower),[17] early began to proclaim the necessity for a change in the teaching of history. In 1922, not content with changes in that subject alone, Rolland wrote a letter to teachers,[18] in which he outlined in a broad and general fashion his concepts of the new education necessary in the new world that he saw being created, willy nilly, by modern man and modern technology. Two articles in *La Vie ouvrière*[19] can add much to an understanding of his ideas on education. The volumes of *L'Ame enchantée* are studded with ideas about the education of the past and the needs of education for the future. One rather brief study on Rolland and the education of children has been written,[20] but the whole subject of his ideas in this field is much broader than the few pages of this article indicate.

In the first publications of *Jean-Christophe*, in the *Cahiers de la Quinzaine*, there are numerous pages and paragraphs that were omitted in later editions. It seems desirable to bring some of these pages, and summaries of the others, within easy reach of those interested in Rolland. The pages that are reproduced have been placed in the Appendix.

---

[15] "La Renaissance chinoise et l'influence de Romain Rolland," *Europe*, XV (septembre–décembre 1927), 101–108.

[16] *Supra*, p. vi.

[17] Erskine, John, "Romain Rolland, Scholar and Dreamer," *New York Herald Tribune* (January 21, 1945).

[18] "Lettre au Congrès des instituteurs, à Bordeaux," *La Vie ouvrière* (20 août 1920).

[19] *La Vie ouvrière* (23 avril, 7 mai 1920).

[20] Wilker, K., in *Das werdende Zeitalter*, V (1926), 49–52.

I have made no attempt to include unpublished letters. The *Association des amis de Romain Rolland* is now actively engaged in the collection of his correspondence, and hopes to edit and publish it at opportune moments, the first two volumes having already appeared. Letters that Rolland published in such collections as *Quinze ans de combat* and *Par la révolution, la paix*, or in periodicals and newspapers, have been included in the bibliography under the date of writing.

Not all of the articles written about Rolland have been included. Many are of ephemeral interest or are merely summary notices of his works. Many others are written from such an obviously biased point of view that they add little or nothing to our knowledge or understanding of Rolland. In the case of the period of the first World War, however, I have included many of the articles of lesser importance. Rolland received praise and blame—principally blame—and not a few false accusations, from all the belligerents and many of the neutrals. It seemed desirable to include many of these articles in order to show the place Rolland held during this period, and to show the effects of war hysteria on otherwise intelligent people. Likewise, many articles from the period 1920–1930—a period during which Rolland's attitude towards Russia and communism, capitalism and modern society was becoming clarified—have been included; some of them are of scant value, but may provide details useful in the study of the attitudes of various prominent men and writers towards a very sharp and widespread conflict, as well as in an evaluation of Rolland's position and influence.

Both Rolland's writings and the works about him have been arranged chronologically, in two separate divisions. An index will enable the reader to find all the articles that deal with one particular work by Rolland, or all the articles by one writer.

If no place of publication is mentioned, Paris is to be understood. The abbreviation *S.I.M.* stands for the *Bulletin de la Société Internationale de Musique*.

I must express my deep gratitude to Mrs. Stewart Lester, by whose kindness I was given access to the rich collection of titles in the bibliography of her first husband, the late Professor Dwight M. Chapman. Professor Chapman had been greatly interested in Rolland for a number of years and knew him personally. He had subscribed to the Argus clipping agency of Paris, during the years 1930–1932, and had an extensive collection of items by and about Rolland for those years. The critical articles mentioned in Professor Chapman's bibliography have not, however, been included unless the reference was verified. His indications are generally exact, but some errors made it undesirable to include all of them without verification, and in some cases I have been unable to produce the article.

Finally, for the help I have received in the compilation of the bibliography I should like to express my gratitude to Northwestern University Library, to Professor Joseph G. Fucilla for his invaluable help and suggestions, to Northwestern University for financial aid that greatly expedited its completion, to Mme Marie Romain Rolland, and to the Association des Amis de Romain Rolland.

William T. Starr

April 20, 1949

I

ROLLAND'S WORKS

1886–1900

1. «Carnets de jeunesse de Rolland,» *La Nef*, III, 14, 15 (janvier, février 1946).

2. «Souveniers de l'Ecole Normale,» *Revue de Paris*, LIII (mars 1946), 47–55. Extracts from his "Carnets de jeunesse."

3. «Extraits inédits du Journal de Romain Rolland. André Suarès vu à l'Ecole Normale Supérieure,» *Le Figaro littéraire*, (11 septembre 1946), p. 3.

4. *Souvenirs de jeunesse* (1866–1900), pages choisies. Lausanne: La Guilde du Livre, 261 pp., 1947.

5. Letter to Renan, no date, published by Henriette Psichari in *Renan d'après lui-même*, Plon, 1937, pp. 147–149.

1887

6. Letter to Tolstoy, published by Dufrenne, G., «Une lettre inédite et sa réponse. Lettre de Romain Rolland à Tolstoï, copiée au Musée de Tolstoï, le 26 novembre 1935,» *Commune*, III (janvier 1936), 521–523. In a note concerning this letter, written in 1935 (see no. 548), Rolland says: «. . . comme mes jeunes correspondants d'aujourd'hui, je m'ingéniais à trouver son point faible, afin de l'obliger à parler. C'est ainsi que j'envisage aujourd'hui . . . la dépréciation de l'art . . . et la prétendue recherche du travail à vide. Ni l'une ni l'autre ne correspondait sincèrement à mon état d'esprit. . . . Qu'on n'attache donc point à cet insignifiant appel un sens de pensée qu'elle n'a point.» This is Rolland's second letter to Tolstoy. See Wilson, *The Pre-War Biographies of Romain Rolland*, p. 16 (no. 922). In all, there were seven letters to Tolstoy, from 1887 to 1906.

1887

7. «Tolstoï et George Eliot,» *Les Nouvelles littéraires* (7 février 1946). Rolland discusses *Crime and Punishment* and *War and Peace* particularly, and compares and contrasts Tolstoy to Eliot. This extract from his diary is dated mid-September.

1888

8. *Credo quia verum*. This hitherto unpublished text is now being edited by Professor Raouf Kamil, as a "thèse complémentaire" at the University of Paris (April 19, 1948). Previously it was available apparently only in a Bengali translation [see Hans Leo Götzfried, *Romain Rolland, Das Weltbild im Spiegel seiner Werke*, p. 165 (*infra*, no. 846)].

1890

9. *Orsino*. Drame inédit. Malwida von Meysenbug translated this play. Dr. Hans Leo Götzfried, Erlangen, plans to publish Malwida's German translation.

10. Letters to Malwida von Meysenbug. Schleicher, *Ein Briefwechsel. 1890–1891. Romain Rolland und Malwida von Meysenbug*, translated by A. Lubbe and Berta Schleicher, Stuttgart: Engelhorn, 1932, 271 pp. English translation by Thomas J. Wilson, *Letters, 1890–1891, Romain Rolland and Malwida von Meysenbug*, N. Y.: Holt, 1933, 274 pp. See Rolland, "Dankgesang. Erinnerungen an Malwida," in Schleicher, *op. cit.*, p. 31: "Der erste ihrer Briefe ist vom 31. Januar 1890. Der letzte vom 27. Februar 1903. Es sind also etwa 600 Briefe die ich von ihr empfing. Und ebensoviel meinerseits, die man nach ihrem Tode mir wiedergegeben hat."

11. «Le grain de vie,» *Mercure de France*, CCC (1er juin 1947), 201–213. Rolland's private notes, 1890–1891, during the time when he was working on *Orsino*. They reveal something of his processes of literary creation, especially the musical character of this process.

12. *Romain Rolland. Choix de Lettres à Malwida von Meysenbug*. Preface by E. Monod-Herzen. Les Bibliolâtres de France. Premier Cahier. Les Minimes, Brie-comte-Robert (S & M), 1948, 332 pp, and Albin Michel.

1892

13. «Le dernier procès de Louis de Berquin, 1527–1529,» *Mélanges d'Archéologie et d'Histoire de l'Ecole française*, XII, 314–325.

14. "Der französische Geist und das französische Drama," *Bayreuther Blätter*, XV, no. 9 (1892), 297–306. This little-known text by Rolland contains some interesting judgments concerning the classic French theater. The French revolution, he says, ruined the aristocratic society from which the most aristocratic art arose, and nothing permanent has yet replaced either one. The double trait of the French spirit that is most important for the development of the dramatic art is the preference for personality and for social intercourse. This latter trait is discussed then in connection with *salon* life and the development of the universal character of this theater. The love of personality, but a universal and not an individual personality, leads to action. Action is the true essence of classic French tragedy. Other characteristics of this tragedy are also discussed, but, in view of Rolland's later dramas, this is the most interesting idea in this article.

1893–1894

15. «Journal intime. Extraits,» *Commune*, III (avril 1936), 913–919. He expresses his hatred of war and of the prejudices which form the bases of

the society of his time. The ideals of socialism take root in him: «A chacun le nécessaire pour vivre;» «Le travail pour tous.» The artist, he says, must also work for the community. Many of the ideas here expressed were taken up later in *Jean-Christophe.*

1894

16. «Rapport sur les manuscrits réservés par la Commission,» in *Supplément à la Correspondance générale de l'Instruction primaire,* 15 décembre 1894.

1895

17. *Les Origines du théâtre lyrique moderne. Histoire de l'opéra en Europe avant Lully et Scarlatti.* (Bibliothèque des Ecoles françaises d'Athènes et de Rome, 1877–1930, fasc. 71). E. Thorin, 316 pp. and 16 pp. of music. Doctoral dissertation. «Couronné par l'Académie française, prix Kastner Boursault.» «Nouvelle édition, augmentée d'une préface inédite de l'auteur,» Boccard, 1931.

18. *Cur ars picturae apud Italos XVI saeculi deciderit,* E. Thorin. Doctoral dissertation. A résumé was published in the *Revue de Paris,* (1er janvier 1896), pp. 168–202, "La Décadence de la peinture italienne.»

1897

19. «Saint Louis,» *Revue de Paris,* (1er, 15 mars, 1er avril), pp. 87–137, 358–395, 571–593; an edition was published by Ollendorff, 1921, 105 pp, and by A. Michel, [1926], 105 pp. The play was published also in the volume, *Les Tragédies de la foi,* Hachette, 1913. The theme of this "poème dramatique" is the triumph of faith. Those who have faith are triumphant, even though they die. This idea of the "vaincus vainqueurs" reappears in other works of these and later years.

20. *Les Vaincus,* drame en quatre actes. Unpublished fragments of a drama written in October and November, 1897. Antwerp: Roger Avermaete, Editions «Lumière,» 1922, 334 pp. The Introduction is dated July, 1921.

1898

21. «Aërt,» *Revue d'art dramatique,* IV (mai–juillet), 92–135, 187–212, 278–302. The first edition was published by the *Cahiers de la Quinzaine,* (1er août 1898); another edition was published the same year by the *Revue d'art dramatique,* 124 pp. Other editions by Ollendorff, 1921, 76 pp.; A. Michel (1926?), 76 pp. It was published also in the volume *Les Tragédies de la foi,* 1913.

22. «La passion à Salzbach,» *Revue d'art dramatique*, n.s. II (septembre), 445–449.

23. *Les Loups* (Homo homini lupus), par Saint-Juste. Edition Ch. Péguy chez George Bellais, in −8 carré, with the reproduction of a lithograph by Henry de Graux. Published by A. Michel (1925), 94 pp., and in the volume *Le Théâtre de la révolution*, Hachette, 1909. Inspired mainly, but not solely, by the Dreyfus case. (See the letter of Malwida von Meysenbug to Olga Monod, 20 Mai 1898, in *Im Anfang war die Liebe. Briefe an ihre Pflegetochter von Malwida von Meysenbug*, Munich, 1926, p. 281–282.) The scene and action have been transported to the French Revolution. It is essentially a debate between the principle of eternal justice and the needs of the nation.

1898–1900

24. Letters, in *La Nef* (août 1945).

1899

25. «Réponse à l'enquête sur la critique dramatique,» *Revue d'art dramatique*, VI (5 février), 161–162. «La critique est également nuisible à l'art et à l'esprit public.» It should be the humble servant of art, and have a clear view of new ideals, and faith in them. Only a creative artist can do this. Thus the only critics worth reading are creators: Wagner, Schiller, Goethe. Suppress the critic, says Rolland, so that the public can judge by itself. «Toute personnalité saine porte en soi assez de pensée pour vivre et pour juger la vie et l'art.»

26. «Les Oratorios de Don Lorenzo Perosi,» *ibid.*, VI (5 mars), 324–328. The article is partially reproduced in *Musiciens d'aujourd'hui*, 1908. All Rolland's articles about Perosi are very enthusiastic; he sees the musician's faults, but hopes that he is the beginning of a renewal of Italian music.

27. «Don Lorenzo Perosi,» *Revue de Paris* (15 mars), pp. 443–448. This same article has been incorporated into the article in *Musiciens d'aujourd'hui*, 1908. Rolland expresses his hopes that art may become an instrument of moral edification, a language common to all peoples.

28. «Richard Strauss,» *Revue de Paris* (15 juin), pp. 769–789. Revised and enlarged in *Musiciens d'aujourd'hui*, 1908. Rolland praises especially the "flot de vie débordante" and the will of this musician. There is also an interesting judgment about Germany, heroic, intoxicated with her triumphs, her immense riches, her force, who grasps the world in her great arms, dominates it, and stops, broken by her victory, asking, "Why have I conquered?"

29. «Le drame religieux au XVIIe siècle,» *La Tribune de Saint Gervais*, V (juin), 136–144. The *Rappresentazione di Anima e di Corpo* by Emilio

del Cavaliere, 1600. The religious drama is less idealistic and more popular than the oratorio proper.

30. «Le triomphe de la raison,» *Revue d'art dramatique,* VII (5 juillet, 5 août, 5 septembre), 241–257, 345–368, 452–469; VIII (5 octobre), 69–76. First edition published by the *Revue d'art dramatique,* 1899, 94 pp.; later editions: A. Michel, 1899, 68 pp.; Ollendorff, 1921, 68 pp. Published also in the volume *Les Tragédies de la foi,* 1913

31. «Les représentations du théâtre du peuple à Bussang,» *Journal des Débats* (19 août). Concerns the popular theater of Maurice Pottecher.

32. «Le novel oratorio de l'abbé Perosi à Côme,» *La Tribune de Saint Gervais,* V (octobre), 270–273. *Il Natale del Redentore* as presented at the cathedral of Como, September 12, 1899.

33. «Tristan,» *Revue d'art dramatique,* VIII (5 novembre), 171–177. Concerning the *Tristan und Isolde* of Wagner.

34. «Danton,» *Revue d'art dramatique,* VIII (décembre), 325–354, 411–450; IX (janvier, février 1900), 64–78, 150–156. The first edition was published by the *Revue d'art dramatique,* 1900, 124 pp. Later editions by the *Cahiers de la Quinzaine,* 2ᵉ série, 6ᵉ cahier (février 1901), and A. Michel, 1936, 119 pp. Republished also in *Le Théâtre de la révolution,* 1909.

1900

35. Letter to Louis Gillet, *Le Littéraire* (8 juin 1946). Rolland clarifies some of his ideas about Christianity, love, heroism, hypocrisy, and lying; he also affirms his needs for truth and sincerity.

36. «*Louise* de Gustave Charpentier,» *Rivista musicale italiana,* VII, 361–366.

37. «Le Premier congrès international d'histoire de la musique . . . ,» *ibid.,* pp. 822–829. Rolland was one of the organizers and presiding officers of this international conference, which was held July 23–28, 1900, at the Bibliothèque de l'Opéra.

38. «Musique d'Italie,» *Le Temps* (9, 26 mai), dated from Milan, May 1 and 20. Perosi's music, Italian music, and his account of an interview with d'Annunzio are the principal subjects. Rolland mingles social and political ideas with the discussion of music.

39. «Le Poison idéaliste,» *Revue d'art dramatique,* XV (juillet), 661–665. Republished in *Compagnons de route,* 1936. An attack on false idealism—an attitude which he held throughout his later years.

40. Letters to Louis Gillet, *Le Littéraire* (8 juin 1946). The letters are dated November 8, 16, December 5. The first letter concerns the premiere of *L'Assomoir* with Sacha Guitry and Suzanne Després. The second was written in reply to a letter from Gillet who was then very lonely teaching in

Greifswald. The last one is a letter of encouragement for Gillet's projected book on Germany.

41. «Le Roman comique d'un musicien allemand,» *Revue de Paris*, IV, 199–214. Republished later in *Voyage musical aux pays du passé*, 1920. The musician is Kuhnau.

42. «Le Théâtre du peuple et le drame du peuple,» *Revue d'art dramatique*, XV (décembre), 1078-1114. This is the germ of part of his *Théâtre du peuple*, 1903.

1901

43. «Les Fêtes de Beethoven à Mayence,» *Revue de Paris* (15 mars), pp. 431-448. The first of his studies on Beethoven; part of this article was incorporated later in his *Vie de Beethoven*, 1903.

44. «Les salons de 1901,» *Revue de Paris* (1er juin), pp. 591–629. Reveals more about Rolland perhaps than about the Salons. He attacks the lack of energy in the epoch, the coldness of soul revealed, the false idealism, and the lack of contact with the life around the artists. "Le pire danger de l'art, c'est le faux idéalisme. C'est l'erreur des jeunes symbolistes, qui veulent exprimer leur rêve intérieur avant de connaître la vie autour d'eux . . . Le rêve est le terme de l'art; la nature, sa source."

45. «Gandolfi, R.,—*Biblioteca del R. Istituto musicale di Firenze . . .*,» *Revue musicale*, I, 262–264. A review article.

46. «E. Grosse,—*Les débuts de l'art . . .*,» *ibid.*, pp. 450–453. A review of the work, translated from the German by E. Dirr.

47. Three articles on Luigi Rossi and his *Orfeo*. «La représentation d'*Orfeo* et l'opposition religieuse et politique,» *Revue musicale*, I, 10–17; «Note sur l'*Orfeo* de Luigi Rossi et sur les musiciens italiens à Paris sous Mazarin,» *ibid.*, pp. 225–236; «Notes sur le premier opéra joué à Paris, et sur Luigi Rossi,» *ibid.*, pp. 363–372. With some changes and additions, these articles form the basis of the article «Le Premier opéra joué à Paris. L'*Orfeo* de Luigi Rossi,» in the volume *Musiciens d'autrefois*, 1908.

48. «Note sur Martinenche, E., *La Comédie espagnole en France, de Hardy à Racine*,» *Art dramatique et musical en* 1901, I, 187–188.

48A. «Note sur la *Revue d'histoire et de critique musicale*,» *L'Art dramatique et musical en 1901*, I, 207–208.

49. «Note sur Rigal, E., *Le Théâtre français avant la période classique*,» *L'Art dramatique et musical en 1901*, I, 188–189.

50. «Note sur Wotquenne, A., *Libretti d'opéras et d'oratorios italiens du XVIIe siècle*,» *L'Art dramatique et musical en 1901*, I, 190–191. Published also in the *Revue musicale*, I, 122–123.

51. «*Patrie* de V. Sardou,» *L'art dramatique et musical en 1901*, I, 131–133.

52. «Richard Strauss: op. 47; *Cinq Lieder . . . ,*» *Revue musicale,* I, 267. A very short note.

53. «Schola Cantorum.—Trois séances de musique française des XVIIe et XVIIIe siècles,» *L'Art dramatique et musical en 1901,* I, 145–155.

54. «L. Torchi, *La Musica istrumentale in Italia nei secoli XVI–XVIII,*» *Revue musicale,* I, 333–337. In this article, as in others, Rolland emphasizes the fact that the history of the civilization of a people is not confined to that people, but that the reciprocal influences of neighboring peoples form an integral part of their civilizations.

55. «Saint-Saëns et *Les Barbares,*» *Revue de Paris* (1er novembre), pp. 208–225. An article about Saint-Saëns and a critical review of *Les Barbares.* It was republished in *Musiciens d'aujourd'hui,* where the critical account of *Les Barbares* is omitted.

56. «Notes sur l'*Orfeo* de Luigi Rossi et sur les musiciens italiens à Paris, sous Mazarin,» *Congrès d'Histoire de la Musique.* Documents, Mémoires et Voeux, publiés par les soins de M. Jules Combarieu. Paris: Fischbacher, 1901 (300 copies), pp. 193–209. The article is in four parts: 1. «Rapports personnels de Mazarin avec la musique et les musiciens;» 2. «Les Barberini en France et la première représentation de l'opéra italien à Paris;» 3. «Luigi Rossi avant son arrivée en France;» 4. «La Représentation d'Orfeo et l'opposition religieuse et politique à l'opéra.» These form the first four parts of the article «Le Premier opéra joué à Paris, L'*Orfeo* de Luigi Rossi,» in *Musiciens d'autrefois,* 1908.

1902

57. «Siegfried,» *Revue de Paris* (1er février), pp. 188–204. Republished later in *Musiciens d'aujourd'hui,* 1908.

58. «Introduction à une lettre inédite adressée à Romain Rolland, datée du 4 octobre 1887,» *Cahiers de la Quinzaine,* 3e série, 9e cahier (24 février), pp. 7–12. (Péguy published Tolstoy's letter in *Les Cahiers de la Quinzaine,* 3e série, 4e cahier). Published later in *Compagnons de route,* 1936, with some changes; Tolstoy's letter appears in the appendix of the same volume. A résumé of the letter appeared in the *Cahiers de la Quinzaine,* 8e série 1er cahier.

59. «Le Quatorze juillet,» *Cahiers de la Quinzaine,* 3e série, 11e cahier (20 mars), 252 pp. Rolland dates its completion June, 1901. The play was published later by Hachette, 1909, 151 pp., and in *Le Théâtre de la révolution,* Hachette, 1909.

60. «Le Quatorze juillet,» *L'Art du théâtre,* No. 18 (juin), 107–111. A critical article about his own play, rectifying some of the errors of judgment concerning it.

61. «Le *Feuersnot* de Richard Strauss,» *Revue d'art dramatique*, VI (mai), 219–223.

62. Letter to Louis Gillet, *Le Littéraire* (8 juin 1946). Dated April 28. Rolland gives his reasons for optimism concerning the political life of the nation to Gillet, who had apparently been much disturbed by the narrow materialism displayed during a meeting of the Socialist party. Rolland also vigorously affirms his belief in the divinity of the human soul. About liberty he has the following to say: «Depuis le jour où le vent de la liberté a soufflé en moi, il a tout emporté: religion, patrie, famille; et il a fait lever en moi une foi, une patrie, une famille nouvelles.»

63. In this number of *Le Littéraire* there are published also extracts from other letters from Rolland to Gillet. No date is given for them. One is a defense of his *Théâtre de la révolution*, especially *Le Quatorze juillet*. He says that his joy and his duty on earth are to understand as much as possible of the world and to try to defend and preserve reason.

64. Letter to Louis Gillet, *Le Littéraire* (7 juin 1946). Dated May 4. Rolland tells of his first meeting with Gillet, to whom he pays tribute here.

65. «La Musique et l'histoire générale,» *Revue musicale*, II (juin), 249–259. Published also in *Musiciens d'autrefois*, 1908, under the title, «Introduction. La Place de la musique dans l'histoire générale.» An extract from a lecture delivered by Rolland at the *Ecole des Hautes Etudes Sociales*. History must be more than the superficial and exterior review of the political life of a people. It must study the penetration of the past by all the arts, philosophy, and literature. «L'histoire doit toujours avoir pour objet l'unité vivante de l'esprit humain. . . .» Republished in a small collection: *La Musique dans l'histoire générale*: *Grétry*: *Mozart*. Collection: «Ecrivains d'hier et d'aujourd'hui,» edited by W. Golde and M. Van de Kerckhove, Berlin: Weidmannsche Buchhandlung, 1930. The text is in French.

66. «Rossini,» *Revue musicale* (août), 374–381. Partially a review article of various articles in the *Onoranze fiorentine a Gioacchino Rossini inaugurandosi in Santa Croce il monumento al grande maestro*, memorie pubblicate da Riccardo, Firenze.

67. «Note sur *Eugénie Grandet*, pièce en cinq actes, tirée du roman de Balzac, par M. Marcel Bryonne,» *Art dramatique et musical en 1902*, II, 19.

68. «Hugo Goldschmidt, *Studien zur Geschichte der italienischen Oper im 17. Jahrhundert* . . . ,» and continuation, «L'Opéra romain et la représentation de San Alessio,» *Revue musicale*, II, 20–29, 29–36, 74–75.

69. «Les Sonates pour piano de Kuhnau,» *ibid.*, II, 71–74.

70. *François Millet*, Popular Library of Art, London: Duckworth, 212 pp. N. Y.: Dutton, 1903, 200 pp. This booklet has never been published in French.

1903

71. «Réponse à l'Enquête de Jacques Morland sur «l'influence allemande,»» *Mercure de France,* XLV (janvier), 106–110. Influence in music. He denies this influence, but says that France would do well to steep herself occasionally in German music.

72. «Vincent d'Indy,» *Revue de Paris* (15 janvier), 401–420. The article is principally concerned with Vincent d'Indy's *Etranger.*

73. «Une oeuvre inédite de Gluck (la Danza pastorella),» *Revue musicale,* III (janvier), 40–41; music, 42–47. This is the first, Rolland explains, in a series of articles in which is to be published a kind of anthology of the masters of the old opera, a collection of unpublished musical dramas of the seventeenth and eighteenth centuries.

74. «Mozart,» *Revue d'art dramatique,* XVIII (15 janvier, 15 février), 15–26, 49–57. Rolland, in *Musiciens d'autrefois,* p. 295, says: "La *Revue d'art dramatique* a donné, en 1903, le petit portrait de Mozart, qui date, en réalité, d'une douzaine d'années plus tôt."

Beethoven. Vies des hommes illustres. *Cahiers de la Quinzaine,* 4e série, 10e 1,2 cahiers, (24 janvier, 22 septembre). Later editions: Hachette, 1907, viii, 160 pp.; Hachette, 1908; limited edition, illustrated with twelve engravings by Perrichon. Pelletan, 1909, 137 pp.; 3rd ed., Hachette, 1909, 137 pp.; Hachette, 1911; 7th ed., 1914; 9th ed., Hachette, n. d. (1914); Hachette, 1927, 177 pp., portraits and headings, woodcuts by Paul Baudier; 15th ed., Hachette, 1928; 16th ed., Hachette, 1931; Ed. du Sablier, 1930; 18th ed., Hachette, 1944, 186 pp. Printed in Canada, Montréal: Les Editions Variétés; ré-impression, Hachette, 1946. A résumé was published also in the *Cahiers de la Quinzaine,* 6e série, 1er cahier, pp. 206–212.

76. *Le Temps viendra. Cahiers de la Quinzaine,* 4e série, 14e cahier (10 mars), 148 pp. New edition, Ollendorff, 1903, 148 pp.; Ollendorff, 1920, 151 pp.

77. «Les Salons de 1903,» *Revue de Paris* (1er juin), pp. 635–672.

78. «Les Précurseurs du Théâtre du Peuple . . .» *La Revue d'art dramatique,* XVIII (15 juin), 177–188.

79. «Le Dernier opéra de Gluck, *Echo et Narcisse,*» *Revue musicale* (1er juin), 212–225. Concerns the paucity of Gluck's invention; Gluck uses the same musical theme, or even the same music, several times.

80. «Réponse à l'enquête sur la collaboration anonyme,» *La Revue d'art dramatique et musicale,* XVIII (15 juin), 166. The individualist cannot understand such collaboration: «Autant vendre sa femme. . . .»

81. «L'Oeuvre des trente ans de théâtre et les galas populaires,» *ibid.,* XVIII (15 juillet), 205–213.

82. «Lettre (à Alphonse Séché) sur le Théâtre Populaire,» *ibid.,* XVIII (15 septembre), 274. Rolland expresses his desire to see all the arts, includ-

ing the theater, and all intellectual life, take part in the struggle for socialism. «Il faut briser tout ce qui s'oppose à la libre croissance de la pensée moderne.»

83. *Le Théâtre du peuple.* Essai d'esthétique d'un théâtre nouveau. *Cahiers de la Quinzaine*, 5e série, 4e cahier (24 novembre); Hachette, blue cover with imprint, Fischbacher, 1904, 216 pp.; Hachette, 1908; new and enlarged edition, Hachette, 1913, xii, 224 pp.; Hachette, 1913, 10th ed.; Ollendorff, 1921; Michel, 1926. «Le théâtre du peuple. Résumé,» *Cahiers de la Quinzaine*, 6e série, 1er cahier, 277–291.

84. «Concert Colonne,» *Revue musicale*, 139–141, 608–610.

85. «Causerie musicale,» «Chronique musicale,» *Art dramatique et musical en 1903*, III, 11–14, 95–98, 309–316, 357–363, 401–409.

86. «Eugen Hirschberg, *Die Encyclopädisten und die französische Oper im 18. Jahrhundert*,» *Art dramatique et musical en 1903*, III, 446–447. Review article.

87. «M. Steuer—*Zur Musik, geschichtliches, aesthetisches und kritisches*,» «*Titania* de MM. L. Gallet et A. Corneau, musique de Georges Hüe,» *Art dramatique et musical en 1903*, III, 14–15, 448.

88. «Les Origines de l'opéra et les travaux de M. Angelo Solerti,» «Les Maîtres de l'opéra. Le Dernier opéra de Monteverdi,» «Les Origines de l'opéra italien,» *Revue musicale*, 127–129, 178–179, 280–281.

1904

«L'Opéra avant l'opéra,» *Revue de Paris* (1er février), 615–647. Divided into three parts: 1. *Le sacre rappresentazione de Venise*. 2. without a title. 3. Le Drame musical de Torquato Tasso. Republished with only slight changes in the volume *Musiciens d'autrefois*, 1908.

90. *Jean-Christophe*. Première partie. *L'Aube*. *Cahiers de la Quinzaine*, 5e série, 9e cahier (2 février), 180 pp. For later editions, see nos. 100–101, 159.

91. *Ibid.*, Première partie. *Le Matin, Cahiers de la Quinzaine*, 5e série, 10e cahier (16 février), 175 pp. For later editions, see nos. 100, 101, 160.

92. «La Montespan,» drama in three acts, *Revue d'art dramatique et musical*, XIX (février-avril), 49–83, 93–110, 117–138, followed by the «Avertissement», 139–140, in which the author affirms the privileges of art in the interpretation of history. Edition published by the *Revue d'art dramatique*, 1904, 94 pp.

93. «Berlioz,» *Revue de Paris* (1er, 15 mars), 65–88, 331–352. Republished in the volume, *Musiciens d'aujourd'hui*, 1908. There are several ideas that are of particular interest in a study of Rolland; he emphasizes the colossal strength of Berlioz; he places him above Wagner, and he insists that Berlioz has opened the way for a great popular art.

94. «L'Etat actuel de la musique française: Réponse à l'enquête de Paul Landormy,» *Revue bleue: politique et littéraire* (2 avril), 424–425.

95. «Gluck: Une révolution dramatique,» *Revue de Paris* (15 juin), 736–772. Republished, with considerable changes, in the volume, *Musiciens d'autrefois*, 1908, under the title: «Gluck—à propos d'*Alcéste*.»

96. «Chronique musicale,» *Art dramatique et musical en* 1904, IV, 11–15, 49–57, 93–99, 136–141, 171–178. Concerts, Berlioz and Schumann, two letters from Meyerbeer, *Orfeo* by Monteverdi, La fille de Roland, De Schumann à Albert Magnard, Le Quatuor à Joachim, M. Henri Expert et les musiques mesurées à l'antique, Lettres inédites de Berlioz, Le Jongleur de Notre-Dame, Alceste, La Société nationale de musique, De La fondation d'un Salon musical.

97. «L'Etranger de Vincent d'Indy,» *Rivista musicale italiana*, XI, 129–139.

98. «Dietrich Buxtehude, *Abendmusiken und Kirchenkantaten*, publiées par Max Seiffert . . . ,» «Alfred Wotquenne, *Catalogue thématique des oeuvres de Chr.-W.-V. Gluck* . . . ,» *Revue musicale*, IV, 359–361, 357–359.

99. *Paris als Musikstadt*, Berlin: Marquardt. Published later in French in the volume, *Musiciens d'aujourd'hui*, 1908, under the title: «Le Renouveau: Esquisse du mouvement musical à Paris.»

1905

100. *Jean-Christophe*. Première partie. *L'Adolescent. Cahiers de la Quinzaine*, (6ᵉ série, 8ᵉ cahier (10 janvier), 220 pp.

101. *Jean-Christophe*. Première partie. Three volumes. Ollendorff, 1905. *L'Aube*, *Le Matin*, *L'Adolescent*.

102. Letter to Paul Landormy, *Fontaine*, VIII, No. 41, 13–20. Dated February 1, the letter is about *Jean-Christophe*.

103. «Musiques des rues,» *Revue d'art dramatique et musical*, XX (15 février), 81–89.

104. «Hugo Wolf,» *Revue de Paris*, III (15 mai), 401-421; also appeared in the *Revue germanique*, I (mai), 346–351. Published later in *Musiciens d'aujourd'hui*, 1908.

105. «Un Vaudeville de Rameau (*Le Procureur dupe sans le savoir*),» *Mercure musical*, I (15 mai), 19–24.

106. «Une fête musicale en Alsace-Lorraine,» *Revue de Paris*, IV (juillet-octobre), 134–152. Published also in *Musiciens d'aujourd'hui*, 1908, under the title: «Musique française et musique allemande.» Includes criticisms of Gustave Mahler and Richard Strauss.

107. «La musique en Italie au XVIIIᵉ siècle,» *Revue de Paris* (juillet-octobre), 763–790. Published later with some changes in the volume *Voyage musical aux pays du passé*, 1920.

108. «La Musique en Italie,» *Revue musicale*, V, 435–443. A review article concerning *Musique instrumentale en Italie aux XVIe, XVIIe, XVIIIe siècles*, and *L'Arte musicale in Italia* by Luigi Torchi.

109. «Hugo Leichentritt, *Frédéric Chopin* . . . ,» *Revue germanique*, I, 351–352.

110. *Michel-Ange*. Librairie de l'art ancien et moderne, 24 engravings, 178 pp. Rolland studies principally the works of Michael Angelo. For the first of his studies on the man, see his «Michel-Ange,» *Revue de Paris*, 1906.

1906

111. «L'Opéra populaire à Venise: Francesco Cavalli,» *Mercure musical*, II (15 janvier, 15 février),60–70, 151–160. He emphasizes the popular character of these operas, and analyzes *L'Eritrea*, *Le Nozze di Teti e di Peleo*, and *Giasone*.

112. «La musique en Allemagne au XVIIIe siècle,» *Revue de Paris*, XIII (15 février), 852–882. Contains much that appeared later in «Frédéric II musicien,» 1912, *infra*, no. 153. Republished with some changes in the volume, *Voyage musical aux pays du passé*, 1920.

113. «Michel-Ange,» *Revue de Paris* (15 avril), 795–822. A study of the man, this essay forms the nucleus of the study of Michael Angelo which appeared later in the *Cahiers de la Quinzaine*. 1906.

114. *La Vie de Michel-Ange*. Vies des hommes illustres, *Cahiers de la Quinzaine*. I. La Lutte, 7e série, 18e cahier (26 juin), 102 pp. II. L'Abdication, 8e série, 2e cahier (16 octobre), 105–210 pp. Other editions: Hachette, 11 novembre, 1907, in-18 Jésus, 212 pp. et portrait; 2e ed., revue, Hachette, 1908, 211 pp. and portrait; 3rd ed., revue, Hachette, 1911, 211 pp. and portrait; 4th ed., Hachette, 1913; 5th ed., Hachette, 1914; 6th ed., Hachette, 1917; édition illustrée par Paul Baudier, Hachette, 1925, 201 pp.; 10th ed., Hachette, 1926, 212 pp.; an edition listed in 1944 by *Les Livres du mois*, 176 pp., 104 plates; réimpression, Hachette, 1946.

115. «Festival Mozart . . . ,» *Mercure musical*, II^1, 362. Rolland points out particularly the Italian and theatrical qualities of Mozart's music.

116. *Jean Christophe*. Première partie. *La Révolte*, 1. *Sables mouvants*. *Cahiers de la Quinzaine*, 8e série, 4e cahier (13 novembre), 148 pp. 2. *L'Enlisement*. *Cahiers de la Quinzaine*, 8e série, 6e cahier (11 décembre), pp. 153–271. For later editions, see no. 160. This edition of the *Cahiers* contains many passages which are not in subsequent editions. I have included extracts and résumés of these passages in the Appendix.

117. «Musique italienne. Prof. Giuseppe Radiciotti: *Teatro e Musica in Roma nel secondo quarto del secolo XIX* . . . ,» «Musique nouvelle. Les *Heures dolentes* de M. Gabriel Dupont aux Concerts Colonne,» *Mercure musical*, II^2, 417-418, 343–345.

118. «Silhouettes Clamecyçoises de la Révolution, d'après une Histoire de la Révolution dans une petite ville depuis 1789 jusqu'en 1797. Manuscrit inédit du docteur Edme-François Bordet,» *Bulletin de la Société scientifique et artistique de Clamecy*. 30e annee, n.s., t.IV, pp. 27–43.

119. «Les Trois amoureuses,» pièce dramatique en trois actes, *Revue d'art dramatique et musical*, XXI, 169–191, 249–275, 333–348.

1907

120. *Jean-Christophe*. Première partie. *La Révolte*. 3. *La Délivrance*. *Cahiers de la Quinzaine*, 8e série, 9e cahier (2 janvier), 275–411 pp. The three parts of *La Révolte*: Sables mouvants, L'Enlisement, and La Délivrance, were combined in one volume in all the later editions. *La Révolte*, Ollendorff, 1907, 339 pp.

121. «Notes sur Lully,» *Mercure musical*, III (15 janvier), 3–55. Published later in the volume *Musiciens d'autrefois*, where it forms parts III, IV, V, VI of the «Notes sur Lully;» it was changed considerably.

122. Letter to Mme P. Landormy, *Fontaine*, VIII, No. 41 (1945), 13–20. Letter dated February 9.

123. «Lettre en réponse à l'enquête sur le répertoire,» *Revue d'art dramatique et musical*, XXII (20 février), 145. Dated Rome, January 21. The article concerns *Le Théâtre du Peuple*.

124. «Claude Debussy's *Pelléas et Mélisande*,» *Morgen*, I (29 November), 797–802. Republished later, in French, in *Musiciens d'aujourd'hui*, 1908. He points out the importance of the first presentation of *Pelléas et Mélisande* in the reaction against Wagnerism, although he himself does not like the piece. It is perhaps significant that he prefers the France of "l'ivresse de la raison, le rire, la lumière," of Rabelais, Molière, and Diderot, to the France of Debussy.

1908

125. «Lully,» *Revue de Paris* (15 février), 699–722. Published in *Musiciens d'autrefois*, as parts I and II of «Notes sur Lully.»

126. «Grétry,» *Revue de Paris* (15 mars), 305–327. Published in *Musiciens d'autrefois*.

127. *Jean-Christophe*. Deuxième partie. *Jean-Christophe à Paris*. 1. *La Foire sur la place*. *Cahiers de la Quinzaine*, 9e série, 13e and 14e cahiers (17, 24 mars), xxi–xxvii, 131, 133–279 pp. 2. *Antoinette*. *Cahiers de la Quinzaine*, 9e série, 15e cahier (31 mars), 148 pp. Later editions in two volumes, Ollendorff, 1908, 324, 261 pp. *Antoinette*, 10th edition, Ollendorff, 1909, 261 pp. The edition in the *Cahiers de la Quinzaine* contains many pages not in subsequent editions. Following are the most important of these passages. There is first an introductory note: *La Foire sur la place*, *Cahiers*, p. 7, in

which he asks the indulgence of his readers for leaving in the text numerous pages to be removed from later editions. He considers the editions in the *Cahiers* as projects, freer and more complete than later editions will be.

In the *Cahiers*, pp. 74–75 (17th ed., pp. 80–81, éd. déf., p. 71), there are some interesting remarks about music. Music is not a universal language, no matter what is said about it. There are as many kinds of music as of races; it is as varied as poetry. At one time it was an international language, based on Italian music.

In the *Cahiers*, pp. 79–80 (17th ed., p. 85, éd. déf., p. 75), there are criticisms of French orchestras and concert halls. Technical reasons for the poor quality of French musical interpretation and presentation.

Cahiers, pp. 116–117 (17th ed., p. 126, éd. déf., p. 102). Christophe did not understand classic French literature. In so doing he was no worse than Goethe, Schiller, and Lessing, and he was much more discreet. He simply thought that he did not understand. This classic tragedy is foreign to about nine-tenths of Europe.

128. «Paul Dupin,» *S.I.M.*, (15 décembre), pp. 1237–1250.

129. *Musiciens d'aujourd'hui*, Hachette, 286 pp., "Bibliothèque variée;" 2nd and 3rd editions, Hachette, 1908; 5th ed., Hachette, 1912, 286 pp., «Bibliothèque variée. Questions d'art et d'esthétique;» 7th ed., Hachette, 1917, 286 pp.; Hachette, 1919; réimpression, Hachette, 1946. The articles that compose this book are: Camille Saint-Saëns. Vincent d'Indy. Richard Strauss. Hugo Wolf. Don Lorenzo Perosi. Musique française et musique allemande. *Pelléas et Mélisande* de Claude Debussy. Le Renouveau: esquisse du mouvement musical à Paris depuis 1870.

130. *Musiciens d'autrefois*, Hachette, 310 pp. with music; 2nd ed., revised, Hachette, 1908, 310 pp. with music; 3rd ed., Hachette, 1912, «Bibliothèque variée. Questions d'art et d'esthétique;» 4th ed., Hachette, 1915; 6th ed., Hachette, 1919; Hachette, 1921. The articles in this book are: L'Opéra avant l'Opéra. L' «Orfeo» de Luigi Rossi. Lully. Gluck. Grétry. Mozart.

131. «Tiersot, J., *Les Fêtes et les chants de la Révolution française . . .*,» *S.I.M.*, IV², 719–721.

1909

132. Letters to Mme Paul Landormy. *Fontaine*, VIII, No. 41 (1945), 13–20. Dated January 22, March 6, October 23, and November 5. In the first, Rolland says that we must look at life, see its tragic basis, but accept it with courage, peace, and gratitude for the beauties it has to offer us. The second concerns *Jean-Christophe*, and an article in the *Courrier musical* which he hopes Paul Dupin will not read. The third is full of remarks about writers and artists of Paris and his disgust with them. He tells what

he is doing, and makes some very interesting remarks about his book on Beethoven and adds that he will never write again about Beethoven. He affirms his dislike of lecturing. The last one discusses Berlioz principally.

133. «Préface au *Théâtre de la révolution,*» *Cahiers de la Quinzaine*, 10e série, 9e cahier (16 février), xv–xviii, appendix.

134. Letter to Claude Monet, *Regards*, IV (16 avril 1936). He says that his admiration for Monet dates from some twenty years before when he first saw Monet's *Les Rochers battus par la mer*.

135. *Jean-Christophe*. Deuxième partie. *Jean-Christophe à Paris*. 3. *Dans la maison. Cahiers de la Quinzaine,* 10e série, 9e and 10e cahiers (16, 23 février), 110, 114–253 pp. Edition in one volume, Ollendorff, 1909, 282 pp. Various passages of the *Cahiers de la Quinzaine* edition were omitted in subsequent editions. I have given extracts and summaries of these passages in the Appendix.

136. «Société G.-F. Haendel,» «A propos de quelques articles sur Richard Strauss,» *S.I.M.*, V², 73–74, 184–186; 513–528, 625–634.

137. «*Heraklès* de Haendel à la Société G.-F. Haendel,» *ibid.*, V², 613–616. In these articles on Haendel, Rolland invites French critics to see in Haendel the most powerful link between Cavalli and Gluck, and the direct precursor of Gluck and Beethoven.

138. Letter to Jean Bonnerot. Published by Bonnerot in his *Romain Rolland. Extraits de son oeuvre*. Introduction by Bonnerot. Nevers: Les Cahiers Nivernais et du Centre, 13e et 14e fascicules, (octobre–novembre), p. 16.

139. Letters to Paul Landormy. *Fontaine,* VIII, No. 41 (1945), 13–20. Dated November 12 and December 31.

140. *Théâtre de la révolution*. The following plays are here collected: Danton. Le Quatorze juillet. Les Loups. Preface of 1909 and note of 1901, Hachette, VIII, 359 pp.; 2nd ed., Hachette, 1909; 3rd ed., Ollendorff; 4th ed., Ollendorff, 192–; 5th ed., Ollendorff, 1923?; 8th edition, A. Michel, 1926; 11th ed., A. Michel, 1926, VIII, 101, 191, 94 pp., in one volume.

1910

141. *Jean-Christophe*. Troisième partie. *La Fin du voyage*. 1. *Les Amies. Cahiers de la Quinzaine,* 11e série, 7e and 8e cahiers (25 janvier, 8 février), 231 pp., consecutive numbering. One-volume edition, Ollendorff, n.d. (*Bibliographie de la France,* March 20, 1925), 268 pp. «Ouvrage couronné par l'Académie française.»

142. «Haendel,» *Revue de Paris* (15 avril), 791–808. Published later in *Voyage musical aux pays du passé,* 1920, with some changes, and also in *Audition du «Messie» de Haendel . . .*, no. 145.

143. «Discours sur Pierre Aubry,» *Revue musicale* (1er octobre), 485–

487. Letter read at the Meudon cemetery, September 6, 1910, and reproduced in the obituary, pp. 18–20, Paris: Plon-Nourrit, 1911.

144. «Les Origines du style classique dans la musique du XVIIIe siècle,» *S.I.M.*, VI^{1}, 81–99. Opening lecture for the course on the history of music, given at the "Faculté des lettres de Paris," 1909–1910. Rewritten later for *Voyage musical aux pays du passé*, 1920.

145. *Une Audition du «Messie» de Haendel par la Société Haendel de Paris*, ... Etudes par Romain Rolland. Programme. Imprimerie Rasquin, Société Haendel, 8 pp. (20 mai).

146. «Le *Messie* de Haendel au Trocadéro,» «Les Plagiats de Haendel,» *S.I.M.*, VI^{2}, 191, 193; 283–297, 419–443.

147. *Haendel*, Alcan, 251 pp.; 3rd ed., Alcan, 1911; 5th ed., 1924.

1911

148. «Musique,» in the volume *L'Ecole des Hautes Etudes Sociales 1900–1910*, Alcan, 1911. Report and programs, pp. 69–80.

149. «Tolstoi,» *Revue de Paris* (15 février, 1er mars, 15 mars, 1er avril), 673–707, 75–105, 285–313, 533–563. *Vie de Tolstoi*. Vies des hommes illustres, 2nd ed., Hachette, 1911, 208 pp.; 3rd ed., Hachette, 1911; 4th ed., Hachette, 1913; 5th ed., Hachette, 1917, 222 pp.; Hachette, 1928, portraits and headings by Paul Baudier; Hachette, 1929; réimpression, Hachette, 1946.

150. Letter to Louis Gillet. *Le Littéraire* (28 septembre 1946). Letter dated July 9. Rolland, Péguy and a literary prize.

151. *Jean-Christophe*. Troisième partie. *La Fin du voyage. 2. Le Buisson ardent. Cahiers de la Quinzaine*, 13e série, 5e and 6e cahiers (31 octobre, 7 novembre), 264 pp. consecutively numbered.

1912

152. «La Femme et l'art dramatique,» *Le Parthenon* (20 janvier), 1.

153. «Frédéric II, musicien,» *Revue de Paris* (1er février), 507–528.

154. Letters to Paul Seippel, who published extracts from them in his «Jean-Christophe,» *Bibliothèque universelle et Revue suisse*, LXVIII (octobre–décembre 1912), 455–457. Letters dated February 2 and November 9.

155. «La Société des concerts symphoniques populaires,» *S.I.M.*, VIII^{1} (15 mars), pp. 39–44. The serious question now is that of the relationship between art and the people. In the Middle Ages and the Renaissance, these relationships were steady and strong; at present they scarcely exist. It is not a question of attributing virtues to the people, or to an aristocracy, but of determining whether art is a superfluous luxury or a moral force, a light for the spirit, a joy for the intellect, and a benefit for the heart.

156. Letters to J.-R. Bloch, published in *Europe*, XXVI (mai 1948), 10–44. Dated January 14, March 16, April 15, June 26, August 10, 26, September 5.

157. «Métastase précurseur de Gluck,» *ibid.*, VIII[1] (15 avril), 1–10. Published also in the *Voyage musical aux pays du passé*, 1920.

158. «Le Jeune Mozart à Mannheim,» *Revue bleue: politique et littéraire* (avril), 490–494, 519–525.

159. *Jean-Christophe*. Troisième partie. 3. *La Nouvelle journée*. *Cahiers de la Quinzaine*, 14ᵉ série, 2ᵉ and 3ᵉ cahiers (6, 20 octobre), 258 pp., consecutively numbered. Edition in one volume, Ollendorff, n.d., 277 pp.

160. *Jean-Christophe*.

Première partie. *L'Aube*, 125th ed., Ollendorff, 1920–1921. *Le Matin*, 106th ed., Ollendorff, n.d.; *L'Adolescent*, 92nd ed., Ollendorff, n.d.; *La Révolte*, 86th ed., Ollendorff, n.d.

Deuxième partie. *Jean-Christophe à Paris*. *La Foire sur la place*, 84th ed., Ollendorff, n.d.; *Antoinette*, 86th ed., Ollendorff, n.d.; *Dans la maison*, 79th ed., Ollendorff n.d.; 119th ed., A. Michel, 1928.

Troisième partie. *La Fin du voyage*. *Les Amies*, 74th ed., Ollendorff, n.d.; 116th edition, A. Michel, 1934. *Le Buisson ardent*, 74th ed., Ollendorff, n.d.; 111th ed., A Michel, 1926. *La Nouvelle journée*, 58th ed., Ollendorff, n.d.; 120th ed., A. Michel, 1934.

Jean-Christophe. Edition définitive. Four volumes: 1. L'Aube, Le Matin, L'Adolescent, Ollendorff, n.d. (*Bibliographie de la France*, avril 1921). 2. La Révolte, la Foire sur la place, Ollendorff, n.d. (*Bibliographie de la France*, novembre 1921). 3. Antoinette, Dans la maison, Les Amies, Ollendorff, n.d. (*Bibliographie de la France*, mars 1922). 4. Le Buisson ardent. La Nouvelle journée, Ollendorff, n.d. (*Bibliographie de la France*, juin 1922).

Jean-Christophe. Illustré de bois dessinés et gravés par Frans Masereel. A. Michel, 1925–1927. 5 volumes. Edition limited to 2012 copies.

Jean-Christophe. Edition définitive. A. Michel, 1931–1933. Five volumes. "Oeuvres complètes."

Jean-Christophe. A. Michel, 1923–1929. Ten volumes.

L'Aube and *Le Matin* reprinted by the Editions Valiquette, Montréal, Canada, 1944. *L'Aube*. Met aanteek. van M. H. J. Horbach. 7ᵉ uitg. Herz. door A. Kook (Coll. Lectures classiques, 47), 127 pp., 22 pp. ill. 1942. Zwolle (Holland): Tjeenk Willink.

161. «Chronique parisienne,» *Bibliothèque universelle et Revue suisse*, LXVIII (octobre–décembre), 614–627. An interesting article in view of his *Ame enchantée*; it is devoted principally to a discussion of the inadequate portrayal of women and the feminine soul in most literature of the past.

162. *Le «Messie» de G.-F. Haendel (1741). Haendel et le Messie*, par Romain Rolland. *Textes du «Messie.» Plan de l'Oratorio*, par Felix Raugel. Paris: au dépôt de la Société coopérative des compositeurs de musique, 19 pp., with music.

163. *De Jean-Christophe à Colas Breugnon. Pages de Journal*. Preface by Jérôme et Jean Tharaud. Frontispieces and illustrations by Jean Lurçat. Editions du Salon Carré (Coll. «Oeuvres et visages d'aujourd'hui,» I), 1946, 182 pp. Edition of 1,350 copies. These fragments of Rolland's "Journal" cover the period from October 1912 to October 1913.

1913

164. Letter from Rolland, published at the head of the «Enquête sur Romain Rolland et l'influence de *Jean-Christophe*,» *Ombres et Formes*, album mensuel inédit d'art libre et de critique; édité à Saint-Pierre-de-Moutier (Nièvre), III (1912), IV (1913).

165. Preface to Simone Bodève, *Celles qui travaillent*, Ollendorff, xvi, 208 pp. The preface is dated January 1913.

166. «Chronique parisienne,» *Bibliothèque universelle et Revue suisse*, LXIX (janvier–mars), 169–184, 381–394, 602–618. Review of novels by Simone Bodève and other women; modern French painting; of the cubists, especially Picasso and Braque, he says: «La rigoureuse nécessité qui mène l'esprit humain les a fait apparaître, à leur moment marqué, dans l'histoire de l'art.»

167. «Réponse à l'enquête sur «La Guerre des deux rives . . . »,» *Les Marges*, XI (mars), 88–89. *Left Bank* against *boulevard* writers.

168. «A l'occasion du «*Choix de Ballades Françaises*,» (de Paul Fort),» *Vers et prose*, XXXIV (juillet–septembre), 202–203.

169. «Stendhal et la musique,» *La Revue*, CV (15 décembre), 462–482; article dated Novembre 1913. It appeared later also as the preface to the *Vies de Haydn, de Mozart et de Métastase*, by Stendhal, éd. des Oeuvres de Stendhal, E. Champion, 1914.

170. «Les Origines germaniques de Jean-Christophe,» *Le Parthénon* (5 novembre), 67–68. Parts were published also in *Mercure de France*, CVI (novembre–décembre 1913).

171. *Le Triomphe de la liberté* (Scène finale du *14 juillet*). Text by Rolland, music by Albert Doyen. A. Leduc. "Prix de la ville de Paris;" another edition in 1917., A. Leduc, xi, 273 pp. See no. 269.

172. *Les Tragédies de la foi*, Hachette, 255 pp.; 3rd ed., 1913; ed. Ollendorff, 1921, 105, 76, 68 pp.; 9th ed., A. Michel, 1925, preface of 1913. This book contains the plays: *Saint-Louis. Aërt. Le Triomphe de la raison.*

173. «L'Opéra au XVIIIe siècle en Italie,» *Encyclopédie de la Musique et Dictionnaire du Conservatoire*, 1913–1931. Première partie, fascicule 22, 1913, 685–749. Dated 1912 by Rolland.

1914

174. «L'Opéra au XVIIIe siècle,» *ibid.*, fascicule 42, 1914, 1343–1361. Continuation of the first article. Contains: L'Opéra avant l'opéra. Rossi (*Musiciens d'autrefois*). L'Opéra populaire à Venise (*Mercure musical*, 1906). Histoire de l'opéra en Europe avant Lully et Scarlatti (Cf. his doctoral dissertation, 1895). The Encyclopedia articles are much more complete than the originals. They include abundant texts and music of the period. Dated 1912 by Rolland.

175. «Les Origines de l'opéra allemand,» *ibid.*, Première partie, fascicule 29, 1914, 911–928. Only brief fragments of this article have appeared elsewhere. Dated 1912 by Rolland.

176. «L'Opéra anglais au XVIIe siècle,» *ibid.*, Première partie, III (1914), 1881–1894.

177. Letter to Ellen Key. Extracts published by Key, *La Revue* (15 janvier), 171–181, and by Jouve, *Romain Rolland vivant* . . . p. 296, and in *Courrier des revues et des livres*, (10 février 1914).

178. Letter to Frank Abauzit, "sur la religion et les intellectuels," in Abauzit, *Le Sentiment religieux à l'heure actuelle*, J. Vrin, 1919, p. 191. Letter dated February 23: «La foi et la liberté sont les deux grandes ailes de l'âme; . . . et je ne saurais dire celle des deux que je préfère. Si, pourtant: la liberté; car, sans elle, la vie n'aurait plus de prix pour moi.»

179. «Une nouvelle histoire du théâtre musical en France,» *S.I.M.*, X^1 (1er mars), 6–15. Review of *L'Opéra italien en France avant Lully*, and *Ballet de cour . . . avant Benserade*, by Henry Prunières.

180. «En Allemagne, une révolution est-elle possible?» Ch.-Henry Hirsch published Rolland's reply to the question in the *Mercure de France*, CVIII (1er mars), 180–181. It is not only possible, but even necessary, says Rolland, because of the great discrepancy between contemporary thought and the political regime.

181. Letter to P.-J. Jouve. Published by Jouve in *Romain Rolland vivant* . . . , p. 47, in part. Letter dated August 3–4.

182. Letter to Gerhardt Hauptmann, *Journal de Genève* (2 septembre); Rolland also published this letter in *Au-dessus de la mêlée*. He published Hauptmann's reply only in the *Cahiers Vaudois*, No. 2., «Louvain . . .

Reims,» p. 126. The *Journal de Genève*, as an introduction to Rolland's letter, publishes a part of an enthusiastic letter from Stefan Zweig about the tenth volume of *Jean-Christophe* (Rütten & Loening, 1914); the letter had first appeared in the *Berliner Tageblatt* (22.Dezember, 1912).

183. Letter to Elsa Richter; published in the *Berliner Tageblatt* (29.April, 1918). Dated August, 1914.

184. «Inter arma caritas,» *Journal de Genève* (Supplément, 4–6 septembre); published later in *Au-dessus de la mêlée*. The dating of the publication by Rolland is there incorrect.

185. «Au-dessus de la mêlée,» *Journal de Genève* (Supplément, 22–23 septembre); *L'Humanité* (26 octobre, 15 novembre), *Coenobium*, VIII (30 septembre), 26–30; later in the volume of the same name.

186. Letter to Verhaeren, *Revue mensuelle*, XVIII (1918), 293–296, 332–333. Dated November 23.

187. «A la mémoire de Charles Péguy,» *Journal de Genève* (20 septembre), p. 1.

188. «Une protestation hollandaise,» *ibid.* (28 septembre). This is a translation of, and an introduction to a letter from Frederick van Eeden, which had originally appeared in the *Amsterdammer. Weekblad voor Nederland* (6 September).

189. Letters to Louis Gillet, *Le Littéraire* (28 septembre 1946). Dated July 30, October 3, and November 5. Their principal subject is the war and problems connected with it.

190. Letter to Paul Landormy, *Fontaine*, VIII, No. 41 (1945), 13–20. Again, war is the principal subject.

191. Letters to Alphonse Séché, published by Séché, in *Les Nouvelles littéraires* (5 août 1934). The letters, dated October 6 and 29, were written from Geneva, where Rolland was already working at the "Agence Internationale des Prisonniers de Guerre."

192. «De deux maux le moindre: Pangermanisme, Panslavisme,» *Journal de Genève* (12 octobre). Published later in *Au-dessus de la mêlée*, 1915. The dating of the publication by Rolland in the volume is incorrect. Cf. Loyson, *Etes-vous neutres devant le crime?* (Loyson was an ardent nationalist, and some of his statements must be taken with a grain of salt.)

193. «Les Idoles,» *Journal de Genève* (10 décembre). Published in *Au-dessus de la mêlée*, where Rolland gives an incorrect date for its publication in the *Journal de Genève*.

194. «Une protestation d'Arthur Schnitzler,» *Journal de Genève* (21 décembre). Introduction by Rolland to a letter from Schnitzler, of which Rolland publishes the complete translation. Schnitzler protests against false judgments about Belgian, English, French, and Russian literature

which have been attributed to him. Rolland takes this means to help combat the wave of misunderstanding and hate inundating Europe.

195. «Au peuple qui souffre pour la justice,» *King Albert's Book*, published by the *Daily Telegraph*, London, 188 pp. Rolland's letter, without a title, in French and English, pp. 107–108. Published later in *Au-dessus de la mêlée*, 1915. Rolland praises not so much the military heroism of Belgium as its spiritual heroism, in such sharp contrast to the spirit of Germany at that time.

196. «Pro Aris,» in *Louvain . . . Reims*. Editions des Cahiers Vaudois, cahier 10, pp. 13–32, Lausanne: Tarin. This was also published in *L'Humanité*, under the title «Pour nous» (23 février 1915), and also in the volume *Au-dessus de la mêlée*. It was partially published in *La Paix par le droit*, XXV (1915), 162–163.

1915

197. «Manifeste des Amis de l'Unité morale de l'Europe,» *Journal de Genève* (9 janvier). An introduction to the manifesto, and a translation of the document itself; list of signers. Rolland dates his introduction December 31, 1914. This was published later in *Au-dessus de la mêlée*, «Un Manifeste des écrivains et penseurs de Catalogne.»

198. Letter to Frederick van Eeden, published by van Eeden, *De Amsterdammer, Weekblad voor Nederland* (24 Januarie). Published later in *Au-dessus de la mêlée*, 1915.

199. Letter to Louis Gillet, *Le Littéraire* (28 septembre 1946). Dated January 17. German imperialism can be killed only by Germany itself.

200. Letters to Henri Guilbeaux. Guilbeaux published extracts from these two letters, dated January 20 and March 23, in his *Pour Romain Rolland*, pp. 54–55.

201. Letter to the director of the review, *Coenobium*, IX (31 gennaio), partially reproduced. Rolland protests that he cannot abandon humanity, in spite of his disgust.

202. Letter to the *Bund Neues Vaterland*, January 31. Incompletely published in the *Bund*, Abendblatt, Berne (10. Februar), under the title "Zum geistigen Zusammenhang nach dem Krieg. Romain Rolland und der *Bund Neues Vaterland*."

203. Letter to the director of the *Bund*, Berne, "Romain Rolland um das *Neues Vaterland*," *Bund*, Berne (18. Februar). This article is composed of a letter from Rolland to the editor of the *Bund*, of Berne, and of a letter to the *Bund Neues Vaterland*, dated February 9. These three letters reveal very clearly his opposition to Prussian imperialism.

204. «Pour l'Europe. Un appel aux Intellectuels de toutes les nations,»

Journal de Genève (15 février). An introduction to his translation of an appeal made by the *Nederlandsche Anti-Oorlog Raad*. Published later in *Au-dessus de la mêlée*, 1915. Dated February 7 by Rolland.

205. Letter to M. Marius A(ndré), *L'Humanité* (26 mars). Dunois publishes a letter from Rolland to himself, dated March 8, and Rolland's letter to Marius André (vice-consul de France, chargé de mission en Espagne). The letter to André was published also in *Les Hommes du jour* (3 avril).

206. «Notre prochain l'ennemi,» *Journal de Genève* (15 mars). Published also in *Au-dessus de la mêlée*, 1915, and *Coenobium*, IX (31 marzo), 42–43.

207. Letters to the periodical, *Les Hommes du jour* (3 avril, 23 octobre, 13 novembre). An appeal to the intellectuals to remember their true duty, and an explanation of his own attitude.

208. Letter to the newspaper, *Svenska Dagbladet*, of Stockholm. Apparently published only in *Au-dessus de la mêlée*, 1915, where Rolland dates it April 10.

209. Letter to *Wissen und Leben*, *Mercure de France*, CX (1er avril 1915), 842–843. Dated from Geneva, February 11. Robert Faesi, of the staff of *Wissen und Leben* had insinuated that Rolland was taking advantage of the uniform price of 3 fr. 50 per volume set by Swiss publishers, by publishing a novel in ten volumes. Rolland here replies—he first published *Jean-Christophe* and other works in *Cahiers de la Quinzaine* for no material returns.

210. «Littérature de guerre,» *Journal de Genève* (19 avril). Published also in *Coenobium*, IX (aprile–maggio), 31–37, and in *Au-dessus de la mêlée*, 1915.

211. «Réponse de M. Romain Rolland à la question «Est-il admissible que la paix future sanctionne l'annexion de n'importe quel pays contre la volonté de ses habitants?»» *Les Documents du progrès*, IX (avril), 146–147. His reply is an emphatic "no", and he insists on the necessity of a just and durable peace.

212. «Le Meurtre des élites,» *Journal de Genève* (14 juin); also published in *Coenobium*, IX (agosto–settembre), 19–25; in *La Bataille syndicaliste* (30 juillet), where it appeared in a distorted and mutilated form, without a title; and in *Au-dessus de la mêlée*, 1915. He publishes letters found on German soldiers killed in the war, letters from an intellectual *élite*, who are horrified by the war and its cruelties. Among others there are extracts from letters of Dr. Klein. Their publication called forth in 1915 a biting and unjust article by August Messer.

213. Letter to Verhaeren, *Revue mensuelle*, XVIII (1918), 293–296, 332–333. Dated June 14 by Rolland.

214. Open letter to the *Journal de Genève,* in reply to the article «Les Deux cloches,» by Maurice Kufferath. Published in the *Journal de Genève* (Supplément, 27–28 juin). Kufferath had attacked Rolland's «Littérature de guerre.»

215. «Lettre à l'*Internationale Rundschau,*» *Gazette de Lausanne* (26 juillet); *Journal de Genève* (31 juillet); *Coenobium,* IX (giugno–luglio), 114–115; *Internationale Rundschau,* I (August), 158–160. A reply to the article by August Messer, criticising and attacking Rolland's article «Le Meurtre des élites.» Rolland announces that in the face of such complete lack of understanding and lack of opportunity to make his position known, he will retire from public discussions of his stand.

216. «Jaurès,» *Journal de Genève* (2 août); *Coenobium,* IX (giugno–luglio), 1–7, and in *Au-dessus de la mêlée,* 1915. Also appeared, according to Bonnerot, in a brochure, *Jaurès,* with a preface by Amédée Dunois, 16 pp., 1915, La Publication socialiste (Delasalle).

217. Letters to George Pioch, *Les Hommes du jour* (21 août, 13 novembre). The first letter also appeared in *Mercure de France,* CXII (1er octobre, 1915), 316–317. In one, he explains his reasons for retiring from public discussion of his stand; the other letter concerns the Nobel prize.

218. Letter to *L'Ecole de la Fédération* (organe des syndicats des institutrices et instituteurs publics), VI, No. 3 (9 octobre). Dated September 26. Rolland thanks them for taking his defense. He has always found more comprehension among them than among his colleagues of the "Enseignement supérieur." The future, he says, is in their hands.

219. «*Au-dessus de la mêlée. Introduction,*» *Revue mensuelle,* XVI, no. 169 (septembre), 103–105; *Journal de Genève* (4 novembre); *Coenobium,* IX (ottobre–novvembre), 102–103; *Bonnet rouge* (17 novembre 1916). Published also in 1915 in the volume of the same name, in a longer version and with various changes. The passage added in the volume follows the sentence: «Mais je ne savais point que je serais outragé, sans même être entendu.» The passage is as follows: «Pendant plusieurs mois, personne en France n'a pu connaître mes écrits que par des lambeaux de phrases artificieusement découpés, déformés par mes ennemis. C'est une grande lâcheté. Elle a duré presque un an. Si quelques journaux socialistes ou syndicalistes réussirent, ça et là, à faire passer quelques fragments[1], ce n'est qu'au mois de juin 1915 que, pour la première fois, mon principal article, celui qui était l'objet des pires accusations,—*Au-dessus de la mêlée,* —datant de septembre 1914, put être publié intégralement (presque intégralement), grâce au zèle malveillant d'un pamphlétaire maladroit, à qui

[1] Only one article, *Les Idoles,* was published in its entirety, in *La Bataille syndicaliste.*

je suis redevable d'avoir pu faire pénétrer, pour la première fois, ma parole dans le public de France.

Un Français ne juge pas l'adversaire sans l'entendre. Qui le fait, c'est lui-même qu'il juge et qu'il condamne: car il prouve qu'il a peur de la lumière.-» The article "Au-dessus de la mêlée" was first published in France by Henri Massis, in his *Romain Rolland contre la France*, H. Floury, 1915, with some changes; notably, the sentence concerning the Tsarist regime was omitted. Cf. Jouve, *Romain Rolland vivant*, p. 236, *infra*, no. 758.

220. Letter to Paul Seippel, published in part by Seippel, «Romain Rolland pendant la guerre,» *Journal de Genève* (4 octobre).

221. Letter to Alphonse Séché, published by Séché, *Nouvelles littéraires* (25 août 1934). Concerns Séché's *La Guerre d'enfer*.

222. Letter to Renaitour, *L'Ecole de la Fédération*, IV, 6 (30 octobre), 25–36. Rolland defends himself against Loyson, who attacked him for not having joined the *Comité de rapprochement franco-allemand* when invited. Rolland says that he is dubious about the amount of work accomplished by committees; he will continue to work for the same ends as a free individual. The question of Alsace-Lorraine must be solved. It is a crime, but there are other methods than war, which is the supreme injustice, for solving questions of injustice.

223. «Aux femmes d'Europe,» *ibid.*, VI, 12 (11 décembre), 69. Brenn (author of *Yves Madec*, Cahiers de la Quinzaine) sent to this periodical two fine works translated from the English. One is by Rolland, who appeals for the women of Europe, who can profoundly influence men, to use their influence for good. He cites his own case as the product of women's influence, and gives the credit to his mother and to Malwida von Meysenbug.

224. «Ara Pacis,» *Bonnet Rouge* (28 décembre); *Journal de Genève* (24–25 décembre); *Les Tablettes* (juillet 1917). In the *Journal de Genève*, Rolland writes: «*Ara Pacis* est le titre d'un recueil de poèmes et de récits, dont le plan était dessiné avant le commencement de la guerre. La page qui suit a été écrite dans la première année de guerre,—à part quelques retouches récentes. Noël 1915. R.R.» Cf. also the note in *Les Précurseurs*, where these verses appeared, pp. 11–13; the last stanza: «Ainsi que le grillon qui chante dans les champs,» was written in the Fall of 1919.

225. *Au-dessus de la mêlée*, Paris: A l'Emancipatrice. Preface by Amédée Dunois, authorized edition. Sold for the benefit of the «Agence internationale des prisonniers de guerre.» This edition contained: «Au-dessus de la mêlée,» and «Inter Arma caritas.» Fourth edition, Ollendorff, and Neuchâtel: Attinger frères, 1915, 168 pp.; 9th, 15th, 18th, 32nd, 48th, 49th, 62nd, 64th, and 65th editions, Ollendorff, 1915, 164 pp.; A. Michel, 1926, 254 pp.

1916

226. «A l'Antigone éternelle,» *Demain*, Geneva, I (janvier), 20–21. Published later in the volume *Les Précurseurs*, 1919. An appeal to women to combat war by love.

227. «A mon meilleur ami—Shakespeare,» *Book of Homage to Shakespeare*, I. Gollancz, editor, Oxford University Press, pp. 411–416, text in French, dated by Rolland, January, 1916. Published later in *Compagnons de route*, 1936, with the title, «*La Pitié de Shakespeare.*»

228. «La Vérité dans le théâtre de Shakespeare,» *Demain*, I, (15 avril), 193–208, 378, accompanied by a collection of texts; «Shakespeare sur la guerre,» pp. 209–215. Published later in *Compagnons de route*, 1936.

229. «Shakespeare. Pour le Tricentenaire de la mort du poète,» *Journal de Genève* (17 avril); article written for the *Book of Homage to Shakespeare*, according to Rolland. However, this is not the same article as no. 227.

230. «A Mes amis de l'Orient et de l'Occident, par Frédéric van Eeden,» *Demain*, I (15 mai), 298–299. The poem is dedicated to and written for Romain Rolland, who here publishes his translation from the German.

231. Letter to Alphonse Séché, published by Séché, *Nouvelles littéraires* (25 août 1934).

232. «Liberté,» *Demain*, I (15 juin), 403–404; *Avanti*, Milan, (1° maggio); *Les Précurseurs*, 1919.

233. Preface to *Une Voix de femme dans la mêlée*, by Marcelle Capy, Ollendorff. Both the text and the preface were mutilated by the censor. The preface was also published integrally in *Demain*, I (15 juin), 401–403, under the title: «Une Voix de femme dans la mêlée;» later in *Les Précurseurs*, 1919.

234. Letter in reply to the question posed by *La France* about the best method of propaganda and expansion for France, *Demain*, I (15 juillet), 62. His advice is to take care not to imitate the indiscreet means employed by Germany, which often causes a reaction in the wrong direction. The best propaganda is to bring to the world the best that France has to offer, and to leave to the Germans their dream of intellectual imperialism, which has done so much to discredit that nation. He warns that the prime condition for France to shine beneficently on the world is that she have *men*, and the war is costing many lives.

235. Letter, *ibid.*, I (novembre–décembre), 391–393. Concerning the Nobel prize.

236. Letter to Jean Longuet, *Bonnet Rouge* (31 juillet); *Le Populaire*, 24–30 juillet. Homage to Jaurès at the occasion of his commemoration. «Bien loin d'annihiler le rôle de l'individu, le socialisme doit en centupler la force: car il lui faut des hommes qui concentrent en eux toutes les énergies

dispersées des peuples et qui les projettent sur leur route en un puissant faisceau de lumière consciente.»

237. *Au-dessus ou au coeur de la mêlée?* Une polémique républicaine, par J.-B. Renaitour, Stéphane Servant et P.-H. Loyson. Letter from Romain Rolland. Edition de la revue *Essor*, 94 pp. The collection of articles that appeared in the *Bonnet Rouge*, 1914–1916, in the course of a dispute between these men about Rolland.

238. «Aux Peuples assassinés,» *Demain*, I (novembre-décembre), 257–266. Also published in *Les Humbles* (mai 1917), where it was partially censored, in *La Vie ouvrière*, 1ère année (29 octobre 1919), p. 3, and in *Bonnet Rouge* (25 mai 1917), where it was also badly censored (153 lines cut out). Published in an edition by the "Editions des Jeunesses socialistes romandes," La Chaux-de-Fonds, 1917, and again in 1920; and by the "Editions Communistes," Brussels, 1921.

239. Letter to the *Bonnet Rouge* (17 novembre). The letter is dated November 8, 1916. Also published in *Revue mensuelle*, Geneva, Supplément (novembre), 108–109. The writer's duty is to seek truth, and speak it out. Down with the "idoles du passé."

240. Letter to J. de G., published under the title «Romain Rolland et le prix Nobel,» *Journal de Genève* (16 novembre). He affirms his intention of giving the prize money to public welfare organizations.

241. «La Route en lacets qui monte,» *Le Carmel*, Geneva, (décembre). Published also in *Coenobium*, XI (gennaio-febbraio 1917), 1–6; *La Tranchée républicaine* (9–17 mai 1917); *L'Art libre* (Bruxelles), 1ère année (15 juin 1919), 1; *La Vie ouvrière*, n.s. 1ère année (29 octobre 1919), and in the volume *Les Précurseurs*, 1919. History, like a mountain road, circles, but rises slowly at the same time.

1917

242. «A Verhaeren,» *Les Humbles*(1917), 6–7; dated January by Rolland.

243. Letter to American writers; translated by Waldo Frank, it appeared under the title "America and the Arts," *Seven Arts*, N.Y., I (1916–1917, November 1916), 47–51. Also published under the title «Lettre aux écrivains d'Amérique;» *Revue mensuelle*, Geneva (février 1917), supplément, 2–4, and in *Coenobium*, XI (gennaio–febbraio), 109–110; appeared later in *Les Précurseurs*, 1919. A word of encouragement and advice to the writers of a younger, broader land, where the burdens and prejudices of the past are not so great, where the best interests of humanity can be truly served, as in the case of Walt Whitman.

244. «La Passion selon St. Mathieu de Bach à Bâle,» *Revue mensuelle*, Geneva (février–mars), pp. 252–254.

245. «Le Journal d'une escouade (*Le Feu* de Barbusse),» *Journal de Genève* (19 mars). Published later in *Les Précurseurs,* 1919.

246. Journal intime. «Feuilles détachées d'un journal de guerre» (entries for January 17, March 16, April 6 and 12, and for May), *Commune,* II (mars–avril 1935), 673–687, 848–862. He expresses his disgust at the title given to him of "European;" he wishes to belong, not to Europe alone, but to all humanity. He will have neither parties nor nations, but internationalism alone. Parts of these entries are very interesting because of his contacts with the revolutionary leaders in Switzerland, who were preparing to return to Russia.

247. Letter to *Pravda,* Moscow, March 31–April 1. Published by Rolland in «Feuilles détachées d'un journal de guerre. . . ,» *Commune,* II (mars–avril 1935), 673–687. He calls on his Russian brothers to surpass the French revolution by completing its work and giving to the Occident the example of a great and free people who reject and conquer all kinds of imperialism—within and without.

248. Letter to Heinrich Woltheim (Berlin). Dated May 7; published by Rolland in «Feuilles détachées d'un journal de guerre. . . . ,» *Commune,* II (mars–avril 1935), 856–857. This is a reply to a very enthusiastic man who wishes to found an United States of Europe, excluding England, Russia, and the Slavic peoples. Rolland explains his opposition to such an arrangement (he opposed Coudenhove-Kalergi's Pan-Europa for the same reasons, several years later). The idea is essentially a form of imperialism.

249. Letter to the *Gazette de Lausanne,* published in *Coenobium,* XI (marzo–aprile), 57–58. A reply to the attack on him by F. Castets in the *Gazette de Lausanne.* Also published in *Revue mensuelle,* XVIIIe année, pp. 285–286. To prove that neither he nor his thought is isolated, Rolland cites the numerous letters of gratitude and sympathy that he had received in the last two years from French soldiers and officers. His own ideas on war, he says, are not only current in France, but have even been surpassed.

250. «A Maxime Gorki,» *Demain,* II (mai), 6–7: article dated January 30; also published in *Coenobium,* XI (maggio–giugno), 57–58. Collected later in *Les Précurseurs,* 1919.

251. *Salut à la Révolution russe,* par Romain Rolland, P.-J. Jouve, H. Guilbeaux, F. Masereel. Geneva: éd. de la revue *Demain,* 32 pp. Publication announced in *Demain* (mai 1917). Appeared in German, in *Die Friedenswarte,* XIX (Juni), 174–175.

252. «Ave, Caesar, morituri te salutant» (Dédié aux spectateurs héroïques et à l'abri), *Revue mensuelle,* Geneva (mai), 267–271. Dated April by Rolland. Collected later in *Les Précurseurs,* 1919.

253. «Tolstoï: l'esprit libre,» *Les Tablettes,* Tolstoy number (1er juin).

254. Letter to Gorky, fragment published in «Lettres à Maxime Gorki,» *Demain*, II (juin), 83–84.

255. «La Jeunesse suisse,» *Demain*, II (juillet), 69–81, dated June by Rolland. Collected later in *Les Précurseurs*, 1919.

256. Letter to Wullens, director of *Les Humbles*, in *Les Humbles* (juillet), p. 31. Rolland assures Wullens that he is in complete sympathy with the magazine.

257. Letter to M. Gustave Ador, president of the International Committee of the Red Cross. *Bonnet Rouge* (3 juillet). Rolland asks the Red Cross to accept his gift of fifty thousand francs for the "Agence internationale des prisonniers de guerre," and asks that ten thousand be put at the disposition of Dr. Ferrière. He pays high tribute to the work of the Red Cross.

258. «Voix libres d'Amérique,» *Demain*, II (septembre), 272–284; and in *Coenobium*, XI (settembre–dicembre), 18–26, in a text mutilated by the censor. Collected in *Les Précurseurs*, 1919.

259. Letter to Alphonse Séché, published by Séché in *Nouvelles littéraires* (1er septembre 1934).

260. «Jean-Christophe et la musique allemande,» «Voix d'un Européen sur les ruines de l'Europe . . . ,» *Revue mensuelle*, XVIII (septembre), 19–21; (novembre), 82–84. These are extracts from *La Révolte* and *L'Adolescent*.

261. «Ave Caesar . . . ceux qui veulent vivre te saluent,» *Revue mensuelle*, XVIII (octobre), 37–41, and in *Les Précurseurs*, 1919.

262. «Un grand européen,» *Demain*, II (octobre), 337–357; (novembre), 13–30; the article also appeared in the *Avenir international*, (mars–septembre 1918), under the title; «*La Biologie de la guerre* du docteur Nicolaï,» and in the *Revue mensuelle*, XVIII, 129–130, in part. Collected later in *Les Précurseurs*, 1919.

263. «L'homme de douleur. *Menschen im Krieg* par Andreas Latzko,» *Les Tablettes*, Geneva (décembre). Dated November 15 by Rolland. Collected later in *Les Précurseurs*, 1919.

264. Completely censored article, *Coenobium*, XI (settembre–dicembre), 88–89. Under the title "Gli Efetti" there are two blank pages, with the initials R. R. at the end.

265. Letter to E. Platzhoff, published by Platzhoff in "Romain Rolland und der Krieg," *Christliche Welt*, XXXI, No. 39, cols. 704–707. He says that he is working on two books inspired by the war: one the spiritual study of a French thinker, the other a fantastic satire in free dramatic form. The books referred to are *Clerambault* and *Liluli*.

266. Letter to the editor of the *Open Court*, Lydia G. Robinson, *The Open Court*, XXI, 45–50. Translation of part of the letter.

267. Letter to *Demain*, *Demain*, II (novembre), 87. A protest against

the unauthorized publication of his writings, or parts of his writings, by *La Paix*, "Journal politique d'économie sociale," a German publication animated by a spurious pacifism.

268. *A la civilisation*, n.d., 30 pp. This pamphlet contains: «La Route qui monte en lacets,» and «Aux peuples assassinés;» in the appendix: «Le Message de l'Inde au Japon . . . de R. Tagore, traduit de l'anglais par André Jouve d'après la revue américaine: *The Outlook*, N. Y.»

269. *Le Triomphe de la Liberté*, Fête populaire. Poem by Rolland; music by Albert Doyen. A. Leduc, xi, 273 pp. Preface by Rolland, who quotes from Rousseau and others on the subject of "fêtes populaires."

1918

270. Preface to Nicolaï, G.-F., *Die Biologie des Krieges. Betrachtungen eines deutschen Naturforschers*. First edition, Zürich: Orell-Füssli, 1917; incomplete and full of errors. Second edition, 2 vols. (called "erste Original-ausgabe"), Zürich: Orell Füssli, 1918. Rolland's preface, in French and German, on pp. ix, xii. Also published in the *Revue mensuelle*, XIX (1919), 220–222.

271. «Voix chrétiennes contre la guerre,» *Revue mensuelle*, XVIII (février), 177–181. Rolland brings news of what churches or church groups are doing toward international good will, and quotes from various pastors, especially in Germany. There are not many, "Mais, ce n'est pas le nombre qui compte dans le royaume de l'Esprit,—dans le royaume de Dieu,—c'est la pureté du coeur et l'ardeur de la foi." He adds, "Chrétien de race et d'éducation, je me suis . . . détaché, depuis de longues années, de la religon chrétienne, parce que je n'y trouvais plus un flambeau assez brûlant et assez haut pour diriger les pas et réchauffer les coeurs de l'humanité fraternelle."

272. *Empédocle d'Agrigente et l'âge de la haine*. Maison française d'art et d'édition, 48 pp.; and Geneva: *Cahiers du Carmel*, 1ère série, no. 1, 48 pp.

273. Letter to the deputy, Paul-Meunier, director of *Vérité*, published first in *Demain* (février), p. 275. Dated February 4. Its publication in *Vérité* had been forbidden by the censor. Rolland congratulates Paul-Meunier for his lecture on persecution for "délit d'opinion," and on the trial of Hélène Brion.

274. «A Propos d'un Institut des Nations pour une culture universelle,» *La Revue politique internationale*, IX (janvier–juin), 226–232. Collected later in *Les Précurseurs*, 1919, under the title: «Pour l'Internationale de l'Esprit;» dated March 15 by Rolland.

275. Letter to Werner von Heidenstam, published by Jonas Fränkel, "Spitteler und Romain Rolland," *Frankfurter Zeitung* (28. April, 1925). Rolland supported Spitteler for the Nobel prize.

276. «En lisant Auguste Forel,» *Revue mensuelle,* XVIII (août), 386–394. Dated June 1 by Rolland. Collected later in *Les Précurseurs,* 1919.

277. «Pour l'internationale de l'esprit humain,» *Le Populaire* (11 juin). A much shorter version of the article which appeared in *La Revue politique internationale*; *supra,* no. 274.

278. Letter to B. H. Clark. Quotations from the letter were published by Clark in his preface to the translation of *Le Théâtre du peuple,* N. Y.: Holt.

279. Letter to Jean Longuet, *Le Populaire* (15 août). Rolland enquires whether *Le Populaire* is still being sent to him, and congratulates Longuet on the victory of his motion at the Conseil Fédéral de la Seine.

280. «Je fais appel à une Révolution allemande,» *Le Populaire* (29 août); letter to Jean Longuet, dated August 22. This article was announced by Rolland in a telegram to Longuet, which was published in *Le Populaire* (25 août); «Reçu votre numéro du 20 août. Je suis entièrement d'accord avec vous contre Rozier. Ma pensée reste la même. Lettre suit. Romain Rolland.» The article: «Je fais appel à une Révolution allemande,» is partially in reply to *Le Populaire's* report of a dispute in *Wissen und Leben,* especially an article by Fernau ("Romain Rolland und der Weltkrieg"). *Wissen und Leben* for August 15 had appeared a few days late, and had not yet reached Villeneuve from Zürich, when on the 20th the press reported on the article by Fernau. Rolland's article is a reply to the latter, who begged Rolland to extend his sympathy, as a French Republican, to the Republican cause in the German revolution. Rolland continues to assert that he is the enemy of all imperialisms, and consequently of Germany's (Prussia's); but it is up to the German people themselves to get rid of their imperialism. Rolland believes that there can be a durable peace only: (a) if the feudal Prussian cast be abolished; (b) if this be accomplished by the German people themselves. Fernau's article had made Rolland appear to be a "jusquauboutiste," and Arthur Rozier, writing in *France Libre* (20 août), had seized upon this to attempt to discredit both Rolland and *Le Populaire.*

281. Letter to Gerhardt Hauptmann, *Bonnet Rouge* (23 septembre). Germany has been betrayed by her rulers (her men of action and especially Prussia) and by her intellectuals.

282. «Hommage au Dr. A. Forel, pour son soixante-dixième anniversaire (1er septembre),» *Revue mensuelle,* XVIII (octobre), 27–28.

283. «Réponse à l'enquête: Une Révolution allemande est-elle possible?» *Le Populaire* (28 octobre). He points out the great disparity between the German government, feudal in essence, and contemporary German thinking, which is even more free than French thought. «Les âmes qui, en Allemagne (et même en Angleterre, où elles sont moins nombreuses, mais non

moins intrépides), ont une fois brisé le respect de l'autorité,—de toutes les autorités—ont atteint à une audace de liberté politique, sociale et morale, que rien n'arrête plus et qui est prête à saccager et à fouler aux pieds les dernières conventions auxquelles les plus libres d'entre nous Français, restent encore attachés. . . .» If the German revolution is not channelized, says Rolland, by a wise and strong emperor or chancellor who can direct it instead of combatting it, great violence will result. He sends his sympathy to German liberals, for the cause they fight for is the liberty of the world. They must succeed.

284. «Devant la Révolution russe,» *Le Populaire* (16 novembre). «Je ne pense pas qu'il soit utile de définir une fois de plus ma position morale. . . . Elle n'est ni politique ni sociale. Elle est *humaine*. Je suis absolument opposé à la violence, d'où qu'elle vienne . . . je n'appartiens à aucun parti. . . . Je ne suis pas bolchévik. Mais . . .» and he enumerates three principal reasons for his support of the Russian revolution: (a) the willful distortion of news about Russia and the revolution; (b) the attitudes of the Allied governments toward Russia since the revolution,—they have done everything possible to create difficulties and to create violence, in an endeavor to throw Russia into the hands of their worst enemy: Germany; (c) his belief that revolution is born of war, and that, to stop the one, the other must be stopped. But war exists because of the abominable social organization of Europe. To combat error and injustice wherever he finds them is his duty. «Car l'avenir de la civilisation humaine est seulement dans le mutuel amour et l'estime mutuelle.»

285. «Un Appel aux Européens par Georg-Friedrich Nicolaï,» *Wissen und Leben*, XXI (1. November), 66–72. The article is dated October 20 by Rolland. Collected in *Les Précurseurs*, 1919, published also in *Les Ecrits du midi* (25 novembre–10 décembre 1918), and extracts in *Mercure de France*, CXXXI (1er janvier 1919), 123–125.

286. «Lettre ouverte au Président Wilson,» *Le Populaire*, (18 novembre); also in *Amsterdammer Weekblad* (23 november). Letter dated November 9 by Rolland. Collected in *Les Précurseurs*, 1919, and the *Revue mensuelle*, XIX (janvier 1919), 145–146.

287. Letter to Jean Longuet, published in *Le Populaire* (3 décembre). Collected in *Les Précurseurs*, 1919, where Rolland gives an erroneous date for its publication in *Le Populaire* (4 décembre). In support of President Wilson's principles.

288. «Contre les barbares,» letter from Rolland to Louise Bodin, *Le Populaire* (18 décembre). Protests against the implacable reply of the «Conseil national des femmes françaises,» to the entreaties of German women. He publishes a heart-breaking letter from a friend who had just returned from Austria.

289. Letter to Jean Longuet, *Le Populaire* (21 décembre). Letter dated December 12. Collected in *Les Précurseurs*, 1919, under the title: «Contre le Bismarckisme vainqueur.»

290. «Journal des années de l'après-guerre.» Extracts published in *Clarté* (juin, septembre, octobre, novembre 1937).

1919

291. «Sur un martyr (Liebknecht),» *Avenir international*, No. 13 (janvier), 36–38.

292. «La ligue «Nouvelle Patrie» et la Révolution allemande,» *L'Humanité* (27 janvier). Concerns the *Bund Neues Vaterland.*

293. «Janvier sanglant à Berlin,» *L'Humanité* (16, 17, 18 février); collected later in *Quinze ans de combat*, 1935. He points out the counter-revolution in Germany, especially the crushing of the Spartacists, which the Allied governments have stupidly applauded; he foresees a threat to the future peace of the world.

294. «Freistätten des Geistes. Ein Offener Brief von Romain Rolland an Georg Friedrich Nicolaï,» *Das Forum*, III (Januar), 243–249. A résumé was published by Nicolaï in his brochure, *Romain Rollands Manifest und die deutschen Antworten, mit einem Anhang uber den Fall Nicolaï*, Charlottenburg: Mundus Verlagsanstalt, 1921, pp. 13–15. This letter to Nicolaï was written à propos of Nicolaï's *Aufruf an die Europäer*. Rolland emphasizes the importance of idealism at the present time. Men will fight for an ideal, but not for purely material interests. Man must therefore be freed of his "Idoles", especially of those created by his own intellect. The duty of thinkers is to help people to understand others. They must not put their intellect in the service of reaction or of revolution, but of all mankind. «Au lieu de «connais-toi, toi-même»;—«connais les autres».»

295. Letter to Paul Vaillant-Couturier, *Le Populaire* (21 avril). The war, he says, is not over. This gigantic crisis must first come to an end. France must reform its bonds solidly with their friends all over the world, especially with the Slavic peoples. The East is going to become more important. It is very probable that he and his contemporaries may be swept away in the changes that are coming; nevertheless, he welcomes them.

296. Signature to the «Appel et manifeste du groupe Clarté,» *Le Journal du peuple* (19 mai).

297. «Le calvaire d'un poète prolétaire (Alfons Petzold),» *La Vie ouvrière* (21 mai). A friend of Petzold's wrote to Rolland, justifying Petzold in Rolland's eyes (see Rolland, «Littérature de guerre,» in *Les Précurseurs*); most of this article is a résumé by Rolland of the book *Aus dem Leben und der Werkstätte eines Werdenden, Alfons Petzold*, Vienna: Anzengruber, 1913.

298. «Déclaration de l'Indépendance de l'esprit,» *L'Humanité* (26 juin); also in *Das Forum*, III (August), 901–904. Collected later in *Les Précurseurs*, 1919, with a list of signers, and also in *Quinze ans de combat*, 1935.

299. Letter to E. Adam, published under the title: «Romain Rolland et l'Espéranto,» *La Vie ouvrière* (6 août). Letter dated June 25 by Rolland; it appeared also in *Le Journal du peuple* (19 août). This is a word of encouragement and support for esperantists. «Il faut obtenir que dans toutes les écoles primaires d'Europe, l'Espéranto soit officiellement enseigné et rendu obligatoire. Il ne peut être, sans cela, de rapprochement international sérieux et durable. Pour que les peuples s'entendent, il faut d'abord qu'ils *entendent.*»

300. «Vox clamantis . . . *Jérémias*, poème dramatique de Stefan Zweig,» *Coenobium*, XII (1° Luglio), 3–5. Rolland dates its composition November 20, 1917. It was published later with many additions, in *Les Précurseurs*, 1919.

301. «A la Russie libre et libératrice,» *Le Populaire* (22 juillet). The French revolution was one of the great bursts of energy of humanity, but it eventually succumbed to the many obstacles it encountered. Rolland hopes and expects that his younger brothers of Russia will have the energy necessary to carry on this revolution.

302. Article in *La Vie ouvrière* (22 octobre). In answer to Eugène Pictet's criticism of Bolshevism that it is «anarchie gouvernementale sanglante,» Rolland points out that this is even more true of a social state that has, in four years, resulted in the death and mutilation of twenty to thirty millions of people, and that Bolshevism has tried to organise this chaos and tried to bring new social formulae into the moral and material ruins of Europe.

303. «Contre le blocus affameur. Une résurrection certaine. Une lettre de Romain Rolland,» *L'Humanité* (26 octobre). He dates the letter October 23. Published later in *Quinze ans de combat*, 1935. In *L'Humanité* (27 Octobre) he brings a correction to the text as it had appeared the previous day. «Juristes retors» should read «légistes retors.»

304. *Colas Breugnon, bonhomme vit encore!* Ollendorff, iii, 324 pp.; written 1913–1914, printed at the moment when war broke out, and released in the spring of 1919. It ran through 52 editions, Ollendorff, the same year; definitive edition, revised by the author, containing «Commentaires du petit-fils à Colas,» A. Michel, 1919, 317 pp.; «Oeuvres complètes,» reprinted again in 1930; edition, Ollendorff, 1920, in –18, iii, 335 pp.; illustrated edition, wood cuts by Deslignères, ed. Mornay, 1927, vii, 319 pp., Collection «Les Beaux Livres.» In 1945 and 1946 various illustrated editions and deluxe editions appeared: Coll. «Athéna-Luxe». Illustrated with ten illustrations not numbered in the text; edition illustrated by Théo van Elsen; 78 original lithographs, «papier d'Arches.» 15,000 fr. Edition illustrated by André

Collot, engravings by Bracons Duplessis, Coll. «Les meilleurs auteurs contemporains,» an edition selling for 8,000 to 2,500 francs, depending on the paper and the number of illustrations; edition illustrated by Benno Vigny, edit. Jeanniard, distributed by Fatout, 28 original lithographs, selling for from 30,000 to 12,500 francs depending upon the paper and the varying number of illustrations. In addition, *Colas Breugnon* was published serially in *L'Humanité* (10 février—27 mars 1936).

305. *Liluli*, Original edition, 32 wood cuts by F. Masereel. Geneva: Le Sablier, June, 800 copies; Ollendorff, 1920, illustrations after the wood cuts by Masereel, 166 pp.; 16th edition, Ollendorff, 1920; A. Michel, 1926, 218 pp.

306. *Les Précurseurs*, Paris: édition de l'Humanité, 231 pp.; 3rd edition, Ollendorff, 1923, viii, 233 pp.; 11th edition, A. Michel, 1931, viii, 237 pp.

307. *Voyage musical aux pays du passé*, plates by D. Galanis. Paris: Edouard-Joseph, 273 pp. Collection «Petites curiosités littéraires;» 2nd edition, Hachette, 1920, 247 pp.

1920

308. «Appel pour le premier Congrès de l'Internationale Intellectuelle,» *Clarté* (24 janvier); in collaboration with Duhamel and Barbusse; also published in *L'Humanité* (25 janvier).

309. «Un livre de Raymond Lefebvre. Le Sacrifice d'Abraham,» *L'Humanité* (19 mars). He particularly admires in Lefebvre the fusion of pessimism of the intelligence, which pierces every illusion, and of the optimism of the will.

310. Introduction to *Poètes contre la guerre*, an anthology by Arcos et Masereel, *La Vie ouvrière* (16 avril); and in *L'Humanité* (15 avril). It appeared later as the introduction to the volume *Les Poètes contre la guerre*. Anthologie de la Poésie française, 1914–1919. Geneva: Kundig, ed. Le Sablier.

311. Letter to E. Adam, under the title: «L'Opinion de Romain Rolland sur l'espéranto,» *La Vie ouvrière* (23 avril). Letter dated April 14 by Rolland. «. . . l'Internationale elle-même . . . ne reste qu'un mot; car les peuples ne peuvent avoir connaissance les uns des autres que par l'intermédiaire de quelques correspondants de journaux. Or, une telle situation est inadmissible pour des démocraties qui revendiquent (justement) le droit de contrôle sur leurs affaires étrangères, et qui doivent pouvoir communiquer directement entre elles. Mon espoir est qu'en ceci comme dans le reste, la République des Soviets décidera et que le socialisme d'Occident suivra. Le cerveau du monde du travail est maintenant à Moscou.»

312. Letter to E. Adam, *ibid.* (7 mai). Dated April 20. He applauds the Soviets for the obligatory teaching of Esperanto in their schools.

313. Letter to Marcel Martinet, *La Vie ouvrière* (8 mai). Rolland extends

his sympathy concerning the measures that have been taken by the State against the *Vie ouvrière*, by means of the arrest of Monatte, the director. «Le mot de 'Démocratie' remplit le monde de son immense duperie: il est le masque dont se couvrent aujourd'hui les pires oppressions.» The letter is dated May 21.

314. Letter to the Communist daily, *Politiken*, of Stockholm, published in *La Vie ouvrière* (16 juillet). The letter is dated April 30. He expresses his admiration for the powerful organizing energy of the Soviets, and points out that there is in Russia a moral cause that pure Marxists fail to take sufficiently into account—«C'est le caractère pour ainsi dire religieux, l'enthousiasme mystique qui anime une partie de la classe ouvrière russe. *Ces hommes croient.*» In a note in the number of July 30, *La Vie ouvrière*, certain mistakes are pointed out in their translation of this letter from the *Politiken*; the letter as published in *Politiken* was itself a translation from the French. Rolland had not written: «Selon moi, seule une révolution communiste peut réussir,» but, «Seule, à l'heure actuelle, la révolution bolchéviste avait chance de réussir.»

315. «Lettre au Congrès des Instituteurs, à Bordeaux,» *La Vie ouvrière* (20 août), p. 1; and *Le Populaire* (19 août), where there are some changes, especially in the first six paragraphs. Letter dated August 6. A continuation, or addition, to this letter appeared in *La Vie ouvrière* (20 août), under the title «La Réforme de l'enseignement,» dated August 7. It is an appeal in favor of Monatte, recently arrested. The first letter was later collected in *Par la révolution, la paix*, 1935.

316. «Pour les militants emprisonnés. Protestation de Romain Rolland,» *L'Humanité* (4 octobre). Protest against the «détention préventive» of various militants and the excessive length of Monatte's emprisonment. «Une république qui n'est capable de répondre à ses adversaires de pensée que par la violence et le bâillon, se condamne elle-même.»

317. «Suprême hommage,» *L'Humanité* (5 décembre). In honor of Raymond Lefebvre, who had recently died in the course of a mission to Russia. The letter was also sent to the director of *Rassegna internazionale*, who published extracts, *Rassegna internazionale*, II (1920–1921), 635. «Ce destin n'avait rien de mélancolique. . . . Ce jeune homme, beau, riant . . . à qui un avenir lumineux était promis, aimait passionément la vie. Le don qu'il en faisait d'avance n'était pas un acte de désespoir. C'était l'ivresse sacrée de la nature au printemps, cette largesse de vie qui se répand des plantes et des arbres dans l'air, en millions de germes féconds. En s'offrant à la mort, il se donnait à la vie; à une vie plus haute, plus large que la sienne, à l'humanité heureuse et délivrée.»

318. «Au nom de Beethoven,» *Le Populaire* (18 décembre). Written at the request of Longuet, for the 150th anniversary of Beethoven's birth,

which is being celebrated even in ruined and starving postwar Vienna. He pleads for human and sensible treatment of Austria.

319. «Pour le cinquantenaire d'André Marty,» *Commune*, IV (décembre 1936), 385–388. Extracts from Rolland's Journal, originally written at the time that he had received various documents from the two brothers of Lieutenant Marty, who had been condemned to twenty years of forced labor for his part in the revolt of the French sailors in the Black Sea. This was published also in *L'Humanité* (10 décembre 1936).

320. *Clerambault*, histoire d'une conscience libre pendant la guerre, Ollendorff, 378 pp. The work reached the 19th edition, Ollendorff, 1920; 41st edition, A. Michel, 1930, in −16, 319 pp.

321. *Pierre et Luce*, Original edition, 16 woodcuts by Frans Masereel, Geneva: Le Sablier, 177 pp.; 2nd to 10th editions, Ollendorff, copyright 1918; 11th edition, Ollendorff, 1921, with four hors-textes and 29 woodcuts by Gabriel Belot, 191 pp.; ed. Carnet Critique, 1921; 25th ed., illustrated with woodcuts by Gabriel Belot, in −16, A. Michel, 1925, 197 pp.; 47th ed., A. Michel, 1928, 190 pp.

1921

322. «Monatte,» *La Vie ouvrière* (25 février); published also in *Rassegna internazionale*, III (maggio), 146–149. Monatte and Rolland, the latter explains, work, by different means, for the same goals: international faith, truth without frontiers, free criticism of all nations, union of all the peoples of the world. Monatte works on the plane of action, Rolland on the plane of the intellect. And Rolland refuses to join any party. He intends to work as an idealistic individual. «Pas plus qu'à la Nation, je ne crois au Prolétaire (avec une majuscule); . . . Patriotisme de race, patriotisme de classe, jamais je ne veux d'aucun patriotisme, il ne me faut pas moins que toute l'humanité.»

323. «Lettre à la défense, en faveur de Monatte,» *La Vie ouvrière* (11 mars). He flays the crimes and errors of governments. Justice is the first necessity. «Veut-on mettre fin aux révoltes? Il n'est qu'un seul moyen: mettre fin aux injustices. Il est à la portée de tous les gouvernements.»

324. «Per un martire,» *Rassegna internazionale*, III (marzo), 45–48. French text. A preface for the posthumous work of Marc de Larréguy de Civrieux, published in Paris, Société mutuelle d'édition, 1920. Larréguy de Civrieux, killed at Verdun, had, like Rolland, penetrated the lies of «La Patrie,» etc. Rolland hails a thought which had gone the same way as his own. (Cf. Rolland's «Les Idoles,» and what he said concerning the effect of war upon thought in the «Prologue» and «Panorama» of *Quinze ans de combat.*)

325. Letter to Lucidi, director of the *Rassegna internazionale*, extracts

published by Lucidi, *Rassegna internazionale*, III (maggio), 131–149. Concerns Rolland's discussion with Barbusse and the group *Clarté*. Rolland does not wish his principles and claims to be confused with *Clarté's* claims and principles. The question of violence, even temporary, separates them. Rolland explains his unconditional opposition to violence.

326. «Contre la loi super-scélérate. Une lettre de Romain Rolland,» *L'Humanité* (3 juillet), p. 1. Dated June 29. Written at the occasion of certain reactionary laws, which were being urged by the forces of reaction in France; this open letter displays a very solid optimism concerning the death and disappearance of nationalism. «Pour nous, toutes les lois 'scélérates' ne font qu'affirmer davantage la scélératesse de la guerre. Au reste je ne suis nullement en peine pour la liberté de pensée. Elle se sauvera beaucoup plus sûrement que les millions de pauvres diables qui ont laissé leur peau pour une cause illusoire. Historien de profession, je sais que jamais un fanatisme n'est plus intolérant que lorsqu'il se sent en danger. . . . Attendons sans trouble. Ce qui doit mourir mourra. Les idoles meurtrières du passé, l'une après l'autre, s'écroulent. Ce n'est jamais sans victimes. Mais ces victimes-là, du moins, seront pour le Droit, et pour la Liberté.»

327. Introduction to *Les Vaincus* (drame inédit), dated July, 1921, by the author. Cf. *Les Vaincus*, 1897. «Un nouveau devoir s'imposait à moi, une voie de salut pour tous, qui n'était ni l'acceptation de la violence, ni le renoncement à la vie, mais l'affirmation de l'âme libre, qui se refuse à transiger avec toute tyrannie, et dont la mission propre est de défendre contre les Réactions, comme contre les Révolutions, l'idéal sacré de la Liberté de l'Esprit,—libre de tous les pouvoirs laïques et religieux, libre de toutes les Eglises, libre de toutes les Patries, libre de toutes les frontières nationales et sociales,—et fraternel à toutes les âmes libres du monde entier.» To show the continuity of his thinking, he publishes some notes of 1897 which reveal the similarity between his state of mind then and now.

328. Telegram to Jean Longuet, *Le Populaire* (2 octobre). Rolland expresses his desire to share in the manifestation of sympathy for André Marty.

329. Letter to Ludwig Hatvany («Über Pazifismus und Bolschewismus»), *Frankfurter Zeitung* (13. November), 3. Concerns Hatvany's *Das Verwundete Land*. Rolland says that Pan-Humanism, or, in its narrower form, Pan-Europeanism, has not become, and cannot become a reality for a long time. The essence of a great belief or ideal is to outstrip the present. Those who think they can bring about an ideal in the present, damage the ideal; they have no conception of the great efforts that are necessary. This is the error that Clerambault made. Rolland is not a pacifist in the current sense of the word; life is tragic as Jean-Christophe knew.

330. «Pour le centenaire de Flaubert,» *Rassegna internazionale*, III

(dicembre), 1171–1172; dated December 12 by Rolland. Rolland's Flaubert is a free individualist who does not allow himself to be shut up in the cage of any dogma or prejudice.

331. Letter to J.-R. Bloch, published by Bloch in his *Destin du Siècle.* Seconds essais pour mieux comprendre mon temps. Rieder, 1931, pp. 244–245. Another satirical attack against «le poison idéaliste.»

332. Letter to a Russian revolutionary, published in part in *L'Art libre,* Brussels, IV (janvier 1922), 2.

333. Preface to F.-J. Bonjean, *Une histoire de douze heures,* Rieder, 230 pp.

334. Preface to Frederick van Eeden, *Le Petit Jean,* tr. by S. Harper-Monnier, Rieder, 1921. This work with the preface also appeared in Spanish translation: *Juan y el elfo,* Buenos Aires: Librería y editorial El «Ateneo» de Pedro García, 1942. Rolland praises Eeden and his work for his virile optimism, the joy that radiates from his pages, the sun that penetrates the pages and scenes of his book. Rolland says that when he first read Eeden,—the autobiographical *Happy Humanity,*—he had the impression of discovering the purest social conscience, since Tolstoy, in European art.

335. Preface to Nadel, H. (i.e., Henri Joseph Vendel), *Sous le pressoir.* Société mutuelle d'édition, 188 pp.

1922

336. «Lettre ouverte à Henri Barbusse,» *Clarté,* n.s., No. 6 (1er février), 126–127; first published in *L'Art libre,* Brussels (janvier). Reply to an article by Barbusse: «L'Autre moitié du devoir. A propos du Rollandisme,» *Clarté,* n.s., No. 2 (3 décembre 1921), 25–28. Barbusse replied to Rolland's letter, «Lettre à Romain Rolland. A propos du Rollandisme,» *ibid.* (1er février), 127–128.

337. Letter to Barbusse, published by the latter, «A Propos du Rollandisme,» *ibid.*, n.s., No. 10 (1er avril), 221–225. Rolland's reply to the last of the above articles by Barbusse. Barbusse replied in the same article. The complete discussion was also published in *Rassegna internazionale,* IV (1922), 5–13, 14–17, 17–18, 180–181. Rolland later published his own letters in this polemic in *Quinze ans de combat,* 1935. This is a clear refusal to associate himself with communism, although he sees its good and necessary aspects. He explains his refusal to associate with the group *Clarté*; the questions of violence, of the ends and the means, and of free criticism, are the main reasons for his refusal. In his second letter he extols non-acceptance (not non-resistance), for this is a supreme resistance—it is a very great moral force.

338. Letter to Amédée Dunois, *L'Humanité* (12 mars). Rolland calls for

a society in which there shall be no privileged classes,—either above or below—, in the face of supreme human values.

339. «La Révolution et les intellectuels,» *L'Art libre*, Brussels (avril). Continues the ideas and beliefs expressed in the polemic between Barbusse and Rolland.

340. Letter to J. Gondry. Fragments published by M. Huebner, «Belgischer Brief,» *Das Literarische Echo*, XXIV (1. April), cols. 812–815. Rolland praises the efforts toward Flemish independence, but hopes that they will first conquer spiritual and moral independence and liberate themselves from the past, and even from the present.

341. Letters to Dilip Kumar Roy, published by Roy, *Among the Great*, Bombay, 1945, pp. 66–69, 6–7, 69–71. Dated March 20, July 7, and November. The translations are apparently by Roy. In the first Rolland says that there is no gulf between the musical art of Europe and Asia; all is part of the same unity. There are some interesting remarks about the nature of genius. In the second letter: "I am persuaded that an art is never great but that it appeals to the most ignorant. Certainly not completely, nor with its supreme appeal. But a great creation in art must contain enough wherewith to satisfy the spiritual hunger of all. . . ." In the third letter Rolland says that Tolstoy is a bad guide, a statement he further explains and clarifies. Rolland also points out the necessity of recognizing two essential elements in man's nature: the social man and the individual man.

342. Letter to Amédée Dunois, published under the title «Le Banditisme du capital aux Etats-Unis. Une lettre de Romain Rolland,» *L'Humanité* (15 juin). Letter concerning the post-war reaction in America, especially of anti-labor groups. Rolland had received documents from friends in the United States.

343. «L'Elite européenne et la Terreur,» letter from Rolland to Albert Mathiez, *Clarté*, n.s., No. 16 (1er juillet), 372–374. In reply to Mathiez' article: «L'Elite européenne et la Terreur,» *ibid.*, (1er juin); Mathiez' reply to Rolland's letter, *ibid.*, (1er juillet), 373–374. The discussion concerns principally Wordsworth and his attitude toward the Terror. See *Quinze ans de combat*, 1935, p. 55.

344. *L'Ame enchantée*. I. *Annette et Sylvie*. Ollendorff, 6th edition, 1922, 282 pp. The Introduction is dated August, 1922. The volume was also published separately in 1946, Editions Hier et Aujourd'hui. Désir de lire. Nouvelle collection populaire.

345. Preface to Ananda Coomaraswamy, *La Danse de Çiva*, Quatorze essais sur l'Inde. Translated from the English by Madeleine Rolland. Rieder, in –16, 259 pp. Rolland emphasizes the need of better knowledge of oriental philosophy and civilization, especially those of India, so that humanity may work its way toward the unity necessary for its salvation.

1923

346. «Ne res judicata pro veritate habeatur,» *The New Student,* II (January 27), 1, 2. Arguments for a pan-humanistic education.

347. «Mahatma Gandhi,» *Europe,* I (février–mai), 129–163, 267–310, 427–454; dated February by Rolland. Included later in his *Mahatma Gandhi,* 1924.

348. Article in *Rassegna internazionale,* V (maggio), 345; collected later in his *Quinze ans de combat,* 1935, under the title: «Sur l'occupation de la Ruhr.» This fatal policy of the conquerors will have for inevitable consequence further war between France and Germany.

349. «Une réunion internationale d'écrivains à Londres,» *Europe,* II (juin–septembre), 102–106. Collected later in *Quinze ans de combat,* 1935, under the title: «Pour la réconciliation franco-allemande. 1. Au P.E.N. Club de Londres (pour la première réunion internationale du Club international des écrivains).» The original article contains eight more paragraphs than the article in *Quinze ans de combat.*

350. «Une réunion internationale des écrivains à Londres,» *Rassegna internazionale,* V (giugno–luglio), 632–642. Among various topics he discusses are: the universality of thought and literature; Hardy, Spitteler, and his own *Jean-Christophe.* Reviews of some of the addresses. This is a résumé of his lecture. Dated by Rolland May, 1923.

351. «Le Conflit de deux générations: Toqueville et Gobineau,» *Europe,* III (octobre–décembre), 68–80; published later in *Compagnons de route,* 1936. Dated by Rolland July 1.

352. «Un Gorki balkanique,» *Europe,* II (juin–septembre), 257–259. Concerns Panaït Istrati. Published later as the preface to *Kyra Kyralina* by Istrati, J. Ferenczi et fils, «Le Livre moderne illustré,» 1932. How Rolland came to know Istrati, and the latter's suicide attempt.

353. Postface to Rauze, Marianne, *L'Anti-guerre,* essai d'une doctrine et d'une philosophie de l'anti-militarisme en 1923. Postface by Rolland. Prefaces by W. Wellock and Dr. H. Stoecker. Niort: Impr. du «Progrès,» in –16, xii, 200 pp.

354. Introduction to *La Montespan,* for American readers, translated by Helen Van Brugh de Kay, N. Y.: B. W. Huebsch. Text in French and English. He claims the right for the dramatic author to falsify historic events somewhat in his dramas, providing that he reproduces, by means of details that are true, the moral and spiritual atmosphere of the epoch. The truth of the moral atmosphere will make a truer work than will an unimaginative, uninspired imitation of facts.

355. Article about Léon Werth, *Les Cahiers d'aujourd'hui,* No. 11. Appeared also in *Mercure de France,* CLXII (1er mai 1923), 765–768.

1924

356. «Pour les affamés d'Allemagne,» *Europe*, IV (janvier–avril), 233–234; dated December, 1923. Published also in *Rassegna internazionale*, VI (febbraio–maggio), 266–267; and in *Quinze ans de combat*, 1935, under the title: «Appel aux Français pour venir en aide aux malheureux d'Allemagne.»

357. «Paroles de Renan à un adolescent,» *Europe*, IV (janvier-avril), 257–266; dated December 26, 1923, by Rolland. Also published in an edition, Paris: ed. de la Belle Page, 1930, in −16, and collected later in *Compagnons de route*, 1936.

358. Address sent by Rolland to the meeting organized by the French section of the Women's International League for Peace and Freedom, January 15, at Geneva. Women's International League for Peace and Freedom, *Pamphlets on Peace*, No. 79, 4 pp. Published later in *Par la révolution, la paix*, 1935. The peoples of the world must maintain cordial international relations, in spite of the sinister manipulators of politics and finance, who wish to keep the peoples separated for selfish reasons. Mutual help is one means, and an effective one.

359. «L'Inde depuis la libération de Gandhi,» *Europe*, IV (janvier–avril), 507–514; dated end of March by Rolland. In a note on p. 507, Rolland writes: «Ces pages paraissent en *post-face* à la vingt-et-unième édition du volume *Mahatma Gandhi*, publié chez Stock.»

360. Open letter, *La Vie ouvrière*, I.S.R. (bulletin bimensuel, édité par le Bureau de l'Internationale Rouge . . .), No. 26 (16 mai), 3. He joins the appeal in favor of the teachers who have been dismissed for «délit d'opinion,» but refuses to request amnesty for them, for amnesty means that there was originally guilt, and actually there was none. The spirit of solidarity among teachers must be developed.

361. Letter to Dilip K. Roy, in Roy, *Among the Great*, Bombay, 1945, pp. 71–73. Dated October 1. Rolland finds certain of his own ideas in a book by Sri Aurobindo; a further proof of affinity between the Aryan of the Occident and the Orient.

362. *L'Ame enchantée*. II. *L'Été*, Ollendorff, 362 pp.; 6th ed., A. Michel, 1926, 356 pp.

363. *Mahatma Gandhi*, Librairie Stock, 186 pp.; it went through 17 editions; new edition, revised, corrected and enlarged, postface, Delamain, Boutelleau et Cie, 1924, 48th ed., according to the cover; this edition was republished by Stock, Delamain et Boutelleau, 1926, 1929, 1930, and 1946, 212 pp.

364. Introduction to *La Jeune Inde* (Recueil d'articles de Mahatma Gandhi, 1919–1922), translated by Mlle Hélène Hart, Stock, xxi, 381 pp. The introduction appeared also in *La Revue européenne*, IV (1924), 1–15.

365. Preface to Jean de Saint-Prix, *Lettres* 1917–1919, Rieder, 264 pp.

1925

366. «Souvenirs et entretiens de Carl Spitteler,» *Europe*, VIII (15 mai), 61–76; dated April by Rolland. Collected later in *Compagnons de route*, 1936. It also appeared in German translation in the volume, *Carl Spitteler. In Memoriam*, by H. Burte, J. Fränkel, and A. Steffen. Jena: E. Diedrichs, 1925, 35 pp., Rolland, "Unser Homer."

367. *Le Jeu de l'amour et de la mort*, Ed. Le Sablier, 163 pp.; ed. A. Michel, 1925, 256 pp.; and in *La Petite illustration*, No. 373. Théâtre No. 202 (10 mars 1928). The play was given for the first time at Paris, January 29, 1928, at the Odéon. Edited for school use by Albert D. Menut and Dwight Chapman, N. Y. and London: Century Co., 1928; and London: Longman's Modern French Plays, 1929.

368. "Music and Life," translated by Dr. Kalidas Nag, *Visva Bharati Quarterly*, III (1925–1926), 64–66. Concerning music in his childhood and youth.

369. «Réponse de M. Romain Rolland à l'enquête «Que pensez-vous de la guerre du Maroc?»,» *Clarté*, IV (15 juillet), 273. «Je ne juge pas utile de m'étendre à ce sujet, car chacun sait que je suis opposé à toute guerre. . . . Celle-ci a de particulier que, même au point de vue national, il faudrait la condamner. Elle est ruineuse pour la France. . . . J'accuse les gouvernements de la France et de l'Angleterre (pour ne point parler des moindres puissances d'Occident) de déchaîner sur l'Europe, par leur obtuse politique, par leur impérialisme brutal et cupide, par leurs provocations continues, l'immense insurrection des races d'Asie et d'Afrique.

«. . . Quant aux communistes, qui ne voient dans ce soulèvement des peuples que la ruine de l'impérialisme, je les avertis que les forces déchaînées ne distingueront pas entre l'impérialisme et le communisme d'Europe et que sous le rouleau d'Asie, le bolchévisme de Moscou, un jour, sera anéanti.»

370. Reply to an address given at the Russian State Academy of Sciences and Arts. Letter dated October 20. Rolland published a short extract in *Quinze ans de combat*, 1935, p. xxxvii.

371. Introduction to Tagore, R., *A Quatre voix*, translated by Madeleine Rolland. Simon Kra, in −16, 223 pp., and portrait. Collection de la *Revue européenne*, no. 12. The introduction is a study of Tagore.

372. Letter to Philippe Soupault; extracts published by Soupault, «Confiance en Romain Rolland,» *Europe*, X (1926), 231–233. «Voici onze ans que j'ai vu cette guerre insensée ébranler les piliers de la civilisation d'Europe . . . je vois le destin. Et le destin est sage quand les peuples sont fous. . . .»

373. Letter to Toshihiko Katayama (Tokyo). Extracts published in the *Bulletin de l'Association des Amis de Romain Rolland* (janvier 1948), 34–36.

1926

374. Letter to Henry Torrès «. . . pour être lue comme témoignage à décharge, dans le procès de la rue Damrémont (bagarres entre fascistes français et communistes), 23 avril 1926,» published in his *Quinze ans de combat*, 1935, p. 67, under the title «Vita sine libertate nihil.»

375. «Ignavia est jacere,» *Zürcher Student* (April), 28–33. Collected later in *Par la révolution, la paix*, 1935.

376. «Extraits des lettres de R. Tagore à diverses personnes,» *Europe*, XI (15 août), 490–491. Tagore denounces Italian fascism. See *Quinze ans de combat*, 1935, p. xli.

377. Letter to A. M. Curtius. Extracts in German translation in "Romain Rolland und die deutsche Musik . . . ," by Curtius, *Neue Zeitschrift für Musik*, XCIII, pp. 13–15. Cf. "Music and Life," translated by Kalidas Nag, 1925, and *Souvenirs d'enfance*, by Rolland, where he tells what music meant to him in his childhood.

378. Letter to Jean Guéhenno, in *Hommage à Romain Rolland*, Lausanne: Ed. du Mont-Blanc, 1945, pp. 149–152. Dated December 22 and concerns a lecture by Guéhenno, some considerations of European affairs, and some remarks about Catalonian songs.

379. Letter to Joe Newman, translator of *Souvenirs d'une révolutionnaire*, by Irène Kachowskaia, Rieder. Fragments of the letter are published in the preface.

380. *Pâques fleuries*. Original edition. Le Sablier; Geneva: Kundig, 173 pp.; ed. A. Michel, 1926, 255 pp.

381. Preface to J.-R. Bloch, *Simler & Co.* German translation from the French by Paul Amann, Zürich: Rotapfel Verlag, 399 pp. Preface to the English translation, "— *& Co.*," by C. K. Moncrieff, N. Y.: Simon & Shuster, 1929. The Introduction by Rolland is not in the French «édition définitive.»

382. Preface and letter to Virgilio Brocchi, *Selon mon coeur*, translated by M. P. Ronzy, E. Flammarion, 284 pp.

383. Preface to Charles de Coster, *La Légende d'Ulenspiegel et de Lamme Goedzak au pays des Flandres et ailleurs*. German edition, Munich: Kurt Wolff, illustrations by Frans Masereel; ed. Le Sablier, 1936; edition illustrated by F. Rops, Editions sociales internationales, 1937; edition published in Moscow: Coopérative d'éditions des ouvriers étrangers en U.R.S.S., 1936, xxx, 574 pp., preface by Boris Pourichev; study by Romain Rolland. Rolland's study appeared also in *Europe*, XIII (15 janvier 1927), 5–22, and in *Compagnons de route*, 1936; and partially in *Les Humbles* (9 janvier 1937).

384. Preface to Marc de Larréguy de Civrieux, *La muse de sang . . . poèmes et légendes*, Librairie du travail, 63 pp.

385. Preface to Frans Masereel, *Bilder der Grossstadt*, 112 engravings and preface, Dresden: C. Reiszner, 128 pp.

386. Preface to Stefan Zweig, *Amok*, ou Le fou de malaisie, translated from the German by Alzir Hella and Olivier Bournac. Original woodcuts by Michel Jacquot. J. Ferenczi et fils, 1939, 158 pp. «Le Livre moderne illustré;» and ed. at Le Cabinet Cosmopolite (No. 13), 1927.

387. *Le Voyage intérieur*, chapters from, for 1926–1940. *Le Périple* (1926–1940), Editeur, Emile Paul, 1946.

1927

388. Letter to Marcel Fourrier, published by Fourrier, «M. Romain Rolland prend position,» *Clarté*, VI (15 janvier), 158. Fourrier had accused Rolland of not having taken a definite stand concerning the questions which agitate the modern world (*Clarté*, V [octobre–décembre 1926] p. 124). Rolland replied in this letter to Fourrier: «Mais si . . . j'ai «pris position»—et depuis longtemps, je suis *contre* tous les assassins—fascistes ou révolutionnaires. . . . Je ne ménage personne. Je ne fais alliance avec personne. Je suis seul. . . .»

389. *L'Ame enchantée*. III. *Mère et fils*, 2 volumes, A. Michel, vol. I, 334 pp.; Vol. 2, 256 pp. (24 février).

390. «Beethoven. Pour le Centenaire de sa mort» (extraits de son *Beethoven. Les Grandes époques créatrices* . . .), *Europe*, XIII (janvier–avril), 289–315.

391. «Actions de grâces à Beethoven,» *Revue musicale* (1er avril), pp. 3–14. These pages were read at Vienna, at the centenary Festival, by Rolland. Published also in German translation in *Beethovenzentenarfeier*, Festbericht, Vienna, 1927, pp. 66–74.

392. «Les Fêtes du centenaire de Beethoven à Vienne (26 mars–2 avril 1927),» *Europe*, XIV (mai–août), 115–118; dated April by Rolland. Reports of the meetings.

393. «Fonti Fortitudinis ac Fidei,» *Deutsches Beethoven Fest, vom* 21. *bis* 31. *Mai* 1927, Bonn: Hofbuchdrückerei Carthaus, 144 pp. Rolland, pp. 57–78. An authorized translation. Rolland pays tribute, not to the great musician, but to the great man, the individual.

394. Telegram in defense of Sacco and Vanzetti, *Le Populaire*, (12 avril). Telegram to Coolidge, signed by Barbusse, Rolland, and Einstein.

395. Letter to Filippo Turati, May 11. Partially published in *Quinze ans de combat*, 1935.

396. Letter to Gaetano Salvemini, May 28. See *Quinze ans de combat*, 1935, p. lxxiv. Rolland flatly denies that he is a communist.

397. «Goethe et Beethoven,» *Europe*, XIV (avril–juin), 5–32, 184–212;

appeared later in the volume of the same title, rearranged and enlarged; it is the first essay in the volume.

398. «Lettre au *Libertaire* sur son enquête sur la répression en Russie,» *Europe*, XV (15 octobre), 270–271. Reproduced in *Quinze ans de combat*, 1935. Rolland blames Moscow for the abuse of force, but points out the gravity of the situation for Russia. Moreover, the Russian revolution is the greatest and most fecund effort of modern Europe, and is the hope of the world. Jean Brecot, *La Vie ouvrière* (17 juin), blames Rolland severely for replying to this query of an anti-communist paper—and blames Rolland for not taking a more active part in the communists' struggle.

399. Letter to Lunacharskii, *Europe*, XV (septembre–décembre), 272. Rolland's reply to an invitation addressed by Lounatcharskii to associate himself with the newspaper *Pravda*, *Europe*, XV, pp. 271–272. Rolland's reply was published later in *Quinze ans de combat*, 1935.

400. Letter to Lucien Price. «Lettre à un ami américain,» *Europe*, XV (septembre–décembre), 238–242. Published later in *Quinze ans de combat*, under the title «Lettre à un ami américain sur le meurtre judiciaire de Sacco et Vanzetti.» Dated August 24.

401. «La Lettre à l'Immortelle Aimée,» *Revue musicale*, VIII (octobre), 193–207. Rolland tries to determine the date of the letter from Beethoven to his unknown beloved.

402. «Note de Romain Rolland à la lettre d'un ami américain, James H. Powers, au sujet de l'exécution de Sacco et Vanzetti,» *Europe*, XV (septembre–décembre), 526–527. Rolland also published the letter from Mr. Powers, *ibid.*, 524–525.

403. Letter to *Peuple* (Brussels), *Le Populaire* (3 octobre). Concerning Mme Matteotti.

404. Letter to Me. Mauranges, defender of Georges Chevé, condemned to six months imprisonment for refusing military service; published by Relgis, E., in *L'Internationale pacifiste*, Appendix B., pp. 145–147.

405. «La jeunesse et la révolution,» published in French and English in *Vox Studentium*, The International Student Magazine, Geneva, V (November), 1–2, 3–4, and later in *Par la révolution, la paix*, 1935.

406. «Réponse à l'invitation adressée par *Voks*, pour les fêtes du Xe Anniversaire de la Révolution d'Octobre,» *L'Humanité* (7 novembre); collected later in *Quinze ans de combat*, 1935.

1928

407. «Réponse à Constantin Balmont et à Ivan Bounine,» *Europe*, XVI (janvier–juin), 246–252; dated January 20. This is the reply to «Le Martyre des écrivains russes. A Romain Rolland—Un appel désespéré de

Constantin Balmont et d'Ivan Bounine,» *L'Avenir* (12 janvier). Rolland published his reply also in *Quinze ans de combat*, 1935.

408. Letters to Hans Leo Götzfried, January 6, February 21, June 23, July 5, November 13. Extracts in Götzfried, *Romain Rolland. Das Weltbild im Spiegel seiner Werke*, 1931.

409. «Romain Rolland. Extrait inédit de son journal,» *Rhythmes du Monde* (Lyon), No. 2 (1948), 8–11. Extracts dated January, February, March 7. Gandhi and the Berthallon brothers who refused military service. Gandhi's criticism—and Rolland's criticism of Gandhi. Rolland publishes a letter he wrote to Mira (Madeleine Slade), January 21, on this subject. In the entry for February he summarizes Gandhi's reply to his letter of January 21, and the last extract is from a letter to Gandhi concerning Gandhi's participation in the World War, 1914–18.

410. *Beethoven. Les Grandes époques créatrices*. I and II. *De l'Héroïque à l'Appassionata*. Ed. originale, Geneva: Albert Kundig; Paris: Ed. du Sablier, 21 janvier. 2 vols. 1–251, 252–441 pp. 1283 copies printed; 2nd ed., Le Sablier, one vol., 378 pp., 1929.

411. «Les Léonides,» *Europe*, XVI (15 février), 153–158; dated October 28, 1927. This appears as the preface of the volume of the same name.

412. *Les Léonides*. Original edition. Wood-cuts by Lucien Boucher. Le Sablier, 207 pp.; A. Michel, 1928, 252 pp.

413. *L'Enfance de Jean-Christophe*, pages choisies par l'auteur. Saumur: l'École Émancipée. Editions de la jeunesse. Publication mensuelle, vol. 1 (avril), vol. 2 (2 juin), in –12, 72 pp.

414. «Léonore,» *Revue musicale*, IX (1er juillet), 225–259; extract from *Beethoven. Les Grandes époques créatrices.*

415. «La Réponse de l'Asie à Tolstoï,» *Europe*, XVII (15 juillet), 338–357, accompanied by a letter written by Tolstoy, two months before his death, to Gandhi, pp. 357–360. According to a footnote: «Cette étude forme un chapitre d'une nouvelle édition de la *Vie de Tolstoï* par Romain Rolland, que va publier la librairie Hachette, à l'occasion du Centenaire.»

416. «Beethoven. Les Soeurs Brunsvik et leur cousine du «Clair de lune»,» *Revue musicale*, IX (1er octobre), 417–444; from *Beethoven. Les Grandes époques créatrices.*

417. Message to *La Volonté de paix*, *La Volonté de paix*, No. 5 (octobre–novembre–décembre); also published in *Par la révolution, la paix*, 1935.

418. Letter to D. K. Roy, in Roy, *Among the Great*, Bombay, 1945, pp. 64–66. Corrections to Roy's manuscript account of their interview. There are some interesting observations on progress, Christ, genius, the effect of great art.

419. «Adresse au Congrès National de toute l'Inde,» *Europe*, XVIII

(décembre), 583–584. He expresses his wish that India may escape the nationalist stage in its development toward a modern state.

420. «L'Inde en marche,» *ibid.*, 473–490; an extract from the *Essai sur l'action et la mystique de l'Inde nouvelle*. Similar ideas to the preceding article.

421. Preface to Wladimir Astrow, *Rudolf Maria Holzapfel der Schöpfer des Panideal. Ein Neues Leben*. Jena: E. Diedrichs, xxiv, 74 pp.

422. *Souvenirs d'enfance*. La Charité-sur-Loire: imprimerie A. Delayance, in –32, 22 pp. Collection Blanche. (*Bibliographie de la France*, 30 mars 1930). Beckwith, *op. cit.*, pp. 7–8, quotes from these memoires, of which he gives the date as 1927. A large part had already appeared in Rolland's letter to A. M. Curtius.

423. «Der Sturm der Gewalt fegt über die Welt,» *Gewalt und Gewaltlosigkeit*, Handbuch des aktiven pazifismus. Edited by Franz Kobler, Zürich and Leipzig: Rotapfel Verlag, n.d. [before 1929], 388 pp. Rolland, pp. 17–18; extract from his *Mahatma Gandhi*.

424. «Vivekananda et Paul Deussen,» *Fünfzehntes Jahrbuch* (1928) *der Schopenhauer-gesellschaft*, pp. 143–165. Rolland published estracts of the *Life of the Swami Vivekananda by Eastern and Western Disciples*, pp. 153–158; and an article, «Lassen, Deussen, et Max Müller,» pp. 158–163.

1929

425. Extracts from his *Essai sur la mystique et l'action de l'Inde vivante* (Ramakrishna and Vivekananda), *Europe*, XIX (janvier–avril), 153–181, 305–336, 465–500; XX (mai–août), 31–63, 497–537; XXI (novembre), 337–356.

426. Article in *Le Cri des Peuples* (10 février). The article concerns the Versailles treaties. «Quand un traité de paix (?) crée partout, en Europe, un état de guerre,—disjoignant ce qui est fait pour vivre ensemble,—et ligotant ensemble ce qui s'entredévore,—il ne faut pas s'étonner que surgisse la dictature. Elle est le fruit de l'arbre que la France de la Victoire a planté. Qui sème le vent récolte la tempête. Le vent est semé.»

427. «Feuilles d'herbe. A Léon Bazalgette,» *Europe*, XX (mai–août), 143–157; dated February by Rolland.

428. «La Piraterie de la paix,» *ibid.*, XXI (septembre–décembre), 431–435. Collected later in *Par la révolution, la paix*, 1935, with various changes. Since he is opposed to all forms of imperialism, he is opposed to the "Pan-Europa" movement which will exclude Russia. A discussion of the secret motives behind such pan-european plans makes his stand clear.

429. Letter to the director of *Asia*, in *Asia*, XXIX (October), 761. Part of the letter is published in English translation.

430. *Essai sur la mystique et l'action de l'Inde vivante.* I. *La Vie de Ramakrishna.* Librairie Stock, Delamain et Boutelleau, 2 décembre, in –16, 319 pp.

431. II. *La Vie de Vivekananda et l'Evangile universel,* 2 vols., Librairie Stock, Delamain et Boutelleau, 20 janvier 1930, in –16, 191 and 253 pp., portrait.

432. Introduction to Henry T. Schnittkind, *The Story of Eugene Debs.* Boston: National Education Committee of Independent Workmen's Circle, 204 pp. The Introduction bears the title: "The Supreme Energy—the Energy of Peace and Love," pp. 15–21.

433. Letter and Message in Relgis, E., *L'Internationale pacifiste,* A. Delpeuch, copyright 1929, 151 pp.

1930

434. «Avec le grand peuple russe! Deux voix lancent l'appel contre les forces de réaction,» *Monde,* Paris, III (19 avril), 3. Theodore Dreiser and Romain Rolland. See *Quinze ans de combat,* 1935, «Pour la défense de l'U.R.S.S.,» and p. xlviii.

435. «Bettine,» *La Revue des vivants,* IV (avril–juillet), 762–768, 944–957. This is the fifth chapter of *Goethe and Beethoven.*

436. «Goethe musicien,» *Europe,* XXIII (mai–août), 324–353, 498–516; extract from his *Goethe et Beethoven,* 1930.

437. Letter to D. K. Roy, in Roy, *Among the Great,* Bombay, 1945, pp. 73–74. Letter dated June 3.

438. Reply to a questionnaire: «Quelle sera votre attitude en cas d'aggression contre l'Union soviétique?» *L'Humanité* (9 juillet). Rolland again denies that he is a communist, but affirms that he has great faith in Russia and in her beneficial effect on existing social orders.

439. Letter to Eugène Relgis, dated October 20; partially published by Rolland in *Quinze ans de combat,* 1935, p. lxxv, 102–111.

440. *Goethe et Beethoven.* Edition originale. Le Sablier; Geneva: Albert Kundig, 287 pp., engravings and facsimile; Le Sablier, 1930, in –16, illustrations and engravings; Le Sablier, 1931, 4 p. (13) –311 pp. Contents: Prélude. Goethe et Beethoven. Le Silence de Goethe. Goethe musicien. Bettine. Annexes: La Marseillaise en Allemagne; Lettre de Bettine sur la musique.

441. Preface to L. Rai, *L'Inde malheureuse.* Rieder, 365 pp.

442. «Zum Gedenkfeier für Rudolf Maria Holzapfel,» in *Rudolf Maria Holzapfel zum Gedächtnis,* Basel: B. Schwabe & Co., 48 pp.; Rolland, p. 5. See Preface to Astrow, W., 1928.

1931

443. Letters to V.O.K.S., January 29 and February 4, *Quinze ans de combat*, pp. xlviii, lxxv; partially reproduced.

444. Letter to Mr. Dwight Chapman, February 8; translated in "Tribute to Professor Chapman," *Bostonia*, Alumnus Magazine, Boston University (February, 1934), p. 9.

445. Letter to Feodor Nikolaevitch Petrov, *La Revue des indépendants*, (1er novembre); and *Das Neue Russland*, VIII No. 4/5 (Mai–Juni), 33. Insists that the long article «Adieu au passé» (1931), in which is generally seen his first break with the past, is only a symbol, and that he had reached that point as early as 1917.

446. Correspondence with Runham Brown about Einstein's declaration concerning refusal of military service. Published in *Par la révolution, la paix*, 1935.

447. «Europe, élargis-toi, ou meurs! Réponse à Gaston Riou,» *Nouvelle revue mondiale*, No. 2 (février). Riou's article «Les Etats-Unis de l'Europe ou les Etats-Unis du monde» had appeared, *ibid.*, No. 1 (janvier). Riou answered Rolland's article, *ibid.*, No. 3 (mars). Riou called upon Rolland to aid in the creation of the new league, France-Europe. Rolland replied that this league would only be a mask for the old imperialism. He will work for it only when three conditions are fulfilled: 1. previous revision of the peace treaties, which guarantee the imperialism of 1914–1919; 2. Russian participation; 3. justice for the Orient.

448. «Suite à Europe, élargis-toi, ou meurs!» *La Paix mondiale*, No. 4 (avril–mai). Reply to Riou's second article. Rolland published both of his own articles in *Quinze ans de combat*, 1935. They appeared also in *La Révolution prolétarienne* (5 avril), and *Tunis socialiste* (5, 6, 7 octobre).

449. Letter to Georges Pioch, partially published in translation by Dr. Hans Götzfried, in an article about Rolland in the *Kölnische Zeitung*, No. 62 (3. März). Calls for revision of the peace treaties.

450. "Three Conversations. Tagore talks with Einstein, with Rolland, and with Wells," *Asia*, XXXI (March), 139–143. Rolland, pp. 142–143.

451. Letter to Jean Guéhenno, published in *Hommages à Romain Rolland*, ed. du Mont-Blanc, 1945, pp. 152–158. Dated March 14. Rolland comments on his ideas of the 20's.

452. Letter to Serge Radine, March 19; partially reproduced in *Quinze ans de combat*, 1935. He insists that men must not be judged by the ideas they profess, but by their deeds and actions.

453. «Lettre ouverte. Le cancer,» *Libertaire* (16 avril). A protest against the French military service law, following an appeal by *Libertaire*.

454. Letter to Henri de Noter, who published it in his *Guirlande d'Epines*

See the article «Romain Rolland et la *Guirlande d'Epines,*» *Voix de Femmes* (1er mai).

455. Letter to Edmond Privat, May 5. Published by Rolland in *Par la révolution, la paix,* 1935.

456. «Lettre ouverte à Fernand Després,» *L'Humanité* (12 mai); dated from Villeneuve, May 9. A discussion of the imperialist activities in French Indo-China.

457. Letter to the meeting for the liberation of Tao, and for the independence of Indo-China, *L'Humanité* (20 mai).

458. Letter to Lunacharskii, published in *Das Neue Russland,* VIII, 4–5 (Mai–Juni), 33; first published in *Izvestia,* March 23.

459. «Adieu au passé,» *Europe,* XXVI (juin), 161–202; fragments of an introduction originally written for foreign editions of *Au-dessus de la mêlée* and *Les Précurseurs.* He published this article also in *Quinze ans de combat,* 1935. Rolland says that in order to write this introduction, he had to review his thinking of the period 1914–1931, and his ideas then took form in a chapter which will probably be included in the autobiographical *Le Voyage intérieur.* Parts of this article also appeared in the *Cri du peuple,* Paris (24 juin).

460. Letter to the «*Ligue Anti-Impérialiste,*» for a meeting in the salle Bullier at Paris. See Romain Rolland, «Politique coloniale,» *L'OEuvre sociale* (18 juillet). He again expresses his unalterable opposition to Pan-Europa, in which he sees an association of the capitalism of France, Germany, and the other "big business" democracies.

461. Review of *Une jeune Chinoise à l'armée révolutionnaire,* by Pin Yin, translated into French by Ouang Té Yio, Valois, in *L'Intransigeant* (18 juillet).

462. Letter to Gladkov and Selvinsky, February; reproduced in «La Liberté individuelle,» *Lu,* Paris (7 août). The article appeared also in *Quinze ans de combat,* 1935.

463. Letter to Soviet newspapers. Published also in *La Métropole,* Antwerp (9 août). Because of his poor health Rolland refuses Kalatov's invitation to pass the summer in Russia. He must, he says, continue to live, since he is almost the only man in Europe to defend the U.S.S.R.

464. Preface to the *Vie de M.-K. Gandhi, écrite par lui-même, Europe,* XXV (janvier–avril), 465–490; and partially in *L'Horizon,* Brussels (19 septembre); preface to the translation from the English by Georgette Camille, Rieder, xlvii, 412 pp.

465. «Appel pour l'entr'aide franco-allemande,» *Europe,* XXVII (septembre–décembre), 98–99.

466. «Message au meeting pour le Désarmement, organisé à Genève le 30 octobre 1931 par la *Ligue Internationale de Femmes pour la Paix et la*

Liberté,» *Europe*, XXVII (septembre–décembre), 599–600. Collected in *Par la révolution, la paix*, 1935, under the title: «Il faut reviser les traités.»

467. «Appel à la lutte révolutionnaire,» *L'Humanité* (4 novembre). A revolutionary change in the existing social orders is the only way possible to attain true peace. He particularly directs his attention to China and Japan.

468. Telegram in the name of «L'Union du Balkan libre» to Muchanow, prime minister of Bulgaria, «La terreur sanglante en Bulgarie,» *L'Humanité* (11 novembre). Signed by Rolland, Karin Michaelis, and Arthur Hollischer.

469. *Empédocle d'Agrigente, suivi de l'Eclair de Spinoza*, Le Sablier, 134 pp. Édition définitive of *Empédocle d'Agrigente*. The *Éclair de Spinoza* is part of his "Confessions" or «Mémoires.» Much of it reappears in *Le Voyage intérieur*, 1945.

470. Preface to Gorki, *Eux et nous*. Published in *L'Humanité* (6 décembre); preface to the volume *Eux et nous*, Éditions sociales internationales, 1931, 304 pp., and later in *Quinze ans de combat*, 1935, under the title: «Au premier *oudarnik* de la République universel du Travail, salut d'un compagnon français.»

1932

471. «Goethe: «Meurs et deviens»!» *Europe*, XXVIII (15 avril), 509–533; dated December 31. Published later in *Compagnons de route*, 1935.

472. Letter to Gérard Lacaze-Duthiers, January 15. Published in *Par la révolution, la paix*, 1935.

473. «Courrier de l'Inde. (1) La déclaration de guerre de l'Angleterre à l'Inde,» (2) «Échec au Roi!» *Europe*, XXVIII (janvier–avril), 250–260, 416–427. Articles dated January 25 and February 25.

474. Letter to Mr. Dwight Chapman, February 17. Published in English translation, "Tribute to Professor Chapman," *Bostonia*. Boston University (February, 1934), p. 9.

475. «Nous en appelons . . .!» *Europe*, XXVIII (janvier–avril), 472. Appeal to aid anti-fascists against the rapidly developing fascism in Japan.

476. Letter to the periodical, *India Bulletin*, I (February), 10–11, in part.

476A. Preface to Zilzer, G., *Gaz*. Avant-propos de Romain Rolland. Paris: Editions du Phare; Grande Librairie universelle, 1932 (20 juin), in-folio, 4 pp. et 24 planches.

477. "Goethe en U.R.S.S.," *Europe*, XXIX (mai–août), 150–151; dated April 20. A very short résumé of Russian articles on Goethe which had appeared in *Izvestia* or *L'Héritage littéraire*.

478. «Appel pour le front uni des travilleurs intellectuels et manuels. Rassemblement! . . . La Patrie (notre patrie internationale) est en danger,»

L'Humanité (1er mai); also in *Quinze ans de combat*, 1935, and *Par la révolution, la paix*, 1935.

479. Letter to Richard Gerber, May 28. Published in part in Gerber, *Romain Rolland als Dramatiker*, pp. 19, 22, etc.

480. Letter, dated from Villeneuve, June 1, published in «Romēna Rollāna en Anri Barbisa *Uzsaukums*,» *Pret Kaŗu*. Fakti un materiali. Krājums iznākzem Vispasaules Pretkaŗu Kongressa (Amsterdam, 1932) Starptautiskas Iniciatives Komitejas godu redakcijas: Rolland, Barbusse, etc. (Contre la guerre, faits et documents), published in honor of the International Committee of the World Congress against War.

481. Letter to Paul Graber (Swiss conseiller national, director of *La Sentinelle*, socialist daily, La Chaux-de-Fonds), July 24; published in Europe, XXX (septembre–décembre), 151–152. A protest against an article by Graber (*La Sentinelle*, 22 juillet), in which he had tried to weaken the World Congress against War.

482. «Courrier de l'Inde. III «Révolution», le chef invisible,» *Europe*, XXIX (mai–août), 108–119; dated April 20 by Rolland. A discussion of the progress of the spirit of non-violent revolution in India after the arrest of Gandhi and the illegal suppression of the Indian National Congress.

483. "A Declaration by Romain Rolland" (read for him at the opening session of the Congress by Mme Duchene, Rolland being too ill to attend). *The World Congress against War. Report on the Congress*, opening address by Rolland, and the Manifesto adopted at Amsterdam, August 27–29, published for the American Committee for Struggle against War, N. Y.

484. «Un congrès de tous les partis contre la guerre,» *Europe*, XXIX (mai–août), 477–478. An appeal to all the peoples of all races, all nations, to organize a great congress for a powerful manifestation against war, and an appeal to send representatives to an organizing committee. Dated by Rolland June 5.

485. «Déclaration de Romain Rolland lue à la première séance du Congrès mondial . . . à Amsterdam, le 27 août . . . ;» «Le Congrès mondial d'Amsterdam contre la guerre;» «Réponse de Romain Rolland à la lettre du 16 juillet de Albert de Jong, Bureau International Antimilitariste, Haarlem . . . ,» *Europe*, XXX (septembre–décembre), 148–151, 249–255, 302–304. Also published in *Par la révolution, la paix*, 1935. Extracts in *Quinze ans de combat*, pp. lxxv-lxxvi, dated August 27, September 20, and July 31 respectively.

486. «A Jacques Robertfrance. Au compagnon de nos combats d'hier et de demain,» *Europe*, XXX (septembre–décembre), 305–312.

487. An article in *Dos Naye Wort* (Jewish monthly of the Independent Workmen's Circle), Lawrence, Mass., XIX, No. 9 (August).

488. «La Guerre est entre les mains du peuple ouvrier. Déclaration de

Romain Rolland lue à la première séance du Congrès (d'Amsterdam),» *L'Humanité* (28 août).

489. Message to Barbusse, read at the Congrès d'Amsterdam by Guy Jerram. Rolland was not present. *L'Humanité* (3 septembre). Calls for the "Front unique" and action.

490. Letter to Henri Barbusse; published in *Par la révolution, la paix*, 1935, pp. 61–64. Concerning the place which should be made for the Conscientious Objectors and Gandhistes, in the revolutionary movement developed at the World Congress against War at Amsterdam.

491. «Pour Henri Guilbeaux,» *Europe*, XXX (septembre–décembre), 471–472. A protest against the irregular action of the State, which accuses Guilbeaux of Bolshevik activities after 1919–1920, when Guilbeaux asked for a revision of the trial of 1918–1920.

492. «Tagore et Gandhi pendant le jeûne,» *ibid.*, 448–451. Rolland publishes information furnished him by C. F. Andrews, and telegrams exchanged between these men and others concerning Gandhi's fast. Very brief comments.

493. «Dankgesang. Erinnerungen an Malwida von Meysenbug,» Introduction to *Malwida von Meysenbug. Ein Briefwechsel* 1890–1891. Edited and translated by Berta Schleicher. The Introduction was translated by Axel Lübke. Stuttgart: Engelhorn; the Introduction, pp. 7–43. This appeared in an English translation: *Letters of Romain Rolland and Malwida von Meysenbug*, 1933, N. Y.: Holt. The Introduction appeared also in *Europe*, XXXIV (15 mars 1934), 305–335. For the correspondence with Malwida von Meysenbug see *supra*, no. 12.

494. *Revolt of the Machines;* or Invention run wild; a motion picture fantasy, translated by W. A. Drake, illustrated with wood cuts by Frans Masereel, Ithaca, N. Y.: The Dragon Press, 60 pp. *La Révolte des machines ou la pensée déchaînée*, Pierre Vorms, 1948.

1933

495. «Vers l'unité de l'Inde par l'entente hindoue-musulmane,» «L'Acquittement d'Henri Guilbeaux,» *Europe*, XXXI (janvier–avril), 107–110, 280. The second article is dated January 29.

496. «Les propos de Gandhi à Romain Rolland. Extraits inédits du 'Journal' de Romain Rolland,» *Figaro littéraire* (7 février 1948). Gandhi's visit to Rolland, December 1932. Rolland's description of Gandhi is very interesting. Various questions are discussed: art and truth, Christianity, violence; Gandhi's visit to fascist Italy.

497. *L'Ame enchantée*. IV. *L'Annonciatrice, Anna Nuncia*, 1. *La Mort d'un monde* (15 décembre), A. Michel, 370 pp.

498 *L'Ame enchantée.* IV. *L'Annonciatrice.* 2. *L'Enfantement,* 2 vols., A. Michel, 314 pp.

499. *L'Ame enchantée.* Edition définitive. *OEuvres complètes.* A. Michel, 1934, 4 vols., 544, 381, 489, 412 pp.; ed. Ollendorff, copyright 1922–1933, 7 vols., vols. 2–7 with the imprint, Paris: A. Michel. I. *Annette et Sylvie.* II. *L'Eté.* III. *Mère et fils,* 2 vols. IV. *L'Annonciatrice.* 1. *La Mort d'un monde.* 2. *L'Enfantement.*

500. Preface to Bosis, Lauro de, *Icare,* poème, translated by A.-F. Hérold. Paris: Claude Aveline, hors commerce. Edition limited to one thousand copies. Rolland's preface, «Euphorion,» dated February 15, pp. 9–23; another edition, Aulard, 1933. The "Euphorion" also appeared in *Europe,* XXXII (mai–août), 5–15, «Introduction à l'*Icare*. . . .»

501. «Documents sur l'Inde. I. Déclaration de Gandhi, au sujet de son jeûne pour les intouchables. II. Notes sur la place tenue par les Musulmans dans le mouvement national indien;» «Les Résolutions du Congrès national de toute l'Inde à Calcutta (mai 1933),» *Europe,* XXXI (janvier–avril), 254–257; XXXII (mai–août), 273–276.

502. «A propos du fascisme allemand,» «Pour les condamnés de Meerut, aux Indes anglaises, et contre le terrorisme colonial,» «Lettre ouverte à la *Kölnische Zeitung,*» «Appel à la jeunesse,» *Europe,* XXXI (janvier–avril), 440; 593–597; XXXII (mai–août), 288–289, 290–291. All were collected later in *Quinze ans de combat,* 1935. «Pour les condamnés de Meerut . . .» and «Appel à la jeunesse» also appeared in *L'Humanité* (18 mars, 25 juillet).

503. Letter to E. Bauchet, March 18; published in *Par la révolution, la paix,* 1935. Bauchet, general secretary of the «Comité d'organisation du Congrès de la Ligue Internationale des Combattants de la Paix,» had said that there are two wars: the war that the peoples make for their masters, and the war that the peoples make against their masters. Rolland replies that there is a third kind of war, the war that the masters make against the people—and this is fascism.

504. Interview with Rolland. P.-L. Darnar, «Chez Romain Rolland,» *L'Humanité* (26 mai). Rolland expressed confidence in the independence of India, in U.S.S.R. (he would like to participate in its work, if it were possible for him to do so). He discusses Panaït Istrati, whom he calls a counter-revolutionary agent.

505. «Pacifisme et Revolution: Adresse au Congrès mondial de Pâques de la Ligue internationale des combattants de la paix, 15 mars 1933.» Collected later in *Par la révolution, la paix,* 1935. It also appeared in German translation, "Pazifismus und Revolution," *Die Neue Weltbühne,* Paris, Prague, Zürich, XXXII (Februar 1936), 180–184.

506. Letter to Georges Pioch, President of the «Ligue Internationale des

Combattants de la Paix,» April 13; published in *Par la Révolution, la paix*, 1935. Against all fascisms. He ridicules the idea that Mussolini wishes to preserve the peace.

507. Letter to Reginald A. Reynolds, General Secretary of No More War Movement, July 12; published in *Par la révolution, la paix*, 1935.

508. Letter to Roger Bodard, published by Bodard in «Une lettre de Romain Rolland, ou Jean-Christophe dans la mêlée,» *Combat*, hebdomadaire belge, (1er septembre 1936). The letter from Rolland is dated October 12, 1933. Bodard could not understand Rolland's swing towards revolutionary materialism, so he wrote to Rolland, who replied in the letter here published. «Je vous disais que j'ai dépassé—non le grand coeur—mais l'humble destin et les limites étroites de l'oncle Gottfried . . . Gottfried n'était, ne pouvait être (for Christophe) . . . qu'un point de départ. Ce point de départ est essentiel. Mais il est essentiel d'en sortir. . . . L'honnête Gottfried ne dirait jamais: «Fais ce que je fais!»—mais «Je fais ce que je peux, fais tout ce que tu peux». Et qui fait «tout» ce qu'il peut, celui-là seul est un «héros». . . . Le premier bien est celui que l'on fait à son prochain le plus proche. Aucun homme n'a le droit de s'en désintéresser. . . . La politique, que vous dépréciez, n'est rien autre que l'action pour le prochain, lointain et proche, pour la défense et le progrès de tous les hommes. . . . Je ne reconnais à aucun homme, doué d'intelligence et de quelques loisirs, le droit de se désintéresser de la politique: car c'est se désintéresser des épreuves des autres hommes, de leurs souffrances et de leurs luttes. Et c'est d'ailleurs faire montre d'un égoïsme bien borné: car la grande vague de ces souffrances retombera sur ces autruches. . . . Je ne dis point de mal de la retraite, où je passe une part de mes journées. Mais se retirer, pour se concentrer,—et puis après, projeter dehors ses énergies. Au dehors? Non! au dedans! au dedans plus large, au plus grand Moi; le Soi du monde et ses combats. Le cours d'un fleuve est un combat. La vie est fleuve, et non étang. . . .»

509. «Appel pour Torgler,» *L'Humanité* (22 décembre), and *Quinze ans de Combat*, 1935.

510. Letter to Jean Guéhenno, December 23, in *Hommages à Romain Rolland*, Lausanne: Ed. du Mont-Blanc, 1945, p. 159.

511. «L'Appel de Romain Rolland au peuple d'Allemagne pour l'acquittement de Dimitrov et de ses compagnons,» *Monde*, Paris, VI (23 décembre), 3. Collected in *Quinze ans de combat*, 1935.

511A. Journal, Fragment for 1933, *Europe* (janvier 1946), 4–25.

512. Preface to Henri Prunières, *Nouvelle histoire de la musique*, published first in *Europe*, XXXIII (septembre–décembre), 319–325. Later in the volume, published by Rieder, 2 vols., 1934–1936. The preface as published in *Europe* contains numerous errors.

1934

513. «Lénine, l'art et l'action,» *Europe*, XXXIV (janvier–avril), 5–14. Also in *Compagnons de route*, 1936. Parts were also published, «Sur Lénine,» *Commune*, I (janvier–février), 562–563. Lénine and Goethe combined dream and action, both of which are necessary for the man of action and the artist.

514. Address sent by Rolland to the «Ecrivains révolutionnaires de l'U.R.S.S.,» upon the occasion of their international congress, August, 1934. Rolland published extracts under the title «Du Rôle de l'écrivain dans la société d'aujourd'hui,» *Commune*, II (mai 1935), 935–936. This article contains ideas that are very important for the understanding of his last works, such as *L'Ame enchantée. L'Annonciatrice, L'enfantement*. Collected in *Par la révolution, la paix*, 1935.

515. Letter to *International Literature* (Organ of the International Union of Revolutionary Writers), No. 6 (March), 153. Concerns the French issue of *International Literature;* a review of certain labor novels, which frequently lack one or the other of two necessary things: tension of a subjective conception, collision of characters. He counsels the publication of letters and diaries of young men and women workers, of such men as Aragon, who felt deep excitement at some moments of Soviet construction. It is important to know the attitudes of intellectuals, scientists, etc., towards the Revolution, towards proletarian labor; it is important to know how the honest among them were driven out of their conservatism by the very force of events.

516. "Kreuz und Rutenbündel," preface to *Österreich, Brandherd Europas*, Zürich: Genossenschaft Universumbücherei, 400 pp.; published later, in French, in *Quinze ans de combat*, «La Croix et le faisceau.»

517. «Appel au président Roosevelt. Pour Norris et Patterson!» *L'Humanité* (18 août); the Scottsboro case.

518. Letter to Maurice Thorez, *L'Humanité* (15 septembre). A very short letter in honor of Cachin.

519. «Pour sauver ceux qui meurent dans les prisons du Duce,» *L'Humanité* (27 octobre). Rolland's name heads the list of signers. The appeal was partly drawn up by Gabriel Péri.

520. *Die in den Gefängnissen Mussolinis sterben*, November. Zürich: Mopr-Verlag, 12 pp. Matteotti, Gramsci and others are the subjects of this brochure. Gramsci's life is briefly outlined. Rolland points up the differences between Hitler and Mussolini. Hitler is led by his ideas, his manias; Mussolini is not. Mussolini's ideas serve him. He knows and understands; in order to destroy, he denies (but he does not fail to understand); consequently he is above and worse than Hitler.

1935

521. «Quinze ans de combat. Prologue,» *Europe,* XXXVII (janvier–avril), 5–36, 153–175, 305–328; dated November 1, 1934. Published as the prologue and panorama of *Quinze ans de combat,* 1935.

522. Letter to the Minister of Justice of Bulgaria, *L'Humanité* (14 janvier). Georges Dimitrov and Rolland arise to defend the Bulgarian revolutionaries in danger of death. Letter from Dimitrov to Rolland. 520 military and civil proceedings against anti-fascist and anti-militaristic fighters. More than eighty death sentences have been pronounced.

523. "Clamecy-Moskva", fragment of his mémoires, published in *Literaturnaya Gazeta,* Moscow (28 Fevral).

524. Letters to Lode Roelandt, January 15 and 28. Published by Rolland, along with an introduction, in Raden Mas Noto Souroto, *La Chanson du Wayang.* Translated from the Dutch by Lode Roelandt. Les Cahiers du «Journal des poètes,» No. 26 (5 janvier 1937).

525. Letter to Noto Souroto, January 28. Published in Noto Souroto, *La Chanson du Wayang, supra.,* no. 524. The letter concerns Noto Souroto's book; Rolland expresses his own aspiration towards harmony of the spirit, the balance between Dream and Action. He criticizes the book, however, because «. . . le visage du temps présent n'y paraisse point sous des traits plus précis . . . notre âge . . . veut . . . lutte, . . . se sacrifie, pour la libération des opprimés de la terre entière, pour la justice universelle, pour l'établissement d'un ordre social qui apporte à tous le droit à vivre, égal et fraternal—. . . .»

526. Letter to a Nazi student, published in Russian translation "Pis'mo Nemetzkomu Soldatu," in *Literaturnaya Gazeta,* Moscow (28 Fevral).

527. «Feuilles détachées d'un journal des années de guerre,» notes and additions of 1935, *Commune,* II (mars–avril), 673–687, 848–862. He has chosen these pages, he says, to show his own errors, as for example, his adverse judgments about the return of the Russian leaders in exile.

528. «Dans la mêlée,» *Monde,* VIII (3 mai), 6–7.

529. «Le vieux Orphée,» *Europe,* numéro spécial consacré à Victor Hugo, XXXVIII (mai–août), 157–174; dated April 20 by Rolland. Collected in *Compagnons de route,* 1936. The special number of *Europe* was also published as a separate edition, Rieder, 1935, in which the article by Rolland is on pp. 5–22.

530. «Du rôle de l'écrivain dans la société d'aujourd'hui,» *Commune,* II (mai), 929–935. For those who wish to write for the masses, the first duty is to speak a language accessible to all; they must discover new fields, and yet be of their (and of all) times. The artist sees better what is coming, and

he lives more intensely everything that others live and see. Thus he is in a position to form a true élite able to lead the proletariat. The true question now is really: «Du rôle de l'artiste dans une société en état de guerre.» This is an important essay for a complete understanding of Rolland's ideas concerning the function of art and the artist, especially in the modern world.

531. «Romain Rolland en U.R.S.S.,» *L'Humanité* (1er juillet). At Moscow, June 30, Rolland wrote in the visitor's book in the State Museum, «En parcourant les . . . salles du musée . . . j'ai eu la surprise et l'émotion d'y retrouver quelques-unes des plus belles toiles qui ravirent ma jeunesse: des Renoir, des Claude Monet . . . des Cézanne. . . . J'ai vécu cette riche période de l'art français, qui fut un des âges les plus glorieux de la peinture. Je suis heureux de voir fleurir cette abondante et diverse symphonie française sous le ciel ami de l'U.R.S.S.»

532. «Romain Rolland au moment de quitter l'U.R.S.S. proclame, dans une lettre à Staline, la nécessité de la défendre,» *L'Humanité* (22 juillet), with a photograph of Gorki and Rolland. From the letter: «Je suis entré en contact puissant avec un peuple qui, au cours d'une lutte inlassable, crée sous la direction du parti communiste, dans un élan héroïque et réglé, un monde nouveau. . . . Je pressentais en arrivant ici que le seul véritable progrès du monde est indissolublement lié aux destinées de l'U.R.S.S., que l'U.R.S.S. est le foyer ardent de l'internationale prolétarienne, qui doit être et sera l'humanité tout entière, que le devoir absolu dans tous les pays est de la défendre contre tous les ennemis menaçant son essor. Vous savez, cher camarade, que je n'ai jamais reculé devant ce devoir et que je ne reculerai jamais. . . .»

533. «La jeunesse soviétique rend visite à Romain Rolland,» *L'Humanité* (17 juillet). Thanking Kossarev for his speech, Rolland replied: «Jean-Christophe et Colas Breugnon sont nés dans le camp ennemi, mais ils sont arrivés maintenant dans votre camp et je suis heureux de voir qu'ils trouvent tant d'amis parmi la jeunesse soviétique. Je donnerai toutes les forces qui me restent au service de l'oeuvre pour laquelle nous luttons. . . .»

534. *Quinze ans de combat*, 1919–1934, Rieder, in −16, lxxx, 244 pp. (27 juillet); 9th ed., Rieder, 1935.

535. «A la mémoire de Henri Barbusse,» *Europe*, XXXIX (septembre-décembre), 255–256; dated August 30.

536. «Retour de Moscou,» *Commune*, III (octobre), 129–133; dated September. Rolland says, in a footnote, that these words are fragments of a more complete study. I have been unable to discover any further such study in his published works. In this article, which praises Russia and Stalin, he relates his impressions of the vital, powerful life which inspires everyone in the U.S.S.R.; it is, he says, a collective psychosis of a great moment of history in which a new era of the world is arising; theirs is a faith which has the character of a scientific hypothesis; their universe turns on

materialistic dynamism towards a social ideal of justice and of panhumanism.

537. «Adieu à Barbusse,» «Jurons de vaincre,» «Aux calomniateurs,» *L'Humanité* (8, 9 septembre, 23 octobre). In the first he calls for the union of all to continue the battle. «A vous, nos camarades communistes et socialistes, . . . Notre chef de file, Henri Barbusse est mort. . . . Mais l'armée que sa voix rassembla en un Front mondial continue la bataille. Et elle la poursuivra jusqu'à la victoire finale. Car elle doit vaincre et elle vaincra! Elle vaincra l'impérialisme et la guerre. La Vie vaincra la mort!» The second is also a call for the unity of all parties against war and fascism, the unity and the fight that had been started three years previously at the Amsterdam Congress. The third was written after his return from Moscow, and attempts to set right some of the false ideas that his enemies had been spreading concerning the trip and his ideas.

538. «L'esprit européen,» *Les Nouvelles littéraires* (23 novembre). Europe cannot be isolated from the rest of the world. The idea of a «Pan-Europa», or a European federation, is only a larger and more dangerous nation.

539. «Romain Rolland pour Thaelmann,» *L'Humanité* (4 décembre). The «Comité Thaelmann» sends to *Humanité* an extract from a letter of Romain Rolland, November 22.

540. «Les propos de table de Beethoven,» *Commune*, III (décembre), 391–399; extracts from the *Cahiers de conversation de Beethoven*, the publication of which was begun by Walther Nohl. Rolland insists on the more or less revolutionary ideas of Beethoven, his hostility toward the aristocracy, toward the Church, and toward the police, in the service of the Church; and on his admiration for English parliamentary government.

541. "What Romain Rolland thinks," conversation between Rolland and S. C. Bose, *The Modern Review*, Calcutta, LVIII, pp. 319–324. The article was revised by Rolland. He explains his fundamental principles: internationalism; equal rights for all races; justice for exploited workers—that is, a society in which there will be neither exploited workers nor exploiters, in which all will work for the community; liberty for oppressed nationalities; equal rights for women. Interestingly enough, he says here that non-violence cannot be the central point of all social action; it is only a means, and it is still largely experimental.

542. "*Volki*. Pervoe predstavlenie moeĭ P'esy v teatre *Tvorchestvo*," *Teatr i Dramatirgiia*, III[9], pp. 7–10. Concerning the "Tvorchestvo" theater; translated from the French.

543. «Message,» in *Souvenirs sur la colonisation*, by Felicien Challaye, Picart, 210 pp. A preface to Challaye's book.

544. *Par la révolution, la paix*. Éditions sociales internationales (Collection: Commune), 175 pp.

545. «Le Plus grand danger. Pour la Conférence Plénière du Mouvement

Mondial contre la guerre et le fascisme, Réunie à Paris, le 23–29 novembre 1935.» An address by Rolland, published in *Comment empêcher la guerre*, 1936, pp. 7–11. The greatest danger is fascist Germany. Peace can exist only between all peoples and nations. If one column of the edifice is shaken, the whole structure is in danger. Russia is now the most important column.

546. «In Memoriam Leon Tolstoy,» published only in *Compagnons de route*, 1936. Written in 1935 upon the anniversary of his death.

547. Introduction to *Compagnons de Route*, 1936; dated Octobre, 1935.

1936

548. «Note de Romain Rolland à sa lettre de 1887,» *Commune*, III (janvier), 523–525; note dated December, 1935. See the «Introduction à une lettre de Tolstoï,» *ibid.*, 525–529. This Introduction appeared also in *Compagnons de route*, 1936.

549. «Réponse à une enquête de *Vendémiaire* sur «le déclin des idées de liberté et de progrès»,» *Europe*, XL (janvier–avril), 104–107. This is a misleading question, says Rolland. There is no decline, for true liberty has never existed, because of the nature of the present and past social orders. But the U.S.S.R. is working towards that end. As to progress, there is no need to discuss it, any more than it is necessary to discuss movement. It is proved by going forward.

550. «Pour l'indivisible paix,» *Vendredi* (24 janvier). Extracts were published in *Commune*, III (mars), 907–908, in *L'Humanité* (29 janvier), and in *Comment empêcher la guerre*, 1936. War approaches; for France, the only danger is Germany; this war of aggression must be prepared for. A close accord between France, England, and Russia is the sole means of preserving peace.

551. Letter to the Communist Party (for their VIIIth Congress), *L'Humanité* (27 janvier); dated January 25. He expresses his pleasure at finding himself, after a lifetime of struggles to free himself, «. . . enfin sur la grande voie des peuples qui montent à la victoire, sur les ruines du passé, établissant un ordre de raison, de justice et de pleine humanité.»

552. «Musiciens d'aujourd'hui—*Tristan*,» *Les Nouvelles littéraires* (1er février), p. 7. Wagner's *Tristan*.

553. «Pour la défense de la paix,» *Vendredi* (26 février). Extracts were published in *Commune*, III (avril), 1019–1020, and *L'Humanité* (7 mars); complete text published in *Comment empêcher la guerre*, 1936. Fascism is war; in order to guarantee a true peace, fascism must be broken. The best way to crush naziism is by peace, by a peace imposed by a close alliance of France, England, and Russia. War is not the worst thing; the worst of all evils is debasement and degradation.

554. «Voyage autour de ma chambre,» *L'Humanité* (26 juin); first published in Dutch in *Communisme. Maandschrift voor Politiek en Cultur*, Amsterdam (Maart). A brief review of his background, some of the main events of his life, and the high points of his development. He concludes by saying that the two most important things that he has learned in his seventy years are: the unity of all human life, all peoples and races; and the indissoluble bond that exists between thought and action.

555. Interview with Aragon. Published in *Les Cahiers du Bolchévisme* (15 mars), and partially published also in *Commune*, III (mai), 1138–1139. There is no peace in the case of individuals; the struggle is eternal. But war between nations is absurd. To arrive at this conclusion, he says, Tolstoy's influence was not necessary; he came to it by examining all man's experiments: the European, the Indian, Gandhi's, the class struggle, fascisms. It is necessary to impose peace on the world; to do this there is only one way: the «International du Travail,» by means of the present struggle of the «Front populaire» on an international scale.

556. «Pour un théâtre du peuple,» *Regards* (2 avril). Rolland's reply to Paul Gsell's question. The bourgeois theater is at the end of its rope. The theater and the cinema today are the reflection of a class that is numerous, but which lacks vigor and life. When he first wrote his *Théâtre du peuple*, there was no «peuple»; there is now. The theater has now but to gain new blood from the energies and passions of the people. He agrees with Nizan that revolutionary literature is the modern form of the tragedy: it is the combat between human will and the resistance of an intolerable world. This conflict releases the values of danger, struggle, heroism—and he would add joy to this list, joy of love, love of cause and party. But the conservative state opposes this eruption of mass emotion and revolutionary energies in the theater. Once again he is forced to the same conclusion, no matter what avenues of thought he may travel . . . «tout renouvellement du monde présent a comme nécessité préalable la Révolution. . . . *Par la Révolution, la Paix . . . Par la Révolution le Théâtre du Peuple, l'Art nouveau.*»

557. «Mon ami le plus cher,» *L'Humanité* (21 juin). The death of Gorki.

558. «Adieu à Gorki,» «Une lettre de Maxime Gorki à Romain Rolland,» with several paragraphs of introduction by Rolland, *Europe*, XLI (mai–août), 289–290, 433–435. The first article also appeared in *Commune*, III (juillet), 1297–1299, and *Regards*, IV (25 juin).

559. «La Couronne de Gorki,» *Commune*, III (août), 1447–1464; contributions by Rolland and others; Rolland, pp. 1449–1450.

560. «Quatorze juillet. 1789–1936,» *Europe*, XLI (mai–août), 293–297. A real «Front populaire» was formed on that morning in 1789; the Bastille was taken by an invisible, invincible force, which ruins old and condemned

states: a bad conscience. It is working for us today, he says. And he calls on his comrades to lead the assault on all the remaining Bastilles. Also published in *Regards*, IV (8 juillet).

561. «A Henri Barbusse toujours vivant et combattant,» *L'Humanité* (30 août); dated August 28.

562. «Un Message de Romain Rolland . . . Faisons face à l'ennemi,» *L'Humanité* (6, 11 septembre). This is his address to the Brussels Peace Congress. Published in English in *Labour Monthly*, XVIII (October), 625–628.

563. «XIXe anniversaire de la révolution,» *Regards*, No. 148 (11 novembre). What strikes Rolland most about Russia is its vitality, its interest in life, its racial equality, its optimism. There is no unemployment, and there is a place for everybody to work.

564. «Appel. A tous les peuples, au secours des victimes d'Espagne,» *Europe*, XLII (septembre–décembre), 565–566, and in *L'Humanité* (22 novembre).

565. *Comment empêcher la guerre*. Bureau d'éditions, 30 pp. This brochure consists of three articles: 1. Adresse à l'Assemblée du Comité mondial contre la guerre et le fascisme; 2. Pour l'indivisible paix; and 3. Pour la défense de la paix. Second edition, Bureau d'éditions, 1937. Collection: «Stratégie et tactique de la lutte contre la guerre et le fascisme.»

566. *Compagnons de route* (essais littéraires), Le Sablier, 227 pp. A collection of essays previously published, one as early as 1902. The introduction and a short note about Tolstoy were written in the fall of 1935.

1937

567. Preface to Nicolas Ostrovski, *Et l'acier fut trempé*, translated from the Russian by V. Feldman, Editions sociales internationales; Editions Hier et Aujourd'hui, 1946, 300 pp. See the review articles by René Lalou, *Commune*, V (septembre 1937), 108–109, and Georges Sadoul, *L'Humanité* (18 septembre 1937). The preface was also published in *L'Humanité* (12 juin 1937).

568. *Le Peuple allemand accuse*. (Das Deutsche Volk klagt an). Appel à la conscience du monde. Preface by Rolland. Ed. du Carrefour (4 février), 335 pp. See the review article by Claude Morgan, *Commune*, IV (juin 1937), 1246–1248.

569. «Adresse à la conférence nationale du Parti Communiste Français,» *L'Humanité* (25 janvier). Letter dated from Villeneuve, January 20. An expression of confidence in the French Communist Party.

570. «Le Message du grand Romain Rolland,» *L'Humanité* (5 janvier). New Year's message for the U.S.S.R., expressing his faith in and adherence to what the revolution stands for.

571. Letter to Henri Lesieur, published under the title, "Rolland nous dit comment il a écrit *Les Loups*,» *L'Humanité*, (14 janvier). The first presentation; Colonel Picquart was present. These passions are eternal. And he adds: «Et en vérité, nous vivons tous . . . une Iliade—un âge de combat, puissant et cruel, . . . Partout j'entends rugir la grande déesse, comme une lionne assaillie, blessée, offensée et indomptable: la *justice*; elle triomphera.»

572. «L'U.R.S.S. en a vu bien d'autres. Une lettre de Romain Rolland à propos du livre d'André Gide,» *L'Humanité* (17 janvier). He expresses his confidence in the French Communist Party which represents the sane and living portion of the French people, and in the ultimate victory and creation of a better social order.

573. A salute to the Spain of the «Frente popular», *France-Espagne*, No. 1. A very short paragraph.

574. «Brief an einen Australier,» *Die Neue Weltbühne*, XXXI (11. Februar), 219. Concerning the increase of anti-Semitism.

575. Greetings to a Conference of the «Maison de la Culture,» *L'Humanité* (25 février). A call for the use of the critical spirit and intelligence to preserve liberty.

576. «Notre Gramsci n'est pas un mort, ni un vaincu,» *L'Humanité* (24 mai). The spirit of such fighters against fascism will outlive their tyrants.

577. «Appel pour sauver Rembte et Stamm,» *L'Humanité* (12 juin). Adolf Rembte, Robert Stamm, Max Maddalena, condemned by Hitler's government.

578. «Aux jeunes,» *Cahiers de la jeunesse*, No. 1 (15 juillet), 4–5. «Mon premier mot aux jeunes est: «*Agir*». Et le premier ennemi que je combats, c'est l'«A quoi bon?» . . . Il y a deux sortes d'«A quoi bon?»: l'un par orgueil: l'autre, par faiblesse. Tous les deux sont impuissance. Mais le plus pernicieux est le premier, car de son vice il fait vanité.» In his own youth, heroic individualism was the reaction against the weaknesses of the times. But this had to be replaced by another kind of individualism. The new one realizes the dreams of the idealists of the past, Beethoven and Schiller, in action and social service: «. . . ce panhumanisme qui couronne le front de notre Révolution. . . . Donc, soyons ferme dans la tempête . . . chacun de nous est l'immense armée, qui livre assaut aux forces obscures de la bêtise, de l'injustice et de la férocité, qui asservissent, exploitent et martyrisent l'humanité.»

579. «Sauvez de la hache les otages allemands de la paix,» «Romain Rolland salue le IXe Congrès du Parti Communiste Français,» *L'Humanité* (11 octobre, 25 décembre). In the first article: «. . . le Führer . . . compte sur le silence et sur l'oubli des démocraties d'Occident, trahies par la faiblesse

pusillanime de leurs gouvernements. Mais il se trompe. . . . Nous n'oublierons jamais. . . . L'opposition allemande emprisonnée . . . constitue la principale garantie de paix qui subsiste encore en Allemagne contre l'État totalitaire et militaire. Il faut sauver des menaces hitlériennes les otages de la paix.» In the second: «Le grand parti qui se réclame de Marx et de Lénine est, à mes yeux, le représentant le plus logique et le plus ferme de la justice sociale. Je me sens lié à lui, par la raison et par le coeur.»

580. «Hommage à Élie Faure,» *Europe*, XLV (15 novembre), 442.

581. *Beethoven. Les grandes époques créatrices. Le Chant de la Résurrection* (*La Messe solennelle et les dernières sonates*), First edition, Le Sablier, 2 vols., 617 pp., figures, music, illustrations, portraits, and facsimiles; reissued in 1947.

582. Preface to a book on Gorki by René Plaud. Unpublished until 1948. Rolland's preface published in *Les Lettres françaises*, VIII (24 juin 1948). It is an excellent portrait of Gorki.

1938

583. «Beethoven vivant (Introduction à un Essai d'analyse du Subconscient et du Conscient dans la création musicale),» *Europe*, XLVI (15 janvier), 5–19.

584. «Un appel de Romain Rolland,» *L'Humanité* (31 mars). Rolland calls for a single front of all parties and of the intellectuals to preserve peace and protect France, one of the last of the bastions of our democracy and civilisation, against the menace that has overwhelmed Spain and Austria and is now at the gates of Czechoslovakia.

585. «Démission ou continuation de la France. Réponse de . . . Romain Rolland,» *Cahiers de la jeunesse*, No. 12 (15 juillet), 15–16. He calls for the union of all intellectual workers, in the face of the rising barbarians of the present, who are armed with a fanatic, Moslem-like hatred of intelligence. We must preserve our heritage, and we must work for fecund peace. «Mais en notre temps—en tous les temps—la paix ne se donne qu'à ceux qui ont le courage de la vouloir et de la défendre.»

586. «Beethoven et l'argent,» *Commune*, VI (mai), 1045–1053. Extracts from *Beethoven . . . Le Chant de la résurrection.*

587. «La «Paix» de Munich est une capitulation dégradante,» *L'Humanité* (14 octobre). He had signed a general protest against war, not attacking any party whatsoever. Now the adversaries of the C.G.T. and the P.C.F. are trying to exploit his name. He reassures them of his loyalty to both of these organizations.

588. «Aux Lycéens,» *Cahiers de la jeunesse*, No. 17 (15 décembre), 17–18; dated October by Rolland. Because you know the dangers which menace your future, your liberty, you must be armed. You must admit discussion

of all political parties in your organisations, study circles, etc. But politics must not dominate your instruction and training. In the difficult times that are approaching, teams of highly trained and well equipped technicians and professional men will become increasingly necessary.

589. *Valmy*. Grand récit historique pour la jeunesse. Editions sociales internationales, 30 pp. Editions Hier et Aujourd'hui, 1946 or 1947. Illustrations by Jean Trubert. Extracts also in *International Literature*, No. 7 (July, 1939), Moscow, 37–44.

590. *Les Pages immortelles de Rousseau*, choisies et expliquées par Romain Rolland. Ed. Corréa, 236 pp. Copyright by Corréa et Cie., Paris, and Longmans, Green & Co., N. Y. Introduction by Rolland, pp. 7–48. Unauthorized edition; see the letter from Rolland to the editor of *Europe*, 1939. *The Living Thoughts of Rousseau*, presented by Romain Rolland, translation by Julie Kernan of Rolland's introduction, New York and Toronto: Longmans, Green & Co., 1939. Authorized edition.

1939

591. «Appel. Du 15 au 22 janvier semaine nationale de solidarité. Un appel de Romain Rolland,» *L'Humanité* (14 janvier). An appeal to offer aid and comfort to those who have defended France by defending Spain.

592. Letter to *Europe*, *Europe*, XLIX (15 janvier), 143. Concerning the unauthorized French edition of *Les Pages immortelles de J.-J. Rousseau.*

593. Letter to the *Union mondiale de la culture juive*, *Commune*, VII (janvier), 125–126.

594. «Adresse de Romain Rolland à la jeunesse française,» *L'Avant-garde* (20 janvier). Against fascism.

595. «Souvenirs sur Péguy,» *Toute l'Edition* (28 janvier). See J. Cassou, «Notes et correspondance. Les souvenirs de Romain Rolland sur Péguy,» *Europe*, XLIX (15 février), 287–288; he publishes extracts from Rolland's article, some of which were omitted from the article in *Toute l'Edition.*

596. «Deuil sur l'Europe,» *Europe*, XLIX (15 avril), 433–434. He castigates the German invasion of Czechoslovakia, and foresees the visitation on Germany of the violence she has used against this brave nation.

597. «Nécessité de la révolution,» *Europe*, numéro spécial, L (15 juillet), 289–302. Revolution is a stage on the road of progress, not a goal. It is the break with epochs of enslavement of man to destiny. In this movement man takes possession of himself and of the world.

598. Letter to Delferière. «Félicitations de Romain Rolland après la création de *Robespierre* à la radio,» *L'Humanité* (16 août).

599. "Message to the International Music Congress, 1939, New York," *Musical Quarterly*, XXV (October, 1939), 510–512. The history of art long ignored music, which is now included on an equal footing with the other

arts. All the arts combined form an integral part of general hisotry. They are the flower and fruit of civilisations and often bear the seed of coming ages. Great artists are frequently forerunners. Musicology also offers tremendous resources for the study of human psychology. Music is the precise and exact language of the subconscious. How research has extended the domain of music.

600. *Robespierre,* drame en trois actes et vingt-quatre tableaux, A. Michel, 319 pp. The last, in order of publication, but not of its place in the cycle, of his «Théâtre de la Révolution.» Extracts were published in *Europe,* XLIX (février–mars), 145–162, 289–298; and in *International Literature* (Moscow), No. 7 (July), 3–8; and *Commune* (janvier–mai), pp. 1–14, 506, 633.

601. Preface to N. Marceau, *L'Allemagne et la Révolution française,* Editions Thaelmann, 224 pp., illustrations.

1940

602. «Gabriele d'Annunzio et La Duse. Souvenirs,» *Les Oeuvres libres,* N.S. No. 20 (246) (1947), pp. 3–50. Finished at Vézelay, July 5, 1940, during the German occupation. This covers the years 1897–1902. Rolland publishes a note from d'Annunzio, 1910, and one from La Duse, 1922. Rolland saw neither of them after 1914.

1940–1941

602A. Letters from Romain Rolland to Elie Walach. Letters dated 1er mars, 12, 25 mai 1940, 12, 22, 27 février 1941. Published in *Lettres de Romain Rolland à un combattant de la Résistance.* Préface de Mme Marie Romain Rolland. L. Rodstein, 1947 (Centre de Documentation auprès de l'U.J.R.E.), 46 pages, no numbering. The preface by Mme Rolland is the principal interest of the brochure.

603. «A Rilke. Souvenir de son voisin,» in *Rilke et la France.* Textes et poèmes inédits. . . . Essais et souvenirs de Edmond Jaloux. . . . Romain Rolland . . . etc. Plon, Coll. «Présences,» 1942. Rolland, pp. 199–206, dated December 1, 1941.

1942

604. *Le Voyage intérieur,* 1942. A. Michel, 241 pp.

1943

605. Letter to Louis Gillet, *Le Littéraire* (15 juillet 1946). The letter is dated July 22, after a visit to Gillet.

606. *Beethoven. Les Grandes époques créatrices.* IV. *La Cathédrale interrompue.* I. *La Neuvième symphonie.* 261 pp. II. *Les Derniers Quatuors.* 315 pp. 8 pls music. Le Sablier.

607. Letter written at Vézelay, November 12, 1943, containing his final instructions. Doisy publishes it in his book *Romain Rolland*, p. 205.

1944

608. Message de Romain Rolland lu pour lui en son absence à la Sorbonne à une séance solennelle de commémoration des intellectuels victimes de l'occupation, le 9 décembre 1944. Published by Doisy, *Romain Rolland*, pp. 203–204; it also appeared under the title «France et Liberté,» *Les Nouvelles littéraires* (5 avril 1945). The effect of France's disaster on the world, on the soul of the French themselves, the miracle of the resistance, and the faith that it gave proof of.

1945

609. «Gruss des zwanzigjahrfeier,» in Hans Mühlestein, *Das Erbe der Sowjetunion*, Zürich, 73, 1 pp. Rolland, p. 7–10.

610. «A la jeunesse, mélodie (chant et piano). Music de P. Arna. (*Bibliographie de la France*, No. 16).

611. *Beethoven. Finita Comoedia. Beethoven, ses grandes époques créatrices. Derniers mois et mort de Beethoven.* Illustrations by Deslignières, Le Sablier.

612. *Péguy*. 2 vols., A. Michel.

613. Preface to Mathilde do Canto, *Doña Josepha*. Liège: Maréchal, 180 pp.

614. Correspondence. *Rolland and Tagore*, edited by Krishna Kripalani, Visva-Bharati, 104, xvi pp.

1946

615. Preface to Alexeï Remizov, *La Maison Bourkov*. Translated from the Russian by Robert and Zénitta Vivier. Ed. du Pavois. 250 pp.

1947

616. «Pages de Journal,» *Horizon*, revue mensuelle (Nancy), no. 2, pp. 3–6.

617. *Le Seuil, précédé du Royaume de T*, Geneva: Ed. du Mont-Blanc, 1946.

1948

618. «Lettres sur l'art,» *La Revue française de l'Elite*, no. 8 (25 mai 1948).

II
ABOUT ROLLAND

1895–1896

619. Stiefel, A. L., *Kritische Jahresbericht über Romanischen Philologie*, IV, 2, pp. 324–325. According to Stiefel, Rolland's thesis is poorly organized and lacks completeness in places.

1898

621. Athis, Alfred, *Revue blanche*, XVI (mai–août), 137–139. A rather careful criticism of *Aërt* and of the first production at the Théâtre de l'OEuvre, with Mlle Laparcerie in the rôle of Aërt. He concludes that the play is better read than seen.

622. Faguet, E., *Journal des débats*, 9 mai. Faguet points out certain faults in the dramatic construction of *Aërt*, which he calls simply an «étude d'âme.»

623. Bauer, H., *La Revue blanche*, II, pp. 221–224. Henri Bauer, dramatic critic of *L'Echo de Paris*, which refused to publish his sympathetic account of *Les Loups*, lost his position when his article appeared in the *Revue blanche*. This is one of the few sympathetic articles at the time of the first presentation. He praises the delineation of character and the power of evocation Rolland displays in this piece.

624. Faguet, E., *Journal des débats*, 23 mai. One of the earliest reviews; a good critical analysis of the good and bad points of the play *Les Loups*.

1899

625. Hérold, A.-F., *Mercure de France*, XXXI (août), 548–550. Rolland has, says Hérold, sacrificed clarity for historical accuracy in *Le Triomphe de la raison* by having the characters pronounce long historical speeches; otherwise the characters are well drawn.

1900

626. Faguet, E., *Journal des débats*, 31 décembre. Faguet's criticisms of *Danton* as a play are adverse; the interest is all psychological, and Rolland aimed only at complete historical accuracy.

627. Larroumet, G., *Le Temps*, 31 décembre. Larroumet's remarks about *Danton* are in general favorable, although he points out weaknesses and defects. There are also some good characterizations of *Aërt* in this article. Rolland is considered a very good playwright by this critic.

1901

628. Picard, A., *La Revue blanche*, XXIV (15 janvier), 146–149. Picard finds that Rolland, in *Danton*, is at an equal distance from history and from the theater because of his very ideas and methods, but is a conscientious workman.

1902

629. Flat, P., *Revue bleue: politique et littéraire*, XVII, 439–441. This account of *Le Quatorze juillet* was written after Gémier's presentation at the «Théâtre de la Renaissance»; the work exists only by the interpretation of the actors. Flat's account is very unfavorable, but many of his adverse criticisms seem to be justifiable.

630. Morel, E., *Art dramatique et musical*, II, 100–105. This interesting review of *Le 14 juillet* is followed by a selection of the opinions of the press and of P. Flat, G. Larroumet, E. Faguet, L. Muhlfeld, and C. Mendès, pp. 105–107.

1905

631. Seippel, P., *Journal de Genève*, 2 juillet, 22 octobre. These are Seippel's first, and among the very first articles, about *Jean-Christophe: Le Matin, L'Adolescent*. Seippel is very favorable and sympathetic in all of his articles.

632. Gillet, L., *Journal des débats*, 17 août. In *L'Aube* Rolland seems to believe in obscure forces which guide the destinies of the characters. «Un panthéisme presque mystique est au fond de ce roman.»

1906

633. Dreyfus, R., «Jean-Christophe ou l'exaltation de la douleur», *Pages libres*, VI (10 mars), 237–252. A good study from the point of view indicated in the title, on the first three volumes of the novel. For Rolland, says Dreyfus, the problem of love is one of problems of suffering. He criticizes Rolland for acting as if Christophe existed independently of him and as if he, Rolland, were serving as an intermediary between Christophe and the reader.

1907

634. Dominici, Pedro Cesar, *De Lutecia, Arte y Crítica*, Ollendorff, iv, 352 pp. Written about Rolland and *Jean-Christophe*, pp. 21–30, after he had read *La Révolte*. It is one of the early essays, and a very enthusiastic one. The author also tells of his delight while reading Rolland's *Beethoven*, and he discusses briefly the novel and the biography.

635. Lecomté, G., *La Grande revue*, XLIII (25 juin), 294–319. The author discusses Rolland and *Jean-Christophe*. Two things, he says, give value to the novel: the profound knowledge which Rolland has of great souls, and the harmony that exists between these souls and Rolland.

636. Seippel, P., *Journal de Genève*, 1er septembre. This interesting review of *La Révolte* bears principally upon Christophe and the «mensonge allemand.»

1908

637. Souday, P., *L'Opinion*, I (18 avril), 23–35. A review of the first nine volumes of *Jean-Christophe*. Souday criticizes the excessive length of the novel, his judgments on French music, his repeated appeal to Life. He admires Rolland's presentation of both sides of a question, not like Renan in a dialogue, but by presenting them as stages in an individual's evolution. He finds a certain dogmatism in the novel.

638. Ecorcheville, J., *S. I. M.*, IV (15 août), 847–853. Ecorcheville establishes some very interesting parallels between *Musiciens d'aujourd'hui* and *Jean-Christophe*.

639. Seippel, P., *Journal de Genève*, 20 septembre. Seippel here writes of *La Foire sur la place* in his usual sympathetic manner.

640. Marnold, J., *Mercure de France*, LXXVI (1er novembre), 148–155. Published later in his volume, *Musique d'autrefois et d'aujourd'hui*, Dorbon aîné (1912?), 366 pp. Principally a study of the intimate and essential relationships between the *Musiciens d'autrefois*, the *Musiciens d'aujourd'hui*, and *Jean-Christophe*. Marnold criticizes Rolland as being a historian rather than a professional musician, and for his subjectivism in the studies on music and musicians.

641. Maubel, *Le Guide musical*, Brussels, No. 17, pp. 347–348. Maubel examines Rolland's *Musiciens d'aujourd'hui* and *Musiciens d'autrefois* from Rolland's own point of view, considering music in its historical and social aspects.

642. I.P., *Rivista Musicale Italiana*, XV, 826–828. I.P. feels that Rolland, in his *Musiciens d'autrefois*, should have studied the mystery plays more, especially in the «Opéra avant l'Opéra».

643. Prezzolini, G., *Rassegna contemporanea*, III, 41–58. This enthusiastic review of the first four volumes of *Jean-Christophe* is interesting principally because Prezzolini publishes a letter from Rolland which describes the latter's education.

644. Séché, A., and Bertaut, J., *Evolution du théâtre contemporain*, éd. de la *Mercure de France*, 304 pp. Rolland's *Le Quatorze juillet*, pp. 131–142. The authors have some interesting ideas concerning the use which Rolland makes of crowds on the stage, as well as the use made by other writers.

1909

645. Bonnerot, J., "Introduction" to *Romain Rolland. Extraits de son oeuvre*, Nevers, 1909; appeared also in the *Cahiers Nivernais et du Centre*, 2e série, 13e and 14e fascicules (octobre–novembre 1909). Bonnerot has here written a good, but not a profound introduction to the works of Rolland that had appeared by that date.

646. Seippel, P., *Journal de Genève*, 18 avril. This is a review of *Dans la maison.*

647. Souday, P., *L'Opinion*, II (juin), 759–761. Souday criticizes *Dans la maison* for certain rhetorical passages, à la Hugo, the perpetual hymn to Life, Christophe's ideas of a "class" art.

648. de Jong, D., *Onze Eeuw*, IV, 114–116, 271–285. A general study of Rolland's works to that date, very good for the musical works: *Beethoven*, *Musiciens d'aujourd'hui*, especially the articles on Berlioz, Wagner, Strauss, and Mahler.

1910

649. Borgese, G. A., *La Vita e il libro*, Vol. 3, Turin: F. Boca. «Jean-Christophe», pp. 30–57, dated 1910; «Un evangelista di Tolstoï», pp. 60–64. These are mostly unfavorable criticisms, of the character of Christophe, of the contents of *La Foire sur la place*, of *Jean-Christophe à Paris*. He gives his approval to *Antoinette*.

650. Souday, P., *L'Opinion*, III (23 avril), 533–534. «Médiocre logicien, esthéticien chimérique et faible, M. Romain Rolland est un grand poète du coeur.» He should try, says Souday, to found a new religion instead of trying to create a new esthetic (collective art, democratic, accessible to all).

651. S., *Revue musicale*, No. 15–16, pp. 370–374. A thorough review of Rolland's *Haendel* in which certain errors of detail are pointed out.

1911

652. Seippel, P., *Bibliothèque universelle et Revue suisse*, LXIV (octobre), 5–28. Seippel gives the main facts of Rolland's life, his writings, his early unpublished dramas of the Italian renascence. Rolland's interest in the Théâtre du Jarat; the founder, Morax, is Rolland's friend and disciple, says Seippel. There is also a rather good analysis of *Jean-Christophe* as a musically conceived work of literature. This article is the nucleus of Seippel's later book on Rolland.

1912

653. Séché, Alphonse, *Romain Rolland. L'Humble vie héroïque, pensées choisies*. Introduction by Séché, Sansot, 96 pp. Introduction, pp. 5–14.

Séché pays glowing tribute to Rolland, the artist and thinker, whose clarity is so plainly French.

654. Bertaut, J., *Les Romanciers du nouveau siècle*, 1ère série. Sansot. Rolland, pp. 159–195. An interesting judgment of Rolland and *Jean-Christophe* by a writer whose conception of what an artist is agrees with that held by Rolland. In Rolland and in Christophe, Bertaut sees a rebel, but not a romantic rebel like those of Schiller and de Musset—no sombre despair or exasperation. The revolt is to free himself from his bonds—physical in the case of Rolland, who therefore prefers heroes of a gigantic stature struggling to free themselves too. These are not broad enough, so Rolland creates his own hero. The remarks about the soul, sensitive, but filled with vitality, which Bertaut makes about Christophe, are applicable to both Rolland and his creation.

655. Le Cardonnel, G., *Les Marges*, IX (janvier), 28–37. Le Cardonnel denies Rolland any artistic value, because of his lack of intellect and his excessive emotionalism. His criticisms concern principally *Jean-Christophe.*

656. Souday, P., *Le Temps*, 2–3 janvier, 13 novembre. See also Souday, *Les Livres du temps*, where these two articles appeared later. The purpose of *Jean-Christophe* is true, says Souday, but the thesis is false. Rolland seems to believe that Life is its own goal, and he has made of it the basis of an aesthetics and a system of ethics.

657. Seippel, P., «L'Idéal religieux de Romain Rolland», *Journal de Genève*, 7 avril. A good early account of this aspect of Rolland, in some ways fairer and more just than some later articles.—, *Journal de Genève*, 3 novembre. A review of the last volume of Jean-Christophe. Seippel's accounts continue to be among the best for the breadth of their view, their penetration, and sympathetic understanding of the work and the man. —, *Fortnightly Review*, XCVII (April), 661–674. This article also appeared in *Living Age*, CCLXXIII (May 4), 285–295. Parts III and V, and parts of the other divisions of the article were republished later in *Bibliothèque universelle et Revue suisse*, LXVIII (octobre–décembre), 449–470.

658. Seillière, E., *Internationale Monatsschrift für Wissenschaft*, VI (April), 830–850. Seillière compares Christophe and Peter Schulz with certain pages from Gottfried Keller, and attributes this part of Rolland's novel to the German writer's influence.

659. Guilbeaux, H., *Das Literarische Echo*, XV, 300–307. A good criticism of *Jean-Christophe* and a short study of the most important elements in Rolland's thinking, such as they were understood by a man who was later to be, for a few years, one of the most ardent admirers and defenders of Rolland.

660. Beaunier, A., «Le Testament d'une époque française», *Revue des Deux mondes*, (1er décembre), 685–696. Included later in his volume, *Les*

Idées et les hommes, 1ère série, Plon, 1913, pp. 44–65. Beaunier criticizes Rolland for choosing a German to represent the intellectual and moral martyrdom of a generation of Frenchmen. He analyzes and speaks well of Gottfried, in *Jean-Christophe*, but seems to find Antoinette's sacrifice vain. His analysis of Christophe is good: Christophe is art, and he is humanity. This art is not only for the people, it comes from the great, fertile soul of the people. In spite of certain misunderstandings, Beaunier seems to have penetrated more deeply into the novel than many of his contemporaries. Parts of his criticisms are typical of an older, more conservative generation of critics, such as Souday.

661. *Ombres et formes*, «Enquête». Replies published in *Ombres et formes*, III (1912), IV (1913). The questions: a. What is your opinion about *Jean-Christophe*? b. Do you think the influence of this novel is bad or good? Replies from some thirty-one people, including L. Hennique, E. Fabre, J.-H. Rosny aîné, P. Margueritte, H. Bataille, Han Ryner, J. Clarétie, H. Duvernois, P. Souday, L. Rolmer, P. Fort, R. Lehmann, André Thérive, and A. Cantillon.

1913

662. Seippel, P., *Romain Rolland, l'homme et l'oeuvre*, Ollendorff. This warmly sympathetic book, written by a man who knew Rolland personally, who corresponded and talked with him, gives an extremely interesting and informative account of the background of reading and influences that Rolland was exposed to. Seippel then traces the development of these ideas in Rolland's philosophy and thinking. —, «L'esthétique littéraire de Romain Rolland», *Journal de Genève*, 2 février. He sees certain resemblances between Rolland and Rodin. «L'un et l'autre font surgir d'un bloc de marbre fruste, des figures pantelantes de vie.»

663. Thibaudet, A., *Nouvelle revue française*, IX (1er février), 316–322. Music, the spirit of poetry, and *Jean-Christophe*. This novel is the summit of the Romantic movement, says Thibaudet. He makes some comparisons with *Les Misérables*.

664. *La Flamberge* (Mons, Belgium), No. 11 (mars), pp. 481–543. Articles by Dupierreux, Dominique de Bray, Hautier. «Enquête sur Romain Rolland et son oeuvre (*Jean-Christophe*),» by Arthur Cantillon. Replies by some 32 persons, including S. Zweig, O. Grautoff, N. Beauduin, Willy, J. Bonnerot, Claude Debussy, G. Duhamel, H. Guilbeaux, F. Hellens, Vincent d'Indy, Marius Ary-Leblond, C. Lemonnier, C. Mauclair, P. Margueritte, M. Pottecher, Rachilde, J.-H. Rosny aîné, Han Ryner, E. Verhaeren. The replies and the articles all have to do with *Jean-Christophe*, except the article by de Bray, which is about Rolland and Malwida von Meysenbug.

665. Del Vecchio, Gina, *Rivista d'Italia*, XVI (marzo), 459–468. Principally about *La Nouvelle journée;* there are some good remarks about Georges and Aurora as personifications of the new generation, and about Italy and Italians in the novel.

666. Souday, P., «Les Tragédies de la foi», *Le Temps*, 23 avril; published later in his *Les Livres du temps*, 2e série, II, 457–466. The principal criticism leveled by Souday is that of anti-intellectualism and lack of critical spirit. In *Aërt* the worst kind of dilettantism can be perceived. In *Saint-Louis* Rolland cries out for faith without providing an object for faith. The ultimate conclusion of all three of these plays is to promote Life as an end in itself.

667. Lavisse, E., *Revue de Paris* (15 juin), 724–733. A review of *La Nouvelle journée.* Lavisse warmly commends the author's great sympathy for all forms of life. He finds *Jean-Christophe* an admirable work, rich in ideas and sentiments. He discusses and gives examples of Rolland's masterful handling of traits of French psychology, descriptions (of surroundings, Italian society, country sides, etc.), and discusses the philosophy expressed in the novel.

668. Le Grix, F., *Revue hebdomadaire* (7 juin), 93–113. This article about *Jean-Christophe* contains an interesting discussion of the feeling of genius in the child Christophe, of Christophe and God, and of the three all-important visitations: the Rhine river, love, and pain. Le Grix criticizes the lack of unity (especially *Antoinette*)*;* the occasional lack of life (*La Foire sur la place*, some of the minor figures in *Dans la maison*)*;* the style, the lack of proportion, of harmony. He admits that Rolland writes like an inspired poet, a lyric poet.

669. Key, E., *Ord och Bild*, XXII, 323–336, and a shorter version in *La Revue*, CVI (janvier–février 1914), 171–181, and in *Die Tat*, V (1913), 697–619. Parts also appeared in English in the *Review of Reviews*, XLIX (April 1914), 484–485. The principal subject is *Jean-Christophe* and the «Crédo métaphysique» of Rolland; extracts from a letter concerning his Credo. Jean-Christophe and Beethoven. Psychological intuition. Guyau and «énergie vitale», Bergson and Jean-Christophe.

670. Mondadon, L. de, *Etudes*, CXXXVII, 271–285. This catholic and classicist judges Rolland to be a belated romantic.

671. Morax, R., *Wissen und Leben*, XII, 549–554. Morax studies the classic elements in Rolland's works and character.

672. Sanborne, A. F., *Century*, LXXXVI (August), 512–518. A rather good, early survey of Rolland, his background and principal writings, especially *Jean-Christophe* and his work in music.

673. Seillière, E., *Mysticisme et domination*, Alcan; Rolland, pp. 181–202.

Rolland is not all things to all men, but many men have tried to bend his ideas to fit their own. Seillière too tries to capture Rolland, finds in him his own mystico-imperialistic theories of Democracy.

674. Semeria, B., *Rassegna nazionale*, CXC, 317–325. Romain Rolland, *Jean-Christophe* and the older and younger generation in France.

675. Thérive, A., *Revue critique des idées et des livres*, XXII, 138–154. Thérive's very adverse criticisms cannot be entirely dismissed. They bear upon Rolland's belief that literature is an apostleship, upon his idealism, which is a vague exposition of confused but stimulating ideas and sentimentalism, upon his poor style, his didactic purpose, his vague lyric philosophy. Rolland is in the direct line, not only of Hugo, but also of all the tellers of moral tales of classical periods.

676. Thibaudet, A., *Nouvelle revue française*, X, 807–811. A review of Seippel's work on Romain Rolland. Thibaudet here suggests that the three conditions necessary to be a friend and admirer of Rolland are: to love music above everything else, to be a Protestant, to be a good European. Thibaudet's reasons for each of these conditions are interesting. He denies the influence of the pre-Socratic philosophers on Rolland; rather they furnished musical themes.

1914

677. Bonsels, W., *Das junge Deutschland und der grosse Krieg*. Aus Anlass des Briefwechsels Romain Rollands mit Gerhardt Hauptmann über den Krieg und die Kultur, Munich: Schmidkunz, 33 pp. Bonsels publishes Rolland's letter to Hauptmann, Hauptmann's reply, and Rolland's second letter to Hauptmann. In general the writer is sympathetic to Rolland. Hauptmann's reply was also published in the *Journal de Genève*, 13 septembre, 2nd ed.; the 3rd edition of the same date contains the same reply with two additional paragraphs. Hauptmann says that Rolland is of German blood, that his *Jean-Christophe* will take its place beside *Wilhelm Meister*, but that France is his adoptive country, and that consequently he judges everything through French eyes. This idea will be repeated in a curious fashion in 1936 by Groszhans, no. 914.

678. Grautoff, O., *Romain Rolland*, Frankfurt a.M.: Rütten & Loening, 62 pp. «Bibliographie», pp. 57–61. Rolland's life and works. The biography is good as far as it goes. The chapter on Rolland and Germany is excellent, perhaps the best, after that by Zweig, on this aspect of *Jean-Christophe*.

679. Hochstätter, Max, *Essai sur l'oeuvre de Romain Rolland*, Paris, Geneva, and Basel: Fischbacher. «Bibliographie» at end of volume. This study is also available in Spanish translation: "Ensayo sobre la obra de Romain Rolland," by Barrenechea, *Nosotros*, XVII (enero de 1915), 28–57. The translator also writes a two-page introduction.

680. Zweig, S., *Neue Freie Presse*, Vienna, 20. März, Morgenblatt, pp. 1–4. Romain Rolland and *Jean-Christophe.* Zweig examines, not the artistic worth, but the moral and spiritual values of the novel. He regards the book as the logical result of Rolland's education and development, which he traces in some detail.

681. Dwelshauvers, G., *La Belgique artistique et littéraire*, XXIV, 9e année (1er mai), 132–151. A short biographical sketch, in which Dwelshauvers studies Rolland, especially as a critic and historian of music, as a playwright (and his ideas as expressed in his *Théâtre du peuple*), as a biographer.

682. Herzog, W., *Das Forum*, I, 260–267; 441–445. The first article is a protest against «Au-dessus de la mêlée.» In the second article, Herzog withdraws most of what he had said about Rolland in the preceding one, and points out translations of his works which had appeared in *Wissen und Leben*.

683. Aulard, A., *Le Matin*, 23 octobre. Aulard denounces his former colleague for fear that Rolland may be mistakenly supposed, abroad, to represent French ideas. Aulard's interpretations are erroneous, the quotations from Rolland are partial and tendentious.

684. Gazzolo, A., «Critica e misticismo religioso nell'opera di Romain Rolland», *Coenobium*, VIII (31 ottobre), 16–24; (novvembre–dicembre), 34–40. Principally about *Jean-Christophe,* written on the occasion of Seippel's biography of Rolland and Ellen Key's article in *Ord och Bild.* Gazzolo thinks that Key does not penetrate to the essence of Christophe's soul because of her own philosophy. He sees in *La Nouvelle journée* a Tolstoyan rather than a Goethean influence.

1915

685. Guilbeaux, H., *Pour Romain Rolland,* Geneva: Jeheber; Paris: Librairie P.-M. Delasalle, 64 pp. One of the early and important works in defense of Rolland. Guilbeaux studies point by point the various attacks on Rolland, and disproves them, pointing out the errors and misstatements. —, in *La Guerre mondiale*, I(5 juillet), 2081–2082. Further defense of Rolland. During the trial of Guilbeaux, Rolland was continually mentioned as one of his collaborators. It seems that this "collaboration", or association with Rolland, was one of the principal charges against Guilbeaux. For this curious chapter in the history of ideas and psychology of people during war and war hysteria, see, «Le procès de Guilbeaux . . . ,» *Revue des causes célèbres*, II, Nos. 25–26, 27–28 (9, 23 mars 1919), 47–64, 107–124.

686. Bueno, Javier, *Una crítica del libro de Romain Rolland. «Au-dessus de la mêlée»*, Barcelona: Imprenta moderna, n.d., 48 pp. This pamphlet is in essence an explanation of Rolland's war position in *Au-dessus de la mêlée*, on the premise that Rolland was neither a traitor to France nor a

great friend of Germany; he wanted to defend Germany, says Bueno, but was carried along by the wave of calumny against that nation. Bueno takes up Germany's defense.

687. Stephens, Mrs. Winifred Stephens Whale, *French Novelists of Today*. Second Series, London, New York: John Lane, xl, 302 pp. Rolland, pp. 95–136; a biographical sketch; pp. 137–176, *Jean-Christophe*. Both studies are fairly good, although they add little that is new.

688. Loyson, P. -H., *La Revue*, CXI (mars–juin), 499–507, CXII (juin–septembre), 252–262; 466–486; CXIII (septembre–décembre), 103–112; 446–455; *La Grande revue* (décembre), 193–204. These articles were all collected later in *Etes-vous neutres devant le crime?*, letter-preface by Verhaeren. Paris: Berger-Levrault, 1916, 239 pp. These are bitter attacks, generally unjust. Loyson, in his zeal, overlooks no details; consequently he has rectified some dates of the original publication, erroneously given by Rolland, of articles in *Au-dessus de la mêlée*.

689. Pioch, G., *Les hommes du jour* (24 juillet, 7, 21 août). A defense of Rolland against the accusations made by Massis in his *Romain Rolland contre la France*.

690. Renaitour, J.-M., *Bonnet Rouge* (18 juin, 18 juillet). Renaitour was one of the small group of ardent defenders of Rolland.

691. Souday, P., *Le Temps*, 30 juillet. Souday tries to conciliate the two extremes, and blames Romain Rolland as well as his enemy, Henri Massis, at the same time.

692. Albert, Ch., «Pensée déprimante», *Bataille syndicaliste*, 31 août. See Thiesson's reply in *Les Hommes du jour*, (2 octobre). —, «Lettre», *Les Hommes du jour*, (16 octobre). —, *Au-dessous de la mêlée; Romain Rolland et ses disciples*, M. Rivière et Cie., 1916, 48 pp. A socialist attacks Rolland, who had rather bitterly criticized the position taken by the socialists in the war. This pamphlet reproduces articles by Albert, including «Pensée déprimante.» He criticizes Rolland because Rolland refused to blame Prussia and Prussian imperialism alone for the war. This was also published in an Italian translation, with a letter from H. G. Wells, Milan: edizione del Popolo d'Italia, 1916, 55 pp.

693. Seippel, P., *Journal de Genève*, 4 octobre 1915, and in *Coenobium*, IX (ottobre–novvembre–dicembre), 24–29. Principally concerning the genesis of *Jean-Christophe* and its significance for its epoch.

694. Truc, G., *La Grande revue*, XIC (décembre), 337–341. He criticizes Rolland's style, and calls his thinking «. . . la pseudo-philosophie . . . une espèce de pot-pourri, où s'épanchent, dans une allure néo-romantique, tous les lieux communs de l'anarchisme individuel ou scandinave, et la débile fadeur des cerveaux innocents et chevelus qui n'ont rien compris à Nietzsche et à Ibsen.»

695. Heine, G., *Christliche Welt*, XXIX, 6, Spalte 114–119. *Jean-Christophe*, in its German translation, 1914, Rütten & Loening, is the occasion of this article, which is devoted principally to a discussion of Rolland and Germany. Heine has numerous adverse criticisms to make of the novel in this respect.

696. Meyier, Fenna de, *Onze Eeuw*, III, pp. 75–103. This is one of the best and most complete studies of Jean-Christophe written at that time, although studies of later dates partially replace it. Meyier points out the circle of life in *Jean-Christophe:* the vision which Christophe had when he was a child returns to him at the time of his death.

697. Kammerer, *Christliche Welt*, XXIX, Spalte 426–429. Kammerer reproduces most of «Au-dessus de la mêlée,» and greets enthusiastically Rolland's attempts to effect a Franco-German understanding. Rolland is the first Frenchman in years, he says, to write about Germany and German art without the usual prejudices.

698. Messer, A., *Internationale Rundschau*, I, 154–158. A reply to Rolland's article, «Le Meurtre des élites», and an attack on Rolland from the German side.

699. Papini, G., *Stroncature*, Florence: Libreria della Voce, 1917, 2nd edition. «Romain Rolland», pp. 211–221, dated 1915. A violent attack by a germanophobe.

700. *Les Hommes du jour*, «Le Cas Romain Rolland» (27 novembre, 4, 11, 18 décembre; 1er janvier, 6, 13, 20 mai 1916). Articles and replies to the inquiry by P. Signac, R. Arcos, A. Doyen, J. Marnold, G. Besson, J. Gaument, B. Collin, Han Ryner, G. Dupin, and many others.

701. *Revue de Hollande*. «Enquête sur l'attitude de M. Romain Rolland pendant la guerre» (15 décembre 1915, 15 février 1916). There are several interesting articles. Fontainas, A., pp. 767–774, says that war is hateful, but the Allies are right and Rolland wrong. Eeden, F. van, pp. 774–776, says that France has had great poets, novelists, but her greatest glory is men of unshakeable character, such as Hugo and Romain Rolland. He describes the great effect produced by Rolland on the smaller nations. Gaultier, J. de, II, 1021–1030, attacks Rolland from a carefully prepared logical basis, going, or purporting to go, to the roots of Rolland's philosophy. He says that Rolland's case is typical of late religious crises. The conclusion is that one must regard him as an enemy because he speaks for peace. Letty, J., II, 1038–1042, replies to Charles Bernard's attack, but sees in Rolland an ill-timed idealist. Bernard, Ch., II, 1042–1044, criticizes the dilettantism of Rolland, whose germanism, he says, is undoubtedly what makes him liked by such Dutch admirers as Van Eeden. There are various other articles, signed and unsigned, one by Rémy de Gourmont.

702. *Revue mensuelle*. «Enquête sur M. Romain Rolland», XVI No. 169

(septembre), 153–154, 186–188, 210–213, 244–248, 286–288, 318–320, 343–348, 371–376 (Arcos, Dupin, Martinet, Mauclair among others); XVII, Supplément (novembre 1916), 1–4; Supplément (décembre 1916), 1–4; Supplément (janvier 1917), 1–4 (Gaument, Monod-Herzen, Guilbeaux, Masson among others); Supplément (février 1917), 1–4.

1916

703. Renaitour, J.-M., Servant, S., Loyson, P.-H., *Au-dessus ou au coeur de la mêlée?* Une polémique républicaine, avec une lettre de Romain Rolland. Editions de la revue l'«Essor», 94 pp. This brochure reproduces the articles in the dispute between these men, carried on principally in the *Bonnet Rouge*. Loyson and Servant oppose Renaitour, who defends Romain Rolland.

704. Guérard, Albert L., *Five Masters of French Romance*, London: F. Unwin, 316 pp. Guérard's chapter on Rolland is interesting and some of his criticisms must be seriously considered. He is puzzled by Rolland's attitude during the Dreyfus affair and criticizes for different reasons Rolland's stand during the first World War. Guérard apparently does not see the similarity of Rolland's attitude during these crises. His remarks about Jean-Christophe are very good.

705. *Les Humbles*. Special number dedicated to Rolland. There are articles by some eleven writers. The articles principally concern Rolland's war attitude. The most important are perhaps those by Henri Guilbeaux, Maurice Bataille, and Han Ryner.

706. Séché, A., *La France centre et foyer de la civilisation européenne, lettre ouverte à Romain Rolland, 28 décembre 1916*, Sansot, 6 pp. Ardent militarism and nationalism prevent a former admirer of Rolland's from justly evaluating the latter's writings of the war years.

707. Södermann, Sven, *Romain Rolland*, Stockholm: Norstedt, iv, 63 pp. Södermann writes first, briefly, of Rolland's early life, educational background, and family, then of his early writings, especially in relation to his developing cult of the Hero, and the theme of the heroic life and struggle in *Les Tragédies de la foi*, and *Jean-Christophe*. He points out that the «Drames de la Révolution» were written during the period of Tolstoy's influence. The long study of *Jean-Christophe*, pp. 19–50, is very good. Södermann suggests that the *Buisson ardent* was written because of Rolland's accident—hence its tone and subject. In *La Nouvelle journée* he sees the influence of Goethe.

708. Vogt, William, *A Propos du moins Romain des Rollands furieux. Riposte à l'auteur d'«Au-dessus de la mêlée», et à ses thuriféraires de jadis et d'aujourd'hui*, Paris: chez l'auteur, 31 pp. This attack is more or less typical of the many unfair articles of the war years. In a flippant, allusive

style and Parisian «blague,» Vogt accuses Rolland of being, among various other undesirable things, an excellent strategist in the propagation of his books and pamphlets, and calls him a «bourgeois cossu.»

709. Isaacs, L. M., *Bookman*, N. Y., XLII (January), 549. Principally about *Musiciens d'autrefois.* "One may say of M. Rolland that he approaches musical criticism like a novelist, and novel writing like a musician—with the added statement, of course, that he accomplishes both tasks as one who knows." He considers Rolland the most interesting of living musical critics.

710. Bundock, C. J., "The Book We Have Waited For", *Labour Leader* (March 9), p. 7. An enthusiastic article about *Au-dessus de la mêlée*, recently published in an English translation by Allen and Unwin. Cf. also an unsigned article in the *London Times Literary Supplement* (March 9), p. 110, which upholds Rolland as the true spirit of France and of humanity, while pointing out some minor errors.

711. Barge, H., *Die Hilfe* (30 März), 209–211. Barge approves what Rolland is trying to do, but criticizes his method. Rolland, says Barge, is too partial to France, and he accuses Rolland of pointing out with pride the spirit of aggression in the French army.

712. Farrère, A., *Coenobium*, X(marzo–aprile), 1–19. A study of Rolland's ideas on the subject of individualism during the war.

713. König, G., *Revue de Hongrie*, XVII (janvier–juin), 19–30. An unusually impartial article considering its date. The principal subjects are *Jean-Christophe* and *Au-dessus de la mêlée.* Some of his analysis of the portrayal of a genius in *Jean-Christophe* is very good.

714. Morel, L., *Revue des sciences politiques* (15 août), 127–132. Concerning Rolland's attitude towards the war, Morel says that Germany alone is guilty of the war, and he proceeds to criticize Rolland on this basis. Like all intellectuals, says Morel, Rolland hesitates to lay the blame on any one person or nation, yet Rolland fulminates against sterile intellectuals.

715. Bowler, M. E., *The Nation*, CII (Supplement, February 10), 6–7; CIII (November 23), 484–486. Both articles are a defence of Rolland and a review of his position. Bowler also discusses the attitude of various public and literary men towards Rolland.

716. Heinrici, J., "Die deutsche Tonkünstler des 20. Jahrhunderts, nach Romain Rollands *Jean-Christophe*", *Signale für die Musikalische Welt*, LXXIV, 361–366, 377–382, 395–399. This is perhaps the best article yet written on this subject.

717. Benda, J., *Les Sentiments de Critias*, Emile-Paul Frères, 1917, 284 pp. Benda includes the open letter to Rolland, pp. 269–272, which had appeared first in *L'Opinion*, IX (19 février 1916), 169–170. His criticisms bear almost entirely upon Rolland's lack of intelligence.

1917

718. Violani-Cambi, B., *La Pensée de Romain Rolland et plus particulièrement l'Italie et les Italiens dans son oeuvre*, Prato, 1917, 112 pp.

719. Sapir, E., *Dial*, LXII (May 17), 423–426. Sapir lays emphasis on Rolland's love of humanity, neither maudlin nor intemperate, on his idealism, which has its roots in the actual world of men and women, and consequently is not mere sentimentalism. Sapir regards Christophe as a symbol, as well as tingling flesh and blood, of absolute sincerity in life and in art.

720. Jouve, P. -J., «La pensée présente de Romain Rolland,» *Les Tablettes* (mai). Especially about Rolland's ideas on war and revolution.

721. Heine, G., *Christliche Welt*, XXXI, 49, Spalte 846–847. About *Jean-Christophe à Paris*. Heine is one of the few to recognize at this time that Rolland's bitter criticism of France springs from a wounded but deeply loving heart. Rolland does not penetrate very deeply into the German character according to Heine, who does not back his statement up with detailed examples.

722. Dauzat, A., *Les Cahiers idéalistes français*, pp. 172–175. An enthusiastic article about Rolland's work of the war years, his struggle for freedom of thought, against militarism, for goodness, charity. Rolland is not at all neutral: «Nul n'est resté plus profondément, plus ardemment Français.»

723. Maurel, A., *Mercure de France*, CXXIII (1er septembre), 5–19. Contains three subjects: Maurel's attitude towards *Au-dessus de la mêlée*; his appreciation of *Jean-Christophe* as a work of art; anti-German propaganda. Some of his critical remarks about *Jean-Christophe* are good.

724. Sancerme, Ch., *Les Serviteurs de l'ennemi*, 2nd ed., Paris, 354 pp. Rolland especially, pp. 60, 73–74, 77, 87, 266. Sancerme discusses the dispute carried on in the *Bonnet Rouge*; he rectifies some of the careless statements made about Rolland and the *Bund Neues Vaterland*.

725. Tailhade, L., *Les Livres et les hommes—(1916–1917)*, Crès, pp. 23–32. A polite attack by an enthusiastic arm-chair strategist and warrior, who does not like what he calls a Swiss accent and Lutheran tinge in Rolland's works.

1918

726. Anquetil, G., *Essai sur Romain Rolland. La beauté de son oeuvre et ses erreurs*. ed. «Aux Alliés,» 40 pp. Anquetil admires *Jean-Christophe*, but he condemns Rolland for his stand during the war.

727. Debran, Isabelle, *M. Romain Rolland, initiateur du défaitisme*, Geneva: Henri Jarrys, 3rd ed., 39 pp. This attack borders at times on libel. Isabelle Debran was an American citizen who was living in Switzerland.

See her article «Prisonnière en Allemagne» in the *Journal de Genève* (7 octobre 1915) and her *Prisonnière en Allemagne*, Payot, 62 pp.; also her article in *Le Temps* (22–27 septembre 1915) for more information about her. See also the pamphlet: Servance, G., *Réponse à Mme Isabelle Debran*, Neuchâtel: Comité en faveur d'une paix durable, 1916.

728. Ziegler, J., *Romain Rolland im "Jean-Christophe" über Juden und Judentum*, Vienna: Beck und Sohn. An interesting and sensitive study of this question, written by a Jewish scholar.

729. Toth, K., "Jean-Christophe und die deutsche Kultur," *Deutsche Rundschau*, XLIV (Januar), 57–78. A bitter attack, obviously inflamed by the passions of nationalism. Toth castigates Rolland for having dared to dream of a harmony between European races, of a mixture of pure Germanic blood, the purest of all, with that of degenerate races. Note that this was written in 1918.

730. Weinberg, A. K., "The Dream in *Jean-Christophe*," *Journal of Abnormal Psychology*, XIII (April 1918–February 1919), 12–16. A new and interesting interpretation of Ada's dream, p. 313 of the first volume of the English translation. The article reveals Rolland's profoundly intuitive grasp of psychology, normal and abnormal.

731. Fernau, H., *Wissen und Leben*, XX (1. April–15. September 1918), 297–304. A first-hand account of an interview with Rolland which covered most of the important points of his war-time and postwar thinking: his attitude "au-dessus de la mêlée," his attitude towards the Russian revolution, pacifism, the place of the individual in society, the German revolution, and other points.

732. Heine, A., *Westermanns Illustrierte Deutsche Monatshefte* (November), 290–296. Of especial interest in studying German ideas about France and about Rolland during and immediately after the first World War.

733. Boeck, Ch., *Preussische Jahrbücher*, CLXXI, 38–51. One of Boeck's chief criticisms of Rolland is that of his excessive intellectualism and lack of soul; his characters are not completely alive. For the opposite view concerning Rolland's intellectualism see Benda, Maxence, and Souday.

734. Loyson, P. -H., «La Conversion de Romain Rolland au Bolchévisme,» *La Revue*, CXXVII-CXXIX, 56–69. This critic is not any more kindly disposed towards Rolland's postwar ideas that he was towards his stand during the war.

735. Prilipp, Breda, "Deutschland und Frankreich bei Romain Rolland," *Hochland*, pp. 178–189. Prilipp criticizes Toth's observations concerning Rolland's portrayal of Germany and the Germans, and he studies briefly Rolland's ideas about France, and about universal human unity.

736. Van Tricht, J. S., *Onze Eeuw*, II, 257–298. Van Tricht studies *Jean-Christophe* on the basis of its philosophy. He first discusses the causes and

motives that inspired Rolland to write the novel, then the psychological background (found in various prefaces and in the conclusion of the novel itself): art is a complement to life; it is the projection of an unfulfilled longing, the conquering of suffering, anxiety, or weakness, and finally, in *Jean-Christophe*, it is the proclamation to all men of the liberty that Rolland had found for himself. Christophe's philosophy of life is, he finds, a sort of vitality and sincerity. In later volumes Van Tricht finds that other values appear: sacrifice, spiritual norms. He explains the significance of Grazia in some detail.

1919

737. Colin, P., *La Vertu d'héroïsme et Romain Rolland*, Brussels: Lacomblez; 2nd ed. Brussels: Maurice Lamertin, 24 pp. Rolland's place in the cult of the hero as it has developed in modern trends of thought and literature.

738. Duclaux, Agnes Mary Frances (Robinson), *Twentieth Century Writers. Reviews and Reminiscences*, New York: Scribners; London: W. Collins sons & Co., (1919), xxiii, 258 pp. The first edition was published in 1914. Rolland, pp. 34–50. The author is highly attracted by the energy in the writings of Rolland, especially in *Jean-Christophe*.

739. Küchler, W., *Romain Rolland. Henri Barbusse. Fritz von Unruh*, Würzburg, 86 pp. This is a good study of Rolland, especially about the Germanic and Beethovenian sources of *Jean-Christophe*, and about Hugo Wolf and *Jean-Christophe*.

740. Souday, P., *Le Temps*, 27 mars. According to this review article about *Colas Breugnon*, Romain Rolland, being of the "école de la vie," does not make his books; his books form within him. Souday remarks certain similarities between this novel and the *fabliaux*.

741. Halbwachs, Jeanne, *La Vie ouvrière*, 28 mai. *Colas Breugnon* is the laughter that is the free spirit of man; he is the man of the people, who creates, who lives by his works, who gives all but takes nothing. What Colas has to offer us now: creation and revolution. This is an interesting interpretation from the left!

742. Gide, A., «Réflexions sur l'Allemagne,» in his *Oeuvres complètes*, ed. N.R.F., IX, 115, 119–120. The first of these appeared also in the *Nouvelle revue française*, (1er juin 1919), pp. 35–46. These are very adverse criticisms of *Jean-Christophe* and other works, by a critic who feels that Rolland, in his writing, is more Germanic than French.

743. Bloch, J.-R., *L'Humanité*, 7, 8, 10 juin. A good sketch of the characters of Colas Breugnon, his wife, and his daughter, of the philosophy of the book and its relation to, and differences from, *Jean-Christophe*.

744. Le Cardonnel, G., *La Minerve française* (15 juin), pp. 290–292. Le

Cardonnel criticizes *Colas Breugnon* from a very strict, classical point of view, and draws false conclusions concerning Rolland's philosophy by attributing to *Colas*, which he analyzes only partially, all of Rolland's philosophy.

745. Burke, J. N., "The Democratic Ideal in Music," *Musical Quarterly* (July), pp. 316–328. Burke compares Tolstoy's and Rolland's judgments on music, and their efforts to infuse it with democratic ideals.

746. Gorki, Maxim, Letter to Rolland, *La Vie ouvrière*, 16 juillet. A letter asking Rolland to write the biography of Beethoven, adapted for children.

747. Groussac, P., *La Nación*, Julio 27 y 28. A typical example of rather conservative criticism. It is not always accurate, and the author labors under a good deal of misunderstanding about Rolland and his work.

748. Martinet, M., *La Vie ouvrière*, 20 août. Martinet indicates the true meaning of *Liluli*, and its place in Rolland's thinking, at least as this is seen from the point of view of a militant revolutionist. Martinet also points out the importance of Rolland's *Théâtre du peuple* for those who are working for a renewal of the world.

749. Spiers, A.H.G., *Review*, New York, I (August 30), 342–343. The author distinguishes the man Rolland (who "abandoned France," and whom he does not like) from Rolland the artist. Spiers is more convinced of the artistic value of *Colas Breugnon* than were most of the French critics. He discusses the vital, meaningful qualities of the novel as he understands them. For him, Colas is the epitome of bourgeois qualities.

750. Tíndaro, Jorge Celso, "Hacia la libertad espiritual," *Nosotros*, XXXIII (septiembre), 106–115. Tíndaro believes that the fundamental themes of *Jean-Christophe* are the idiosyncrasies of the genius and the triumph of life. A central purpose is to be found, he says, in the didactic qualities of the work. Christophe and the immortal thought of the Ninth Symphony: *Durch Leiden zur Freude*.

751. Herzog, W., *Das Forum*, III (Oktober), 6–9. Praise for Rolland's war attitude, for his love of truth and of humanity. Rolland and the German revolution.

752. Baudouin, C., *Contemporary Studies*. Translated by E. and C. Paul. London: Allen & Unwin, 1924, 288 pp. Romain Rolland pp. 62–78. First published in *The Word*, The Hague, October 4 and 11, 1919. Rolland had a great influence on Baudouin during his adolescence. Baudouin, like many others who already knew Rolland, first read *Au-dessus de la mêlée* in Massis' pamphlet, *Romain Rolland contre la France*. He here studies Rolland's principal purposes in his different works, the various aspects of his thinking, and the development of these ideas. He finds liberty to be the connecting thread that runs throughout all Rolland's works.

753. Edschmid, C., «I Tedeschi e Romain Rolland,» *Coenobium*, XII

(novembre-dicembre), 3–16. A vigorous defense of Rolland's efforts to bring about unity among men, and a résumé of Rolland's position in Germany at that time, especially among younger writers.

754. Ganz, H., *Wissen und Leben,* XXII (1. Oktober 1919–15. September 1920), 121–138. A very sympathetic and just article. Ganz studies especially Rolland and the theater (*Le Théâtre du peuple, le Théâtre de la Révolution*). He also analyzes briefly Rolland's other works and discusses their relation to Rolland's ideas.

754A. Rosenberg, F., "Franzosen und Deutschen im Romain Rollands *Jean-Christophe,*" *Germanische-romanische Monatsschrift,* VII (1915–1919), 196–213. The author discusses more than is indicated by the title. It is also a study of Rolland's place in the modern world, in humanity's new beliefs.

755. Vandérem, F., *Le Miroir des lettres,* 2e série, vol. II. Flammarion; Rolland, pp. 112–116. Vandérem discusses Rolland's attempt to unite all intellectuals (*Déclaration d'Indépendance de l'Esprit*).

1920

756. Zweig, Stefan, *Romain Rolland, der Mann und das Werk,* Frankfurt a. M.: Rütten & Loening, 279 pp.; 3rd ed., enlarged, 1926. English translation by E. and C. Paul, New York: Seltzer, 1921, 337 pp. French translation by O. Richez, Éditions Pittoresques, 1930. This is one of the best of the biographies of Rolland, although some parts of it have, of course, become out of date.

757. Curtius, E. R., *Drei literarische Wegbereiter des neuen Frankreichs,* 2nd. ed., Potsdam: Kiepenheuer Verlag. Romain Rolland, Part 3. A very good essay on Rolland's life, education, and some of his works. Curtius studies and evaluates rather justly Rolland's position during the war. He makes some interesting observations concerning the relationship of the "heroic biographies" to the various parts of *Jean-Christophe*. Germany and *Jean-Christophe*.

758. Jouve, P.-J., *Romain Rolland vivant 1914–1919,* Ollendorff, 336 pp. An excellent work, by a sincere admirer, about Rolland and his activities during this critical period. Jouve knew Rolland personally in Switzerland. There is a rather summary bibliography of Rolland's works previous to 1914, and a more detailed bibliography of his works after that date. See a good review by L. Bazalgette, *L'Humanité,* 23 novembre 1920.

759. Evrard, E., *Nos Mandarins* (Barrès, Brieux, Lavedan, Rostand, Rolland, France), Tourcoing, 1920, 317 pp. Rolland, pp. 266–290. Written from the point of view of a French classicist and a dogmatic Catholic, the article adds little to the subject. His discussion, rather brief, of the lyric qualities of Rolland's style (Rolland, he says, is above all, a lyric poet) is fair.

760. Richter, E., *Germanische-romanische Monatsheft,* VIII, 299–312.

A stylistic study of *Colas Breugnon*, *Jean-Christophe*, *Le Temps viendra*, *Le Théâtre du peuple*, and *Beethoven*. Richter criticizes Rolland's *Beethoven* because of a lack of objectivity; Rolland wrote the biography solely from out of Beethoven's soul, not out of the soul of the surroundings. She finds Rolland's judgments about Vienna ludicrous occasionally and frequently wrong. She suggests that this may be due to Wagner's dislike of Vienna. This study is a rather general work, but there are some interesting considerations on Rolland and music, and on his historical ideas and perspectives.

761. Lefebvre, R., *Le Populaire*, 11 janvier. Rolland's authority in the socialist movement is doubly great, says Lefebvre, because before the war Rolland was a writer only, and has never had ". . . dans son portefeuille une seule carte rouge. . . ."

762. Souday, P., *Le Temps*, 8 avril. Souday is now more just in his estimation of Rolland than formerly, although his criticisms are all unfavorable. He sees in *Liluli* the complete abdication of Christophe, and Rolland's change of heart about Life. However, he still sees Rolland as an anti-intellectual.—, *Le Temps*, 2 septembre. Rolland makes good use, says Souday, of the contrast between innocence of the two young people and the horror of the war, in *Pierre et Luce*. He then takes Rolland to task for his stand during the war, for his blaming of the munition makers in the novel. He repeats his charge: Rolland is a "peintre du coeur," in whom the heart and sentimentalism outweigh the intelligence.—, *ibid.*, 14 octobre. *Clerambault*, Souday says in this article, should have led logically to Tolstoian non-resistance; but Rolland refused to go that far. The only good thing that Souday can find in the novel is that when Clerambault comes in contact with socialists and revolutionaries he dislikes them.

763. Brugh de Kay, Helen van, *The Nation*, CXI (July 10). About the first presentation of *Danton* at the People's Theater, Jaurès' preliminary remarks, and an account of the presentation of this play by Max Reinhardt in Berlin, 1920.

764. Dunan, R., *Le Populaire*, 6 septembre. A reply to Souday's article of September 2 about *Pierre et Luce*. He defends Rolland especially against the charge of not being an intellectual. Such attacks, he says, are simply part of an effort to halt the spread of Rolland's (and Barbusse's) works. —, *ibid.*, 21 septembre. A good review article about *Clerambault* by a revolutionary, who studies the various reasons for Clerambault's failure to come into real contact with socialist and revolutionary groups.

765. Bodin, L., *L'Humanité*, 13 septembre. Another reply to Souday's article on *Pierre et Luce*. Bodin insists that *Pierre et Luce* is an attack on the bourgeoisie, and that Souday attacked it because he is a bourgeois. Aside from this, there are some good critical remarks about the novel.

766. Seippel, P., *Journal de Genève*, 27 septembre; translated in part in

Living Age, CCCVII (November), 360–362. This article begins and ends with a very favorable criticism of *Pierre et Luce*, the greater part being given over to an attack on Rolland's kind feelings toward Russia, regarded by Seippel as a sort of Genghis Khan. Seippel also discusses Rolland's position in regard to President Wilson.

767. Chapiro, J., *Die Zukunft*, CXI (2. Oktober), 49–56. A good study on the importance of Rolland's thinking for modern man, for whom life in present-day society is so difficult. Chapiro also studies the place of *Les Précurseurs* in the development of Rolland's thinking. In *Au-dessus de la mêlée*, and before, Rolland believed that the value of a man determined the value of his works. After *Les Précurseurs*, he believed that ideas are a man's pride, but that the ideas are made for man, and not man for the ideas.

768. Martinet, M., *La Vie ouvrière*, 15 octobre. A review of *Clerambault*. «Il faut voir ensemble ces deux aspects, de la douleur lucide et de la foi, pour comprendre la pensée et le coeur de Rolland, pour comprendre l'unité de son oeuvre.» This is most clearly revealed in *Clerambault*.

1921

769. Bonnerot, J., *Romain Rolland* (*sa vie, son oeuvre*), Carnet-Critique, «Bibliographie,» pp. 101–139. One of the best and most completely documented studies of Rolland and his works.

770. Hatzfeld, H., *Paul Claudel und Romain Rolland. Neufranzösische Geistigkeit*, Munich: Rösl, 1921, 161 pp. Hatzfeld fails to relate the two men: they are simply two highly important men of two opposing French tendencies: Feudal and Revolutionary. Hatzfeld does not show what part of the French spirit they have in common. See the review by Klemperer, *Archiv für das Studium der Neueren Sprachen*, CXLIII (1922), 309–311.

771. Martinet, M., Introduction and notes to his *Pages choisies de Romain Rolland*, Ollendorff, 2 volumes, 350, 320 pp. «Bibliographie,» II, 309–316. This work does not include *Liluli*, *Clerambault*, or *Pierre et Luce*. It gives a good general explanation and analysis of the more important parts of Rolland's works and his thinking to date.

772. Altamira, Rafael D., *La Nueva literatura pacifista. El "Clerambault" de Romain Rolland*, Madrid: Editorial Reus, 46 pp. Altamira criticizes *Clerambault* on the ground that Rolland frequently forgets that he is a novelist. The novel form is harmful to the dialectic side of *Clerambault*. There are two purposes in the novel which cannot well be harmonized: the attempt to portray the psychological atmosphere of French society during the war; a process of argumentation and discussion on the theme of war, peace, and militarism. Trying to combine the two leads Rolland into various errors, which Altamira discusses at length.

773. Nicolaï, G. F., *Romain Rollands Manifest und die deutschen Antworten, mit einem Anhang über den Fall Nicolaï*, Charlottenburg: Mundus

Verlagsanstalt, 72 pp. Nicolaï publishes a letter from Rolland. The article is interesting for a study of Rolland's influence, for the way the *Déclaration d'Indépendance de l'esprit* was circulated, who, and what percentage of those requested, signed it.

774. Thibaudet, A., *La Nouvelle revue française*, (1er janvier), 67–80. *Clerambault*, says Thibaudet, belongs to the series of works inspired by the Dreyfus case among the writers of 1900, such as *Monsieur Bergeret à Paris* and *Justice*. Rolland said it was not autobiographical, and Thibaudet sees as the reason for this the fact that Rolland believed he already possessed the truth, whereas Clerambault seeks it throughout the novel.

775. Serge, V., *La Vie ouvrière*, 9 avril. Praise for Rolland who "betrayed" the bourgeoisie for the proletariat but whose cult of disinterested intellectualism and aversion for violence are illusory. This is a rather frequent reaction of more militant communists towards Rolland.

776. Dilla, Geraldine P., *North American*, CCXIII (May), 676–680. Most of Dilla's article is to show that *Liluli* is the logical sequence of the tragedy of *Jean-Christophe* and the comedy of *Colas Breugnon*. All three works lead to disillusionment. There is a good analysis and discussion of Rolland's purpose in writing *Liluli*, but Dilla's insistence on the despair and disillusionment is exaggerated.

777. Holmes, J. H., *The World Tomorrow* (October), 305–308. Holmes welcomes with enthusiasm *Clerambault* and the ideas and ideals there expressed. He analyzes the novel and Rolland's position during the war. He finds enduring qualities in *Clerambault*.

778. Bahr, H., *Bilderbuch*, Vienna: Wienerliterarische Anstalt; Rolland, pp. 142–147. This account of Bahr's first knowledge of Rolland and the first reading of *Jean-Christophe* falls short of its promising beginning. For Rolland, says Bahr, all exterior life becomes an inner problem; the fate of every man is the theme of this one man (Christophe); Rolland's men weave their own destinies. This is an "Urdeutsch" work (in the line from *Meister Eckhart* to Goethe). However, there is something new in it, says Bahr, who unfortunately fails to analyze this something new.

779. Wolfsberg, O., "Romain Rolland und die jüdische Gegenwartsgeschichte," *Jeschurun*, Berlin, VIII, 380–391. Wolfsberg shows the place that Rolland has assumed in the minds of the Jewish people. Rolland is really more the pretext than the subject of the article, although there are to be found here some interesting ideas about Rolland and the conquered who are sure to be the victors, and about this idea in relation to Christianity.

1922

780. Maxe, Jean, *Le Bolchévisme littéraire* (Cahiers de l'Anti-France. No. 1) *L'Idole «Européen» Romain Rolland*. Bossard, 91 pp. Published also in his *Anthologie des Défaitistes*. Preface by E. Buré, Bossard, 1925, 2 vol-

umes, xiv, 560, 561–1154 pp. Rolland, pp. 13–91. Other parts: II. L'Alliance du défaitisme et du Bolchévisme en Suisse, 1914–1919, pp. 93–159. III. L'Abbaye et le bolchévisme cultural, pp. 161–238, and X. Le complot Judéo-Bolchévik mondial, pp. 984–1113, also contain some "judicious" remarks about Rolland, who is accused of being one of the centers of these diabolical machinations. Maxe devotes about half of his work on Rolland to proving that Rolland had no will, and was purely emotional; the rest concerns the evil results of Rolland's action and influence. Maxe makes some biased statements, and when he discusses from firsthand information some such interesting question as Rolland and Zimmerwald, he must be read with caution.

781. Grautoff, O., *Preussische Jahrbücher*, CLXXXVII, 2 (Februar), 204–206. Judgments on *Clerambault* and Rolland's stand during the war. The great disappointment of the Germans in Rolland, after the war, was caused by the fact that he left the arena after victory, instead of remaining to combat all the ills that needed to be corrected. Thomas Mann is the only one of Rolland's opponents whom Grautoff considers worthy to criticize Rolland.

782. Bernier, J., *Clarté*, n.s., No. 17 (15 juillet), p. 397. Bernier analyzes Rolland's dilemma, which results from the problem of violence in the modern world, as it is shown in Rolland's fragmentary play, *Les Vaincus*; the heart versus the intelligence is another aspect of this dilemma. This critic too feels that the heart has the chief place in Rolland's personality and thinking.

783. Martinet, M., *L'Humanité*, 14 septembre. Martinet now feels that, although he had formerly believed that Rolland was not at all a neutral, he must have a sort of complete inner neutrality in order to have been able to write *Les Vaincus* in his youth.

784. Houston, P. H., "Romain Rolland and the plea for international brotherhood," *Southwestern Review*, VIII (October), 134–145. A better title for the somewhat summary article about this important aspect of Rolland's thinking might have been, "Romain Rolland and the Romantic spirit;" as such it is rather interesting.

785. Küchler, W., *Preussische Jahrbücher*, CXC (Oktober–Dezember), 29–38. Küchler feels that Rolland the artist suffered greatly, in his works and in his soul, because of his leaning towards both social and artistic criticism, especially because of his leaning towards social criticism and action. Küchler's remarks about Rolland's criticisms of France are less felicitous.

786. Emmel, F., *ibid.*, CLXXXVIII (April), 108–111. A rather brief study of the historical sources of *Les Loups*, and a critical analysis of the play and of its presentation by Berthold Viertel: its dramatic effect in a Germany facing the same choice.

787. Manacorda, G., *Studi e saggi*, Florence: F. Lemonnier. Rolland,

pp. 215–222. When Rolland blames the war on one class, it is not sound, says Manacorda. This is only a way of cataloguing a small part of humanity. Manacorda denies that Rolland is "au-dessus de la mêlée", and says that his work is, probably involuntarily, one of hate.

789. Platz, Hermann, *Geistige Kämpfe im modernen Frankreich*, Munich: Verlag Kösel und Pustet, 672 pp. Rolland, *passim*, especially pp. 180–205. A study by a Catholic writer of modern trends in France. Rolland is placed among them according to Platz's beliefs and prejudices. Somewhat prejudiced, his judgments must be accepted with caution.

1923

790. Schmidt, W. F., *Gral*, XVII (März), 281–282. A good review of *Voyage musical aux pays du passé*, especially about Rolland's method.

791. Baldensperger, F., *Revue de Littérature comparée*, III (avril–juin), 288–294. Baldensperger points out certain similarities between *Jean-Christophe* and *Daniel Vladys* by Camille Selden, which appeared in 1862.

792. Bachmann, F., "Jean-Christophe as a Portrayal of German Character," *Southwestern Review*, IX, 47–63. A study to determine to what extent Rolland's characterization of Germans and Germany is just. Bachmann considers principally Rolland's remarks about the "mensonge allemand"—false idealism, and emphasizes Rolland's knowledge of Germany through his knowledge of German music. The article is neither very profound nor very revealing, and is "sujet à caution."

793. Vasconcelos, José, *Vidas ejemplares. Beethoven. Miguel Angelo. Tolstoi*. Introduction by Vasconcelos. Mexico: Universidad Nacional de México, 440, iv pp. Publicaciones de la Secretaría de Educación Pública. In this short introduction, Vasconcelos explains his appreciation of these biographies, which he calls one of "los libros redentores," like those of Galdós, Tolstoy, Rolland, and Tagore.

794. Rosenfeld, P., *Musical Chronicle 1917–1923*, New York: Harcourt, Brace, 1923, viii, 314 pp. "Rolland and the composers," pp. 11–19. The part played by music in Rolland's youth, and in *Jean-Christophe*. Rolland understands music not as a composition of sevenths and ninths or ascending chords, but as the soul of its creators. Rosenfeld regards *Jean-Christophe* as a sort of *summum* of Rolland's experiences with music.

1924

795. Massis, H., *Jugements*, II, Plon. The basis of Massis' criticism is that Rolland, like Anatole France, is a dilettant, but a dilettant of faith ("fidéisme"), not of scepticism. Rolland, he says, accepts all, and cannot choose. Truth for Rolland is what one feels; he wishes to deny nothing, under the pretext that everything must be respected in human nature.

796. Stöcker, H., *Die Neue Generation*, XX (Januar–Februar). A good review of the *Vie de Gandhi* by an acquaintance and admirer of Rolland.

797. Masson-Oursel, F., «Indianisme . . .», *Mercure de France*, CLXXI (1er mai), 807–808. Rolland, faithful to his method of seeking ideas in typical persons, chose Gandhi and Tagore. Masson-Oursel points out elements in each of the Indians which Rolland cannot agree with, and shows what Rolland does in the work on Gandhi, which he regards as an admirable work and the natural completion of Rolland's *Tolstoï*.

798. Zweig, S., *Dial*, LXXVI (May), 445–448. The *Ame enchantée* is the principal subject of this article. Zweig points out the fight for freedom that is common to all of Rolland's heroes; the deep revolutionary vein they all have. Zweig analyzes this novel, *Colas Breugnon*, and *Clerambault* in this respect.

799. Bazalgette, L., *Europe*, V (juin), 246–249. A good review of the second volume of the *Ame enchantée*, *L'été*. Bazalgette calls Rolland "le maître écrivain."

800. Drake, W. A., *Sewanee Review*, XXXII (October), 386–404. A good general article about Rolland and his work, although it is dated by its time of publication. There is some good criticism of *Jean-Christophe* and other works. Drake stresses the connection between the man and his work. This has been better done by others, by Zweig especially. Drake discusses Malwida, Gabriel Monod, and the latter's wife, in connection with Rolland's background.

1924–1925

801. Fischer, V. A., *Gral*, XVIII, 457–458; XIX, 557–558. Fischer points out in Annette (*L'Ame enchantée*) Germanic characteristics, Roman traits, and occasional Indian mysticism. Annette and the religious necessities of the human soul, for whom the old, revealed religion no longer is satisfactory.

1925

802. Fassbinder, Klara Maria, *Romain Rolland. Der Mann und sein Werk*, Dortmund: Wolfram Verlag, 1925, 123 pp. Volume two of the collection "Dichter des Auslandes." See the review by Muckermann, *Gral*, XX (März 1926), 370–372.

803. Martin du Gard, M., *Nouvelles littéraires* (21 février). —, *Feux tournants*, C. Bloch, 234 pp.; Rolland, *passim*. The remarks about Rolland in both the article and in the volume were written after Martin du Gard's visit to him, and are a very lucid description of the effect that Rolland produced on his visitor. See also pp. 37–44 in *Feux tournants* for an interesting account of the life of Panaït Istrati and his relationship with Rolland.

804. Krause, H., *Gral,* XIX (August), 542–543. An interesting discussion of *Le Quatorze juillet* in post-war Germany. Krause observes that Rolland failed to present in adequate form in this play his ideas of rekindling the people's faith in republican ethics.

805. Basadre, Jorge, *Mercurio peruano,* XV, 175–191. A general discussion of Rolland, the man and his works; his principal ideas and their merits. Basadre also reviews many of the false judgments concerning Rolland, and attempts to rectify them. A shorter version of this article appeared later in *La Pluma,* VIII (Año 2) (septiembre de 1928), 93–97.

806. Nag, Kalidas, "Notes on Romain Rolland's Autobiographical Fragment," *Visva bharati Quarterly,* III, 80–82. A discussion of the part music played in Rolland's boyhood and later life. Nag also discusses *Jean-Christophe* in relation to this musical background. Nag was a personal acquaintance of Rolland's.

807. Marble, Mrs. Annie (Russell), *Nobel Prize Winners in Literature,* New York: Appleton; "Romain Rolland and *Jean-Christophe,*" pp. 175–188. A good survey of Rolland and his works, up to and including volume one of *L'Ame enchantée,* although it leans heavily on Zweig's biography.

1926

808. Alapetite, G., *Romain Rolland Clamecyçois.* Recueil collectif des articles publiés dans les numéros des 2 et 9 mai de l'*Echo de Clamecy,* en l'honneur du 60e anniversaire de la naissance de Romain Rolland, par MM. G. Alapetite, H. Bachelin, J. Bonnerot, J. Gadiou, M. Mignon, A. Renard, A. Du Tessier. Clamecy: impr. A. Lahaussois, 26 pp.

809. Lerch, Eugen, *Romain Rolland und die Erneuerung der Gesinnung,* Munich: M. Huebner, 331 pp. Contains a bibliography, chronological and by subject matter. It is an excellent work, based on Rolland's contribution to the overcoming of the sickly despair, materialism, and lack of faith prevalent in France towards the end of the century. Rolland's answer to the problem, says Lerch, was a sort of activism; it is struggle, but against one's self, not against others, a struggle to overcome evil and darkness. Lerch emphasizes well the religious (not necessarily orthodox) nature of his work: "Gott ist das Güte." This is a much deeper and fairer account of his feeling towards Life than the one-sided accounts of some critics, Souday, Benda, and others. Lerch's discussion of the various works of Rolland and their relation and affinites with Nietzsche and Bergson is very interesting. Rousseau and Rolland. Lerch finds that Rolland's tragedies are an integral part of his work and thinking. His philosophy is that of the struggle in the universe between enemy powers, forces, of equal strength, both equally justified. This is true in his dramas especially. This study should be read to understand Rolland's pacifism. —, *Frankfurter Zeitung,* 31. Januar. Lerch

here points out certain elements in Rolland's work which cause him to be placed among the expressionists.

810. *Liber Amicorum Romain Rolland.* Romain Rolland sexagenario ex innumeralibus amicis paucissimi grates agunt. Published by Gorky, Georges Duhamel, and Stefan Zweig, Zürich: Rotapfel Verlag, 406 pp. This is a collection of letters and tributes from numerous admirers and acquaintances of Rolland in various languages. The book is a moving testimony of his world-wide influence.

811. Price, L., *Atlantic Monthly*, CXXXVII (January), 71–81. Written for the 60th birthday of Rolland, this article is about *Jean-Christophe* principally. Price also studies briefly the other important works. He compares *Jean-Christophe* to *Faust.*

812. Marti, H., *Bund*, Bern, 14. Januar, and *Kleine Bund*, No. 4, and *Bund*, 29. Januar. Written after the presentation at Bern, under the direction of Dr. Hans Kaufmann, of *Le Jeu de l'amour et de la mort.* Marti calls Rolland's plays the "Iliad of the French revolution," which look both to the past and the present. They are the ". . . Echo der Tageskämpfe unter den hallenden Wölbungen der Geschichte. . . ."

813. Muckermann, F., *Gral*, XX (März), 370–372. Muckermann here writes of Rolland's relations with Catholicism, discusses briefly his *Triomphe de la raison*, *Le Jeu de l'amour et de la mort.* He reviews briefly the biographies by Zweig and Fassbinder.

814. Priacel, S., *Regards*, (23 juillet). An account of the presentation of *Danton* at the "Arènes de Lutèce"; the play's implications for present-day political action.

815. *Europe*, X, numéro spécial consacré à Romain Rolland à l'occasion de son soixantième anniversaire. Articles by many writers, pp. 131–316. The following are some of the more important. Gálvez, M., pp. 153–159. This Argentine writer regards Rolland as a summit in French and even world literature. In Rolland the form is of less importance than the essence, the content. Gálvez compares and contrasts Rolland with Stendhal and Bourget, and concludes that Rolland's ideology does not harm the life of his works. Montherlant, H., pp. 181–186. An enemy of Rolland's frankly admits that any true Christian can only take his stand beside Rolland. Frank, Waldo, pp. 151–152. «Rolland . . . est un homme intégral dans un siècle émietté. . . .» He has attained this unity, not by a flight into the past, but by adhering to his time. Gorki, M., pp. 160–164. Tribute to Rolland, sincere, honest, and loyal, in a cynical world. Tribute to his *Colas Breugnon*, and to his new conception of woman. Lichtendorf, T., pp. 172–174. Rolland in Roumania, and a brief discussion of *Colas Breugnon* and *Jean-Christophe.* Lunacharskii, A., pp. 175–180. Rolland and the Russian revolution in the eyes of a revolutionary. He makes both favorable and adverse criti-

cisms of Rolland. Roland-Holst, H., pp. 189–196. A communist explains the relationship between Rolland and modern revolutionary social movements. Rolland's idealism, love, and sacrifice are necessary in the struggle, she says. Haya de la Torre, R., Rolland's influence in South America. This article also appeared in Spanish, in *Amauta*, I, No. 2 (Octubre de 1926), 12–13. Arcos, R., pp. 265–271. Arcos says that in India and a good part of Asia, when one wants to distinguish the best parts of Europe, one calls them: "Romain Rolland's Europe." Alain, pp. 272–278. Alain studies briefly the themes of love and death in *Jean-Christophe*. There are some interesting reflections about Christophe and his music, about the novel as music, about Rolland as a musician, and the style of Jean-Christophe and music. Durtain, L., pp. 285–293. He discusses the biographies of Michael Angelo, Beethoven, Tolstoy, and Gandhi; their differences and their teachings. Martinet, M., pp. 294–299. Martinet's judgments on Rolland's theater differ from those of many critics. He prefers Rolland the dramatist. The real action of a drama, says Martinet, begins before the curtain rises and continues after it has fallen, in the minds of the spectators; it is combat, the playwright must be himself this combat, and Rolland is combat. Prunières, H., pp. 300–306. Prunières points out a duality in Rolland, which appeared even in his works of musical history: the objective study of facts and judgments based on moral criteria. The two are not always in accord in Rolland.

816. Deutsch, O. E., "Dichterische Freiheiten im Romain Rollands *Beethoven*," *Neue Zeitschrift für Musik*, XCIII, 489–492. Deutsch criticizes certain errors, notably, that Rolland makes Beethoven too Flemish.

817. Grautoff, E., and Grautoff, O., *Preussische Jahrbücher*, CCIII, 71–84. The two authors discuss briefly the europeanism of Rolland, its origins and influence; Rolland and Germany. *Liluli*, *Pierre et Luce*, and *Clerambault* arise from his revolt against dejection and despair, say the authors, and therefore have not the same importance as his other works. There are some thought-provoking remarks about *L'Ame enchantée*.

818. Richard-Mounet, L., *Mercure de France*, CLXXXVIII, 163–168. According to this critic, Rolland wrote, in *Le Jeu de l'amour et de la mort*, neither a tragedy, nor a drama, but a historical poem in dialogue. His criticisms are generally well founded, from the point of view of the stage presentation.

819. Stöcker, H., *Die Neue Generation*, XXII, 34–45. Stöcker visited Rolland in the fall of 1917. In this article she discusses at some length his experience with Tolstoy, his idealism, and his new ideals in art (especially the duty of art to bind all men together). Rolland's attitude during the war (1914–1918) as a result of these ideals; their relation to his attitude now towards the U.S.S.R. Rolland and Gandhi.

820. Wilker, K., *Das werdende Zeitalter*, V, 49–52. Wilker sees in Rolland

especially the advocate of a newer and better method of education for children.

1927

821. Brecot, J., «Une enquête du *Libertaire* sur la répression en Russie,» *La Vie ouvrière*, 17 juin. Bitter criticism for even answering *Libertaire's* query. Brecot, a communist, accuses Rolland of remaining "au-dessus de la mêlée," of confusing bourgeois governments, fascist dictatorships, and the dictatorships of the proletariat, because of his passive and pacifistic attitude. Note that this was written at a date when Rolland has been accused of being an avowed and valuable communist.

822. Kin-Yn-Yu, J. B., «La Renaissance chinoise et l'influence de Romain Rolland,» *Europe*, XV (septembre–décembre), 101–108. A very rewarding article for anyone interested in studying the influence of Rolland's thought and personality in the Orient.

823. Durtain, L., *Europe*, XV (septembre–décembre), 372–380. A short article about the influence of Paul Claudel and Rolland on Fritz von Unruh.

824. Sénéchal, Christian, *Europe*, XV (septembre-décembre), 536–542. A critical article about *L'Ame enchantée* by one of the best interpreters of Rolland's works. Bergsonism and the Germanic idea of becoming ("Stirb und werde") have entered French art, thanks to Rolland's novel.

825. Marquez Miranda, Fernando, *Amauta*, II, No. 10 (diciembre), 65–70. The author expresses some general ideas about Rolland, Rolland and music, *Jean-Christophe*, the biographies, Rolland's internationalism, and his religious sentiment.

826. Schüler, G., "Studien zur Romain Rollands *Colas Breugnon*," *Romanische Forschungen*, XL (Mai), 331–457. A lengthy and thorough stylistic study of *Colas Breugnon*. It is divided into two parts: 1. Das musikalische Element in der Sprache. . . . 2. Sprache und Wortschatz. The author finds that a form midway between prose and verse is used, especially in pathetic and important moments of Colas' life. Rhythm is used to reflect feeling, emotion, and character. Other poetic devices, alliteration and rhyme, are also used for similar purposes. Part II studies Rolland's use of proverbs, folklore, literary reminiscences, archaisms, and neologisms.

827. Borgese, G. A., *Ottocento europeo*, Milan: Treves; "Rolland e l'autorità morale," pp. 215–221; "Ame enchantée," pp. 222–228. In the first, the basis of Borgese's judgments of Rolland is that there is no moral authority without a simple, passionate, and rectilinear faith. He discusses Tolstoy and Rolland. In the second, Borgese says that Rolland's belief in the dignity of mankind led him to write about the perfect man, as others wrote about Il Cortegiano, Télémaque.

828. Gabriela, G., "La Visione della guerra in Romain Rolland," *Educazione fascista*, I.

829. Santoro, F., "Romanticismo vecchio e nuovo, Augusto von Platen e Romain Rolland," *Annuario del Reale Liceo ginnasio "Conti Gentili" Alatri*, 1927–1928, pp. 17–46.

830. Lob, Marcel, *Un grand Bourguignon, un grand Européen, Romain Rolland*, Auxerre: Tridon Gallot.

831. Schaezler, K., *Hochland*, XXIV, 2 (März–Oktober), 332–334. Concerns principally *Musiciens d'aujourd'hui*, *Musiciens d'autrefois*, and *Voyage musical aux pays du passé*, although *Beethoven* and *Jean-Christophe* are mentioned. Schaezler is interested by the kind of musicians who attracted Rolland, but he does not examine this subject thoroughly.

1928

832. Glauser, Charles, *Rolland: La Famille et la société*. Textes annotés et précédés d'une étude sur l'oeuvre de Romain Rolland, Hannover: C. Meyer, xxv, 112, 66 pp.

833. Lambert, R. R., *Beethoven Rhenan* (reconnaissance à Jean-Christophe). Les Presses françaises, 78 pp. Lambert records his impressions of Beethoven's house in the Bonngasse, during a stay in Germany during and after the occupation of the Rhineland. He outlines Beethoven's life and some of his work, and picks out the parallels between his life and Christophe's. He also seeks other musical origins of the novel. This aspect of *Jean-Christophe* has been studied in more detail by others.

834. Ostermann, W., "Das Bild des menschen in Goethes *Wilhelm Meister*, Kellers *Grünem Heinrich* und Romain Rollands *Jean-Christophe*," *Neue Heidelberger Jahrbücher*. Dissertation. Bonn. Vol. XV, 116 pp. This is a very interesting study in comparative literature; how the changing values in society are reflected in these novels.

835. Dubech, L., *Revue universelle*, XXXII (janvier–mars), 761–764. One would need to read Rolland's introduction to his *Montespan* before accepting the criticisms that Dubech makes of historical truth in Rolland's play, *Le Jeu de l'amour et de la mort*. More justified is his remark that, «L'auteur donna sa vraie mesure dans cette oeuvre où la vérité simple et la force créatrice manquent.»

836. Abraham, P., *Europe*, XVI (janvier–juin), 254–264. A review of *Le Jeu de l'amour et de la mort*. The article also deals with *Jean-Christophe* and *Au-dessus de la mêlée*. How Abraham became acquainted with Rolland's works.

837. Crémieux, A., *Europe*, XVI (janvier–juin), 252–254. Crémieux lists the European theaters where Rolland's *Jeu de l'amour et da la mort* had been presented from 1925 to 1927.

838. Chamson, A., *Europe*, XVI (janvier–juin), 546–550. A defense of Rolland against Benda.

839. Menut, A., and Chapman, D. I., Introduction to *Le Jeu de l'amour*

et de la mort, edited by Menut and Chapman. New York and London: Century Co. Their introduction, pp. vii–xxi, contains a more or less conventional sketch of the life and principal ideas and works of Rolland. Pages xiv–xxi treat his plays, and the editors have some interesting remarks. Concerning the revolutionary dramas, they express the belief that Rolland may have been influenced by the sociological doctrines of Emile Durckheim (the "collective soul," a benevolent force, etc.). Rolland rebelled against the submission of the individual to the will of the crowd and turned to the heroic biographies. Menut and Chapman point out some inconsistencies in his thinking.

840. Church, H. W., Introduction to *Jean-Christophe. I. L'Aube*, edited by Church, New York: Holt, xxxi, 216 pp. Bibliography, pp. xxx–xxxi. A similar introduction, with necessary changes and additions was published by Church in his edition of *Antoinette*, New York: Holt, 1930. His introduction to *Antoinette* is especially interesting because he publishes parts of a letter from Rolland in answer to a query by Church concerning the origins of Antoinette. Rolland denies the widely attributed source (Henriette Renan). This part of the introduction also appeared in *Modern Philology*, XXVIII (May 1931), 475–478. Both introductions are well done by an enthusiastic and sensitive admirer of Rolland.

841. Benda, J., *The Treason of the Clerks*. Translated by R. Aldington, N. Y.: W. Morrow & Co. Benda repeats essentially the same conclusions that he had expressed about Rolland during the first World War: Rolland scorns intelligence; he lacks logical thinking; he disregards facts; he is all sentiment. See the reply by Canguilhem, G., and Alexandre, M., *Europe*, XXIII (15 juin 1930), 302–304.

842. Guérard, A. L., *World Unity*, I, 309–314. Guérard is rather severe in his judgments, but he insists on two services that Rolland has rendered to the world: his efforts to remedy the lack of international understanding—especially between France and Germany—and the effort to remain above the passions of the day.

843. Mattzahn, H. A. von, *Deutsch-französische Rundschau*, I, 2, 788–790. Only a fair critical article about *Les Léonides*. Mattzahn sees in this play less a dramatic presentation than a framework in which Rolland has expressed his noble and heroic philosophy.

844. Seibt, R., *Zeitschrift für französischen und englischen Unterricht*, XXVII, 161–167. This critic feels that Rolland, instead of having tackled, himself, various problems which lay outside his training and competence, should have used his ideas and spirit to influence those who are qualified for action, especially in the political field. Otherwise he runs the risk of committing errors and of being used by others. This sort of criticism is more or less typical of these years, in which Rolland was elaborating his stand on

Soviet Russia, Communism, and Western Democratic societies. There are, however, other good points in this article.

845. Sikabonyi, Antal, "Romain Rolland levele jókairól," *Magyar Bibliofil szemle*, Budapest, Evfloyam 1, pp. 136–138.

1929

846. Götzfried, Hans Leo (Johannes Leonhard), *Der Heroische Idealismus bei Romain Rolland*. Dissertation. Bonn: Freudenstadt (Schwarzwald): Druck und Verlag von Hans Götzfried. —, *Romain Rolland, das Weltbild im Spiegel seiner Werke*. Dissertation. Bonn. Second ed., changed and enlarged with Rolland's latest works. Stuttgart: Engelhorn, 1931, 175 pp. Götzfried describes very penetratingly the directing principles of Rolland's philosophy; he reduces the principal ideas to two: in metaphysics, the monism of Empedocles, renewed by Spinoza in the direction of pantheism; in the realm of ethics, a dualism tending toward a harmonious synthesis encompassing the opposites: love-hate, being-knowledge, subject-object, body-soul, matter-spirit, etc. Götzfried divides Rolland's ideals into general ideals and particular goals. The first include vigorous affirmations of life, of existence, of absolute sincerity. The second includes spiritual renascence of France, social liberation of all the oppressed, panhumanism. The author emphasizes the aspect of becoming in Rolland's philosophy and its development; he examines Rolland's attitude toward Christianity, towards Christ and the Trinity.

847. Szilard, E., *Romain Rolland et l'Allemagne*, L'Institut français de Pécs (Hungary). In Hungarian.

848. Souday, P., *Les livres du temps*, Emile-Paul Frères, vol. II, «Les Drames philosophiques de M. Romain Rolland,» pp. 457–466. «Romain Rolland,» vol. I, pp. 249–259. Souday accuses Rolland of being guided by two main ideals: faith and sacrifice, regardless of the object of the faith, or the purpose of the sacrifice. This is an extreme position.

849. Beermann, M., *Die Bücherwelt*, XXVI, 89–94. Essential differences between the *Tragédies de la foi* and the *Théâtre de la Révolution*; Claudel and Rolland; Büchner's *Danton* and Rolland's. *Danton* is here studied in relation to the other plays of the cycle.

850. Lehner, F., *Die Schöne Literatur*, XXX, 329. *Les Léonides*; the spirit of fairness and objectivity that inspires Rolland's play causes struggles not only between the antagonists, but also within the protagonists. The result weakens the dramatic tension.

1930

851. Ashokananda, Swami, *The Influence of Indian Thought on the Thought of the West*. (A note on M. Romain Rolland's *The Life of Viveka-*

nanda and the Universal Gospel), published by Swami Vireswarananda, Advaita Ashrama Mayavati, Almora, Calcutta, 45 pp. Some considerations about Rolland's interpretations of Vedantic thought, in relation to his *Life of Vivekananda and the Universal Gospel*.

852. Brandes, Georg. Rung, Gertrud, *Georg Brandes, I Samvaer og Breve*, Copenhagen: Gyldenalski Boghandel, 236 pp. Pp. 166–170 contain an account of an interview between Brandes and Rolland, and reproduce much of their conversation.

853. Hutchens, J., *Theatre Arts Monthly*, XIV (February), 103–104. A write-up of the presentation of *Le Jeu de l'amour et de la mort* by the Theatre Guild, New York. The play is criticized unfavorably as lacking true dramatic construction.

854. Tacke, O., "Romain Rolland, der Europäer. Versuch einer Arbeitsmethod. Einführung in den modernen europäischen Geist," *Zeitschrift für französischen und englischen Unterricht*, XXIX (Februar), 87–92. This is a rather penetrating article. His judgments about *Le Jeu de l'amour et de la mort*, and *Les Loups*, must be seriously considered. The influence of Rolland's philosophy on the younger writers and students. There are some suggestions concerning the use of Rolland's writings for an introduction to the modern European spirit.

855. Montesano Delchi, Arturo, *Nosotros*, LXVII (marzo), 352–381. Critical article about *Ramakrishna* and *Vivekananda*. The principal adverse criticism is that Rolland remains too much of a rationalist when he studies the Vedantic system.

856. Pierre-Quint, L., *Europe*, XXII (15 mars), 443–447. A review article about *Ramakrishna*. Pierre-Quint pays tribute to Rolland's constant endeavour to be just and impartial. —, *ibid.*, XXIII (15 août), 604–607. *Vivekananda*. The writer here is too preoccupied with modern social problems to write an objective critical article.

857. Robertfrance, J., *Europe*, XXIII (15 mai), 114–117. A review of *Les Grandes époques créatrices*, and a comparison of it with the Beethoven of 1903.

858. Price, L., *Yale Review*, n.s. XX (December), 273–292. Interview with Rolland at Villa Olga. Price discusses many of Rolland's ideas.

1931

859. Kaempffer, A., *Romain Rollands Frauengestalten*. Dissertation. Jena. Charlottenburg: Gebr. Hoffman, 103 pp. This dissertation comes very close to being simply a list and a brief description of the principal female characters in Rolland's works. Their psychology is largely ignored or insufficiently treated, and their place in regard to Rolland's personality and

character is not studied. This subject seems still open for treatment, and it is a very interesting aspect of Rolland and his work.

860. Krakowski, B., *La Psychologie des peuples allemands et juifs dans les romans de Romain Rolland.* Toulouse: J. Castellvi & Cie., 154 pp. Krakowski concludes, in this interesting study, that the portrayal of Jews is not as good as that of Germans.

861. Bartlett, R. M., "Conscience of Europe," *World Unity*, VIII (April), 16–23; published again in *The Congregationalist*, (May 28, 1931), and in the volume by Bartlett, *They Dared to Live*, New York: Association Press, 1937, pp. 18–22. This article discusses Rolland's influence in America and his internationalism, and studies briefly the basis for his pacifism.

862. Waltzmann, G., «Romain Rolland pendant la guerre,» *La Paix*, (avril), pp. 79–85. This is a good statement of Rolland's position during the war. It is interesting to see this subject so carefully discussed at this late date.

863. Downes, O., *New York Times*, April 5, p. 8x. Completes, in certain respects, Rolland's *Goethe et Beethoven.*

864. Bonté, Florimond, *L'Humanité*, 11 avril. An organization, the "Entente Pacifiste Internationale," had published Rolland's name in a "Comité d'honneur." Bonté publishes Rolland's denial of his authorization. The rest of the article explains Rolland's espousal of the cause of the U.S.S.R.

865. Laloy, L., *Europe*, XXV (janvier–avril), 569–572. Laloy appreciates the *Goethe et Beethoven* as the work of a poet and a historian.

866. Landormy, P., *La Victoire* (1er, 8, 15 septembre, 27 octobre). According to Landormy, Rolland endeavours in vain, in *Goethe et Beethoven*, to defend Goethe against the charge of selfishness and egoism in his relations with Beethoven. Altogether, these articles constitute a good résumé and critical discussion of this work.

867. Kemp, R., *Le Temps*, 14 juin; *La Liberté*, 27 juillet. Kemp, who later writes with considerable enthusiasm about Rolland's *Péguy*, here writes of *L'Eclair de Spinoza* and *Empédocle d'Agrigente* in a semi-mocking style. His criticisms, both of style and of content, are adverse. In the second article he tries to reduce Rolland's ideas of universal unity to an absurdity.

868. Torrès, Henry, *Gringoire*, 17 juillet. Torrès here writes a good criticism of a presentation of *Le Quatorze juillet*, and points out the historical inaccuracies and some internal paradoxes in the play.

869. Fréville, J., *L'Humanité*, 22 septembre. A communist welcomes Rolland, and gives a good, brief, but somewhat one-sided account of Rolland's movement towards the left.

870. Bloch, J.-R., *Destin du Siècle. Seconds essais pour mieux com-*

prendre mon temps, Rieder, 316 pp. Rolland, *passim*. Bloch discusses Rolland and modern man, Rolland and Stalin, Tolstoy's influence on Rolland, optimism and pessimism in *Liluli*. His remarks about *Liluli* as evidence of Rolland's crumbling faith are interesting, although denied by Rolland.

871. Kraucher, J., "Zur Künstlerischen Gestaltung des *Jean-Christophe*," *Zeitschrift für französische Sprache und Literatur*, 194–218. A stylistic study, rather well done, of the work which has so often been judged on its political or social ideas and on purely factual content.

1932

872. Cossío del Pomar, F., *Con los buscadores del camino*, Madrid: Ediciones Ulises, 214 pp. "Con Romain Rolland," pp. 81–101. Written after an interview with Romain Rolland some years previously. The interview covered such questions as violence in the modern world, nationalism, Soviet Russia, Spain, revolutionary movements in South America (especially Víctor Raoul Haya de la Torre). Cossío publishes a résumé of Rolland's ideas on these questions.

873. Clark, B. H., *New York Times*, January 3, p. 4x. Mr. Clark studied literature under Mlle. Rolland, and took the course in the history of music given by Rolland. Mr. Clark draws a vivid portrait of Rolland the "conférencier." Revised and expanded to include criticisms of *Les Loups*, this article appears as the introduction to the volume, *The Wolves*, translated by Clark, New York: Random House, 1937. Introduction, pp. v–xi.

874. Pozner, Vladimir, «Romain Rolland et l'Académie des Sciences de l'U.R.R.S.,» *Revue des vivants*, VI (avril–juin), 1012–1013. Rolland's election to the Academy as an honorary member.

875. Barbusse, H., *Living Age*, CCCLXII (August), 519–522; translated from the *Frankfurter Zeitung*. Barbusse discusses the merits and errors of Rolland concerning the needs of modern society, and extends his welcome to what he calls the enthusiastic adherence of Rolland to the Soviets.

876. Guéhenno, J., «Littérature prolétarienne. II,» *Europe*, XXVIII (janvier–avril), 111–115. True artists, says Guéhenno, and true savants create liberty: Rolland, Gorky, and even Lenin and Marx. How this applies to Rolland.

1933

877. Dvořak, Robert, *Das Ethische und das Aesthetische bei Romain Rolland*. Dissertation. Münster. Bottrop i.W.: Postberg, vii, 71 pp. A very good and thorough study on the essence of Rolland's esthetic and ethical thinking. Dvořak analyzes it in relation to the background of positivism, naturalism, and the resultant pessimism and despair. His analysis of Rolland's synthesis of aesthetics and ethics is especially good, as is his develop-

ment of Rolland's conception of life as a flux, which has so greatly molded Rolland's thinking and writing.

878. Gerber, Richard, *Romain Rolland als dramatiker*. Dissertation. Arbeiten zur Romanischen Philologie, hsgb. von E. Lerch, No. 3; Münster: Druck H. Pöppinghaus; Paris: E. Droz, v, 122 pp. Gerber studies Rolland the dramatist from various points of view: content, structure, technique, sources. Like Greek tragedies, Rolland's plays are frequently the struggle of two equally justified ideas or forces. The question of non-violence and Rolland's dramas is well discussed. Gerber draws parallels between the dramas and *Jean-Christophe*. Gerber refutes Lerch's assertion (who wanted to contradict Seippel) that Rolland had wanted to celebrate, in *Le Triomphe de la raison*, the blind urge to life, "beyond good and evil." Differences between Bergson's philosophy and Rolland's as seen in these dramas.

879. Jäger, Maria, *Die Erzählungstechnik Romain Rollands im "Jean-Christophe."* Dissertation. Arbeiten zur Romanischen Philologie, hsgb. von E. Lerch, No. 4. Münster: H. Pöppinghaus; Paris: E. Droz, iv, 43 pp. A moderately valuable stylistic study limited to Rolland's narrative technique. The introduction paints Rolland as the prophet of a new France and his works as the expression of a new "Weltanschauung." The body of the thesis treats his narrative technique as compared to that of the naturalists and impressionists, and the use of epic techniques, which Jäger finds especially characteristic of this novel.

880. Sénéchal, Christian, *Romain Rolland*, ed. de la Caravelle, 135 pp. Undoubtedly one of the best books about Rolland written up to that date. Sénéchal's discussion of Rolland and Ramakrishna is especially good. He finds a parallel between the two men. He discusses Rolland's works in relation to the great ideas or currents of thought that are important in that time and in Rolland's works. His discussion of the ideal of universality held by Rolland is very good. He finds that the true mystery of the Trinity in Rolland is: *Amour*, *Connaissance*, *Action*. See also Sénéchal, *Les Grands courants de la littérature française contemporaine*. Société d'éditions littéraires et techniques, 1934, 464 pp. Rolland, pp. 62–65, 94–96, 121–123, 143–146, about Rolland and the people's art, Rolland and Truth.

881. Kraucher, L., "Die französische Gesellschaft des Vorkrieges in den drei groszen Zyklusromanen: *Jean-Christophe*, *A la recherche du temps perdu*, und *Les Thibault*," *Germanische-romanische monatsheft*, XXI, 59–70. Kraucher's study of the picture of society in these three cycles brings out some of the differences between the writers, between the types of society each was interested in. It is a rather interesting article, but perhaps not very profound.

882. Oster, O., "Romain Rolland in der musikalischen Geistesgeschichte," *Schweizerische Musikzeitung*, LXXIII, 680–685. The greatest

merit, according to this critic, of Rolland in musical criticism is that he showed how little value any creative act has unless it is closely connected with, or is part of, its time and place.

883. Fess, G. M., "Jean Bodel and Romain Rolland," *Modern Language Notes*, XLVIII (December), 505–507. A discussion of the song in Act IV of *Saint Louis*. The song and its singers are almost exact duplicates of the song and singers in Jean Bodel's *Jeu de Saint-Nicolas*, but Rolland makes the song an integral part of the action, whereas it is not an essential part of Bodel's work.

1934

884. Fite, A. G., "Romain Rolland as a critic of modern civilization," *Modern Language Forum*, XIX (February), 18–26. Fite discusses the prophetic and interpretative role played by Rolland as a critic of contemporary society, especially in the *Ame enchantée*. The discussion is not in detail, Fite being content to comment only on the more important and noticeable ideas.

885. Sénéchal, C., *Europe*, XXXV (15 mai), 137–142. A review of the last volumes of the *Ame enchantée*; some essential differences between *Jean-Christophe* and the later novel. Sénéchal, who is a very sensitive admirer of Rolland, discusses the meaning of the novel as a whole; the symbol of the river. He says that Rolland saw in Jean de Saint-Prix his Aërt, that is, himself. Marc, who incarnates the author's struggle to free himself from individual liberty, was born from this contact with Saint-Prix. He also discusses Chiarenza's role in the novel.

886. Strauss, H., *New York Times*, Book Review Section, October 28. Strauss criticizes, perhaps erroneously, the ending of *L'Ame enchantée*.

887. Strauch, R., "Sollen wir noch Romain Rolland lesen?" *Neuphilologische Monatsschrift*, V, 141–144. A Nazi suggests that *Jean-Christophe* be used to teach the Nazi theories of racial superiority! Obviously of no value for a study of Rolland, but it is interesting to see how this man and others (especially Grosshans) cannot overlook Rolland, and so try to make him fit their theories.

888. Tagore, Soumyendranath, *Mahatma Gandhi*, N.R.F. Introduction: a dialogue between S. Tagore and Rolland. See the critical article by Françoise Marie, *Commune*, II (novembre), 265–266. The book was written to prove that Gandhi was a counter-revolutionary, and was considered as such by revolutionaries. Rolland's attitude towards Gandhi is severely criticized on this basis.

1935

889. Fest, Otto, *Stilistische Untersuchungen zu Romain Rolland's "Pierre et Luce." Formentwickelung und Deutung*. Dissertation. Jena. Borna: Noske,

166 pp. Fest finds that the basic element of this book is "Pierre und die Aussenwelt," a duality which goes throughout the work. But for such a work of art to be formed, he says, it was necessary that a link, a synthesis, be born from the dissonance, a synthesis leading to harmony; this link is Luce. The artistic thought is that a part of the surrounding and alien world, a part of the great dissonance, was destined to be the fruitful principle and the necessary condition for this harmony. To describe this simple and great Organism, Rolland, says Fest, wrote an artless, pure, simple language, and gave to his tale the musical form of a four part symphony. Fest analyzes this musical form in great detail. The introduction, pp. 1–11, and the "Besondere Bermerkungen," pp. 147–155, contain most of the pertinent material. The remaining part, pp. 25–146, analyzes in outline form the motifs, their elements, and their occurrence.

890. Fite, A. G. *Modern Language Forum*, XX (February–May), 8–15. Written on the occasion of the publication of the last volume of *L'Ame enchantée*. Fite outlines the whole cycle. His article is suggestive for further studies rather than an analysis of the novel: the symbolism of names in the novel, and in Rolland's works, the symmetry of characters and situations, further comparisons with *Jean-Christophe*, education, child psychology, among others.

891. Brunet, G., *Mercure de France*, CCLX (1er juin), 345–349. In this short article on *Quinze ans de combat*, Brunet analyzes Rolland, the eternal rebel, and his inner conflict: idealism—realism (historian) in its relation to this work and to the man.

892. Boukharine, N., *Commune*, II (août), 1431–1434. A speech of welcome to Rolland, who visited Russia in the early part of the summer of 1935.

893. Price, L., *Atlantic Monthly*, CLVI (December), 718–726. Price reports his conversation with Romain Rolland. With some changes this and the preceding article by Price are again published in his *We Northmen*, Boston: Little, Brown & Co., 392 pp. Conversation with Rolland, pp. 312–353.

894. Eishiskina, N., "Romain Rolland: *Ocharovannaia͡ dusha*. Rody Provozvestnit͡sa, Leningrad: Goslitizdat, 1935, 459 pp.," *Khudozhestvennaia Literatura*, V, 10, pp. 35–37. Review of the Russian translation of *L'Ame enchantée*.

1936

895. Beckwith, Wm. Hunter, *The Formation of the Esthetic of Romain Rolland*. Dissertation. New York University, 286 pp. This is a very thorough study of Rolland's aesthetic development. Beckwith analyzes especially well what Rolland means in his constant references to "vérité" and his hatred of "mensonge"; also Rolland's cult of life. This thesis has not been published, but a brief summary of it has been printed and is available.

896. Kopal, J., "Cesta Romaina Rollands," in *Mélanges Prokop M. Haškověr*, Bruenn: Imprimerie Globus, 411 pp. See the review by Edgar Glässer, *Literaturblatt für germanische und romanische Philologie*, LXI (1940), 34–35, who says that Kopal finds that each period is based on a denial of the principles of the preceding period, from *Jean-Christophe* to *Compagnons de route*. This seems to be an exaggerated position.

897. Bloch, J.-R., *Vendredi*, (17 janvier). Tribute to Rolland on his 70th birthday. —, *Commune*, III (janvier), 513–520. More tribute for Rolland's birthday. This article contains the interesting remark: «Les orientaux ont coutume de distinguer deux Europes: la nôtre, et celle de Romain Rolland.»

898. Greetings extended to Rolland by Dimitrov, Gorky, Soyuz Sovetskikh Pisatelei, Prezidium Akademii Nauk S.S.S.R., and a group of Russian writers. *Literaturnaya Gazeta*, Moscow (29 Yanvar).

899. Aragon, *Regards*, IV (30 janvier). Aragon claims Rolland as one of the heroes of communism because of his outspoken criticisms of the society in which he was born, and in which flourished all the art forms he knew and loved, because of the force of his conscience, and because of the reflection in his works of the essential disturbance in the modern world—the forward march of the workers. —, *Les Cahiers du Bolchévisme*, XIII (15 mars), 257–263. This article, which appeared also in part in *Commune*, III (mai), 1138–1139 of the same year, is the report of an interview with Rolland, who is quoted extensively. The topics discussed included peace and pacifism, war, Gandhi and his experiment, and the experiments of fascisms of various sorts.

900. Desprès, F., *Regards*, IV (30 janvier). The effect of *Au-dessus de la mêlée* during the first World War; being unable, because of the censor, to publish all of Rolland's articles in the *Bataille syndicaliste*, and because of bad health, Desprès went to Switzerland, where he had many conversations with Rolland during the years of the first World War.

901. Frank, Waldo, *New Masses*, New York, XVIII (January 21), 19. Frank, on the occasion of Rolland's seventieth birthday, discusses the qualities and ideas of Rolland that are of importance to the Western World.

902. Various articles in *L'Humanité*, tribute to Rolland on his seventieth birthday, 26, 29, 30 janvier, 1er, 2, 3 février. The first article is unsigned; the second is signed by Georges Dimitrov and is the reproduction of a telegram he sent to Rolland; the third is a letter to Rolland from Maxim Gorky; the articles of February 1 and 2 are by Marcel Cachin, the first is a tribute for his birthday, the second concerns a "Soirée Romain Rolland;" the last article is a tribute from the Italian Communist Party.

903. «Hommage à Romain Rolland,» *Commune*, III (mars), 789–801. Tributes for Rolland's seventieth birthday: Maxim Gorky, Waldo Frank, G. Dimitrov, S. Zweig, T. G. Masaryk, E. Benes, Leonid Leonov, Van

Min, revolutionary students of the University of Lisbon. Of especial interest are the articles by Frank, Zweig, and Leonov. Frank aptly characterizes what Rolland stands for. Zweig discusses what he considers to be Rolland's great virtue: to remain free. Leonov bears witness of Rolland's influence on youth in Russia.

904. Nelli, Sandro, «Romain Rolland et le peuple italien,» *L'Humanité*, 29 mars. An expression of gratitude to Rolland for the aid his writings proved to be in freeing Gramsci.

905. Gide, A., *Nouvelle revue française*, XLVI (1er mars), 457–458; this is part of an article by Gide which first appeared in *Vendredi* (24 janvier). «Ceux qui le méprisaient, par patriotisme, le haïssaient le plus alors [at the time of the first World War], doivent reconnaître aujourd'hui que la figure de Romain Rolland est de celles en qui s'incarnent l'honneur et la gloire de la France et de toute l'humanité.»

906. Zweig, S., *Universidad*. Mensual de cultura popular. Mexico, D. F., I (abril), 5–6. Zweig emphasizes particularly Rolland's faith; his only maxim, says Zweig, was faith in one's own faith, whatever it be.

907. Maxence, P., *Gringoire* (5 juillet). Severe criticisms especially of *Compagnons de route*, based in part on Maxence's opposition to Rolland's "anti-intellectualism," because, according to Maxence, emotions and intuition are more important in Rolland and in his works than the intellect. There is some justice in his remarks, but on the whole they ignore many other parts of Rolland's works.

908. Luisi, Luisa, "Romain Rolland—El sentido místico en su vida y en su obra," *Nosotros*, 2a época, I (julio), 273–280. In Rolland, says Luisi, is realized the complete and total man. The unifying thread in Rolland's works is faith, impassioned faith in the superior destiny of man; this faith strengthens and illuminates Rolland. She discusses this aspect of Rolland's character and thinking as shown in his various works, especially in *Jean-Christophe* and the heroic biographies, and in *Gandhi*, *Vivekananda*, and *Ramakrishna*. The discussion of the last three works is inadequate.

909. Gsell, P., *L'Humanité*, 14 juillet. In this short review of *Le Quatorze juillet* and its presentation at the Alhambra theater, Gsell studies the play in relation to Rolland's ideas as expressed in *Le Théâtre du peuple*.

910. Chabannes, J., *Les Nouvelles littéraires* (18 juillet), 8. Chabannes had presented *Le Quatorze juillet* at the Alhambra, and here presents an interesting and enthusiastic account of the play and its presentation.

911. Unik, P., *Regards*, (23 juillet). Unik discusses the question of historical accuracy in *Le Quatorze juillet*; the characters of the play are more often symbols than living beings with strictly and historically defined characters, but "la vérité passionnée de l'ensemble" is there.

912. Two articles about *Les Loups*, *L'Humanité*, 24 décembre, 31 dé-

cembre. The first one, by Vaillant-Couturier, is an account of the presentation by the "Théâtre du peuple" (C. G.T.) at the Renaissance theater. The great lesson of unity which the play presents so well and the triumph of the play itself are Rolland's double victory. The second article, by Priacel, is an account of the same production, and he sees in the piece the lesson of the necessity of justice above all.

913. Savin, M., *Nouvelle revue française*, XLVII, 396–399. Adverse criticisms of *Le Quatorze juillet*. The piece is cold and abstract, although eloquent, says Savin; it is the work of a historian not a poet. It could have been called "La Bastille ne fut pas prise"—it surrendered. This is, he concludes, a tragi-comedy of faith, with occasional movements of an operetta.

914. Groszhans, K., *Romain Rolland und der germanische Geist*. Dissertation. Friederich-Wilhelm Universität. Würzburg: Triltsch, ix, 86 pp. This is a curious example of literary theory and criticism based on the racial theory. It is here included only as an example of what men can be driven or led (or misled) to. Groszhans even publishes Rolland's protest against this prejudiced book, without suffering a single qualm or change of opinion.

915. Gilbeaux, H., *La Fin des Soviets*, Société française d'éditions littéraires et techniques, v, 188 pp. «Le Mariage d'état de Romain Rolland, prisonnier du Kremlin,» pp. 27–48. An obviously unfair chapter, bordering on the libelous, in an equally unfair book. Guilbeaux, the brilliant but unstable admirer of Rolland and the Russian Revolution, has now become equally anti-Russian and anti-Rolland.

916. Kurzweil, Anne E., *La Crise de la famille dans le roman français contemporain*, (Bibliothèque de l'Institut français de Budapest), Budapest, 78 pp. See the review by Heinemann, *Literaturblatt für germanische und romanische Philologie*, LXI (1940), 47–48. Rolland is one of twenty novelists studied.

1937

917. Massis, H., *L'Honneur de servir*, Plon, 1937, iii, 368 pp. Rolland, pp. 107, 134–142, 145, 147–149, 177, 192, 275, 335, etc. He now denies the influence and importance of that part of Rolland's work whose nefarious influence he had blamed so severely during the first World War. Part of these remarks appeared also in the *Revue catholique des livres et des faits*, XI (25 décembre 1931), 25–27.

918. O'Brien, Justin, *The Novel of Adolescence in France: the study of a literary theme*, New York: Columbia University Press, 246 pp. Rolland, pp. 7, 98, 136–137, 164–166, 180. Since Rolland is only one of many authors studied, it was impossible to do justice to this important aspect of Rolland's creative works.

919. Sadoul, G., *L'Humanité*, 11 décembre. A good review, and much more favorable than some of the other reviews, of *Compagnons de route.*

1938

920. Aron, A., "Romain Rolland und Goethe," *Monatshefte für deutschen Unterricht*, XXX, 98–109. An article on the gradual conversion of Rolland to Goethe's ideas, especially to that of "Stirb und werde", and of absolute truth. As the author indicates, certain points related to this question have been purposefully omitted: Rolland's belief that social evolution implied in "Stirb und werde" leads to communism, his invoking of Goethe in connection with his consistent opposition to present political developments (in 1938–1939) in Europe.

921. Rudwin, M., *New Republic*, XCVI (September 7), 132. In answer to the claim that Rolland moved back to Vézelay because he was a broken and discouraged man, Rudwin says that Rolland is not discouraged, is not a broken man. He publishes parts of a letter, in translation, from Rolland, which is his call to the intellectuals to assume their share of action and responsibility in the world.

1939

922. Wilson, R. A., *The Pre-War Biographies of Romain Rolland and Their Place in his Work and the Period*, New York: Oxford University Press, iv, 233 pp. An important study, although I believe that the subject of the place of the biographies in Rolland's development and thinking has not yet been exhausted. Wilson does some meritorious work: for example, he rectifies Zweig's mistake (subsequently repeated by others) that Tolstoy destroyed all that Rolland held most precious at the time of his letter to Tolstoy. (*What is Art?* was not written until 1896; in *What then must we do?* Tolstoy still reveres Beethoven.) He also rectifies the error of Zweig and Bertaut that Rolland abandoned biography in order to devote himself more completely to *Jean-Christophe*. Wilson's chapter on the moral and literary resonance of the biographies after 1914 seems to be merely a skimpy review of the war years. To discuss adequately the biographies, Wilson needed to call more on the short studies published before the biographies appeared. He neglects completely the theme of "le vaincu vainqueur" or "le vainqueur vaincu," which is so important in many of Rolland's works.

923. Starr, W. T., *Romain Rolland's Internationalism*, Dissertation. University of Oregon. Thesis Series, No. 2, Eugene, Oregon, 1939, 106 pp. Bibliography, pp. 85–106. The origins and bases of his internationalism, the influences which aided its growth, influences both within the man and

without, the relation of this internationalism to his political and social ideas. Their development during and after the first World War.

924. Ambrière, F., *Mercure de France*, CCXCIII (1er juillet). In this very short review, short work is made of *Robespierre*. Ambrière judges it to be a failure, no style, few ideas, no color.

925. Morgan, C., *Commune*, VII (août), 1078–1079. This is a favorable review of *Robespierre*, in which Morgan gives us a brief interpretation of the historical event in terms of modern social conflicts.

926. Sénéchal, Christian, An incompleted work on *Jean-Christophe*. See André Spire, *Les Nouvelles littéraires* (12 août 1939), p. 6: «... (il) nous aurait fait entrer plus avant encore dans le détail de la composition ... nous aurait fait connaître, par des centaines de témoignages ... les réactions à cette œuvre....»

927. Isbach, A., «Danton en Bielorussie, *Littérature internationale*,» No. 6, Special number dedicated to the French revolution. A fascinating description of a rather astonishing production of Rolland's *Danton* in 1918 in Russia. Sadoul reproduces the principal portions of the article, *Commune*, VII (août 1939), 1093–1097.

928. Keenan, D'Elbert, *Virginia Quarterly*, XV (Winter), 154–156. There are some good remarks about the *Ame enchantée*. Keenan analyzes the novel especially from the point of view of Annette who (and the novel with her) grows in stature as she meets, fights against, and conquers modern society. This, he says, symbolizes the change in Rolland himself. Marc in turn repeats the quest.

1940

929. Aguirre, Mirta, *Palabras en Juan Cristóbal*, Havana: Imp. "El Siglo XX", A. Múñoz y hno, 62 pp. Aguirre feels the importance of having people read *Jean-Christophe* in order to avoid the recrudescence of hate during World War II. In this connection the main themes of the novel are discussed.

930. Jacinto de Prado Coelho, "Poesia e verdade em Romain Rolland," *Revista da Faculdade de Letras. Universidade de Lisboa*, VII, 1 & 2 (1940–1941), 175–211. Rolland, says this writer, is always a poet, and no matter what his errors may be, as a poet he was always great. There follows a good discussion of Rolland's blending of the various opposing aspects of the nineteenth century: objectivity and subjectivity, physics and metaphysics, reality and beauty, idealism and realism, faith and truth, life and death. For Rolland art finds in humanity its reason for existing, says Prado Coelho, who examines *Jean-Christophe* in this respect. The discussion of Rolland's pantheism is based mainly on Ellen Key's account, in 1914.

1941

931. Torrens, R. W., *The Social and Political Ideas of Romain Rolland.* Dissertation. Cornell, unpublished. This is a well-done thesis on this aspect of Rolland's thought and activity, although certain phases of the subject had already been studied by Starr. Torrens' announced purpose is to note the direction, rhythm, and route of Rolland's social and political ideas, to see them as a whole and to judge them. His analysis of Rolland's early dramas against the background of France of 1870–1910 is very good. Torrens draws some unjustified conclusions, as when he concludes, p. 193, from a quotation taken from *L'Ame enchantée,* III, 198, that Rolland had no longer any objection against the use of violence in behalf of the Soviet Union. It is not quite accurate to see in Marc's denunciation of pacifism Rolland's denunciation and renunciation of his brand of pacifism. Marc does not always represent the author, and he lives his own life (see what Rolland says in this respect in the preface to volume III). Similarly, Torrens says that as the persons of *L'Ame enchantée* renounced individualism, so too did Rolland—a statement that needs to be qualified. Torrens has not made enough use perhaps of Rolland's articles and lesser known writings during 1934–1939. In spite of these reservations, the work is well done.

932. Grossman, Vladimir, *Korichnevye Klopy,* Moscow, 1941, 48 pp.

933. Gorky, M., *Nesobrannyie literaturno-kriticheskie stat'i,* Moscow, 546 pp. Contains many references to Rolland.

1942

934. Levy, A. R., *L'Idéalisme de Romain Rolland,* A. -G. Nizet, 310 pp. Dissertation. A very good work, with some shortcomings, of which the most important is the slightly prejudiced stand on which the writer bases his work: namely, that Rolland found the truest expression of his principles in the doctrine of non-violence, and that after he departed from this ideal, in opposing fascism, he weakened his principles. Nevertheless, it is a good study of this subject, which is so important in Rolland.

935. Fernández, Ramón, *Nouvelle revue française,* LVI (1er juin), 624–627. In Rolland's *Voyage intérieur* Fernández finds the style of Montaigne and the style of romanticism. Rolland, he says, was conscious, overconscious of this duality. Rolland bridges the gap between romanticism and the modern era; *Jean-Christophe* is an essentially romantic theme. He compares Rolland, Roger Martin du Gard, J. Romains, and G. Duhamel.

936. Myron, H. B., *The French Review,* XV (February), 340–342. Myron criticizes unfavorably, but not unjustly, Rolland's interpretation of Rousseau's character, and points out some omissions. His most severe criticism is of Rolland's tendency towards oratory.

1944

937. McClain, W. H., "Goethe as Romain Rolland's *Compagnon de route*," *Germanic Review*, XIX (December), 269–283. As Mr. McClain said, one cannot judge accurately how far Goethean thought played a role in the formation of Rolland's spiritual outlook until the journals and other documents have all been published. However, he shows how Rolland shares with Goethe certain convictions which form the basis of his spiritual make-up. Mr. McClain bases the article on four references made by Rolland to Goethe, each one during a critical period of his development: 1. Rolland's comparison of Christophe's serene outlook in his later years to that of Goethe in 1813; 2. his letter to Hauptmann, in 1914, where he recalls the example of Goethe as one who repudiated hatred among nations; 3. his criticism through Marc in *L'Ame enchantée* of Goethe's unwillingness to allow himself to be disturbed by contemporary social and political upheavals; 4. his reference to Goethe in his article on Goethe and Lenin in *Compagnons de route*. Rolland's changing attitude towards Goethe is clearly shown, although Mr. McClain digresses considerably concerning Rolland's social and political ideals of the war and postwar periods, and his attitude towards Russia. Mr. McClain also wrote a later article on Rolland and Russia, *Romanic Review*, XXXIX (April, 1948), 122–129, which contains various erroneous interpretations. See the answer by Starr, *Romanic Review*, XL (April, 1949), 106–113.

938. Klein, J. W., *Music and Letters*, XXV (January), 13–22. A premature obituary, this is a good article on Rolland, especially about Rolland and music, his musical criticism and his work as historian of music. —, *Musical Opinion*, LXVII (July–August), 313, 346–347. Klein, who writes very sympathetically of Rolland as a musical critic, does not fail to point out some of his defects: Rolland's attitude of hero worship towards Beethoven; his tendency to read too much of Beethoven's character in a few bars of his music. About 1936 Professor Klein presented a thesis on Romain Rolland's dramatic works and theories to the University of London for the degree of Doctor of Philosophy. The thesis has not been published. It contains some interesting material on the reception of the various dramatic works; the development of Rolland's ideas about the people's theater, and his precursors in this movement.

939. Chantraine, Jacqueline, *L'Art de Romain Rolland biographe*. Thèse présentée pour l'obtention du grade de licencié . . . dans les Facultés de Philosophie et Lettres. Année académique 1944–1945. Université de Bruxelles.

940. Lessinnes, Suzanne, *La Musique dans le roman littéraire de «Jean-Christophe» de Romain Rolland*. Thèse présentée pour l'obtention du grade

de licencié. Facultés de Philosophie et Lettres. Année académique 1944–1945. Université de Bruxelles.

1945

941. Doisy, Marcel, *Romain Rolland*, Brussels: Editions La Boétie. A good biography, well-chosen texts, documents of some importance. Doisy insists on the dual nature of Rolland: realist and idealist, faith and lucid intelligence, pessimism and optimism. The author divides his biography into three parts: *La Vie, L'Oeuvre, La Pénsée*. His treatment of Rolland's thinking, in the last part, is perhaps the best. Doisy insists on the Bergsonian and Nietzschean qualities of Rolland's thought.

942. *Hommage à Romain Rolland*, Lausanne: Editions du Mont-Blanc, 164 pp. In this collection of tributes to Rolland, those by Baudouin, Buraud, and Roubakine are especially interesting. Baudouin, pp. 13–27, tells of his two meetings with Rolland, one during the first World War, the other in 1931, at the time of Gandhi's visit. Buraud, pp. 36–48, places Rolland at the very center of modern investigation, scientific and intuitive, of the subconscious; the *L'Ame enchantée* is the center and keynote of all his works. Buraud shows what parts of Rolland's psychology in this novel antedate the discovery of the libido and the mother complex by Freud and Jung. Roubakine's brief article, pp. 69–74, tells why Rolland is liked by the Russians. There are numerous famous names among the contributors, but their tributes are too many and too short to summarize here.

944. Mühlestein, H., *Geist und politik. Romain Rollands politische Sendung;* gedächtnisrede. Zürich, 74 pp. The emphasis of this brochure, a speech delivered by Mühlestein to a workers' meeting, is entirely on the political mission and activities of Rolland, in whom he sees the living bridge between the bourgeois and proletarian revolutions, between the ideals of the French revolution and those of the Soviet Union. He quotes at length from a letter of Rolland, dated March 4, 1934, to the "Internationaler Verband revolutionärer Schriftsteller," tracing his political development, and also from an appeal written in June, 1937, after the murder of the anti-fascist refugees in Paris, the Roselli brothers, by agents of the OVRA.

945. Roy, Dilip Kumar, *Among the Great*, Bombay: N. M. Tripathi ltd., Nalanda publications. Conversation with Rolland, pp. 5–63. There are some interesting remarks especially about what constitutes great art, and its place in the world, according to Rolland. Roy brings direct quotations from Rolland, summarizes other remarks and discussions by Rolland. There are some extremely interesting ideas about Gandhi, Tolstoy, India, etc.

947. Beirnaert, Louis, *Etudes*, CCXLIV (février), 250–256. A fairly good article about Rolland and his religion. It is not an orthodox religion,

part of a church or of an official doctrine, but one of Rolland's own attitudes and beliefs. Rolland's religion in relation to his development is well outlined; Beirnaert makes considerable use of his journals and correspondence, but the subject is not exhausted, and this article is a trifle biased. It disregards entirely Rolland's attacks on organized religion. H. Hogarth, in *London Quarterly Review*, 5th series (January, 1946), 48–50, gives a good résumé of the article.

948. Forster, E. M., "Romain Rolland and the Hero," *The Listener* (published by the British Broadcasting Corporation), March 8, 269–270. An obituary that insists on *Jean-Christophe* and its qualities, music, Rolland's Germany, Rolland and the cult of the Hero.

949. Beirnaert, L., «Dialogues autour de Péguy,» *Etudes*, CCXLIV (mars), 397–405. Concerns the biographies of Péguy by Marcel Péguy, Secrétain, Halévy, P. Doncoeur, Vercors, and Romain Rolland. Rolland is mentioned throughout, and Beirnaert's criticisms are very similar to those by Béguin, no. 951.

950. Kemp, R., *Les Nouvelles littéraires*, (5 avril). Kemp too finds various adverse criticisms to make of Rolland's *Péguy*, because of innate and acquired differences between Rolland and his subject. Kemp knows Rolland personally and admires his work. Nevertheless, he points out what Rolland wanted to do and failed to do in his biography of Péguy.

951. Béguin, A., *Revue de Paris*, No. 3, pp. 87–90. Béguin pays tribute to an excellent work, but fears that it may distort the image of Péguy if taken to be a definitive and perfect explanation of the man and his work. There are too many basic differences between Rolland and Péguy. Béguin's adverse criticisms are based on these differences; for example, Rolland writes *Péguy* in the same spirit as he had written his heroic biographies, a romantic spirit; Péguy draws nurture from tradition, from within a narrow circle of life, whereas Rolland looks afar for adventure—he is cosmopolitan and international; Rolland is an idealist, Péguy a mystic—just the opposite; Péguy is a "paysan français," Rolland a German romantic strongly imbued with ideas from the Orient.

952. Maublanc, R., *La Pensée*, n.s., No. 4 (juillet–août–septembre), 26–28. Maublanc praises Rolland's courageous stand against fascism. The position of their magazine in relation to Rolland is explained. Maublanc's principal criticism of Rolland is that of his disinterestedness, his consistent refusal to enter into action on a material plane.

953. Jourdain, F., «Souvenirs sur Romain Rolland,» *Ibid.*, n.s. no. 4 (juillet–août–septembre), 40–42. Jourdain helped Rolland in certain ways in his political action, especially by verifying the solidity of some campaigns, and by transmitting Rolland's thinking to others. The article is especially

interesting for Rolland's attitude toward and relations with the militants of extreme left-wing groups.

954. Lalou, R., *Revue de Paris*, LII (août), 59–62. Lalou believes that the frequent misunderstandings about Rolland are because of a duality within himself; Rolland wishes to be an independent personality with the same strength that he clings to the masters he chose during adolescence. He has a word of caution about the interpretation of the three "éclairs" Rolland has told about: for example, Rolland accepted Voltaire into his Pantheon only some thirty years after being introduced to his writings. Rolland's preference for Titans rather than Olympians is stressed. Rolland is perhaps, says Lalou, a "grand animateur" of ideas and of emotions, rather than a great writer.

955. Arcos, R., *La Pensée*, n.s., no. 4 (juillet–septembre), 29–39. Souvenirs of Rolland. Arcos says that there is no mysticism in Rolland, and quotes from the *Poison idéaliste* as proof. Rolland's lucid intelligence and opposition to intolerance and sectarianism make him an excellent subject for reading by young people.

956. Erskine, J., *New York Herald Tribune*, January 21, VI, 1–2. This obituary is a rather good brief survey of Rolland's life and writings, although Erskine seems to make Rolland more of a dreamer than he actually perhaps was. The *Ame enchantée* is not mentioned.

957. "Homenaje a Romain Rolland," *Occidente*, México, D. F., I, 3, pp. 9–23. Tribute from Antonio Acevedo Escobedo, Francisco Giner de Los Ríos, Julio Jiménez Rueda, Francisco Monterde, Bernardo Ortiz de Montellano, Gutierre Tibón, and José Vasconcelos; none of them are profound studies, and generally rather brief. The most interesting is the description by Tibón of a visit by Rolland to Tibón's father.

957A. Breitburg, J. M., "Romain Rolland et Gorki," *Novy Mir*, No. 1 (1945).

958. Relgis, Eugen, *Haltes Chez les grands européens*, Bucharest, 1945–1946. Five pages are devoted to Relgis' visit to Rolland at Villeneuve. —, *Romain Rolland et l'Union Soviétique*, Bucharest, Edition Véritas, 1945–1946.

1946

959. Association des Amis de Romain Rolland. *Bulletin*, I, 1 (août). News about this group in various countries, articles relative to its activities and about research on Romain Rolland. Invaluable bibliographical notes for Rolland studies. This *Bulletin* recently published, no. 8 (Juillet 1949).

960. Götzfried, H. L., *Die Erneuerung des deutschen Geistes*, Erlangen: Dipax Verlag. See also his articles, "Der Dichter der Allmenschlichkeit.

. . . ," *Schwäbische Landeszeitung*, II, 9 (29. Januar); "Der grosse Friedensfreund . . . ," *Fränkische Landeszeitung*, I, 25 (17. Juli).

961. Saurat, Denis, *The Listener* (April 4), 427–428. A fairly good estimate of Rolland; Saurat's remarks about Rolland's *Péguy* constitute the best part of the article. In general Saurat neglects other works than *Jean-Christophe*. This article was later incorporated into his book, *Modern French Literature* 1870–1940, London: Dent, Aldine House, Bedford St.

962. Claudel, Paul, «Le *Beethoven* de Romain Rolland,» *Le Littéraire*, (6 avril 1946). A tribute to Beethoven's music, and to Rolland's final volume on Beethoven and his works, *Finita Comoedia*. Claudel quotes from Rolland's volume, and tells something about his own relations with the author of *Jean-Christophe*. It appeared also in the volume by Claudel, *Accompagnements*, N.R.F., Gallimard, 1949, pp. 89–98.

1947

963. Beigbeder, M., «Il n'y a pas eu de Romain Rolland,» *Esprit*, IV (avril), 605–625. One of the needs of the post-war period (1946–1947) was a Romain Rolland, independent as he was during the first World War and the period following. Beigbeder discusses his probable position and influence, basing his surmises on Rolland's attitude and stand during the first World War. The article is as much about the period from 1939 to 1944 as about Rolland.

964. Claudel, P., Discours de réception à L'Académie française. March 13. Extracts in *Le Littéraire* (15 mars). Louis Gillet and Romain Rolland. This appeared *in extenso* in *Une Semaine dans le monde*, (22 mars 1947), 7, 8.

964A. *Estudiantina*, Nos. 5 & 6 (febrero de 1947). Number entirely dedicated to Rolland.

1948

965. Descotes, Maurice, *Romain Rolland*. Ed. du Temps présent. Coll. «Artistes et écrivains du temps présent.» Descotes groups his discussions of Rolland around *Le Voyage intérieur*, *Péguy*, *Le Théâtre du peuple*, *Robespierre*, *Jean-Christophe*, and *Au-dessus de la mêlée* (in that order), which the author considers the summits of Rolland's work. The discussion of the "Heroic biographies", based on *Péguy*, another of the conquered heroes, is very good; these *Lives* are the life of Rolland himself. Descotes' analysis and evaluation of *Jean-Christophe* is particularly satisfactory. There are some questionable statements: Descotes sees the influence of Indian thought in *Aërt* (the date of publication of this play, and Rolland's mentions of it in his correspondence with Malwida von Meysenbug [whom Descotes calls Meysenburg] make this seem little likely); his claim that Rolland ". . . en 1938, s'était rallié au Communisme depuis plusieurs années déjà . . ." needs qualification. Indeed Descotes' treatment of Rolland, Russia and Com-

munism is quite inadequate, and lacks the objective treatment and balance of the rest of the book.

966. Weiss, Hans G., *Romain Rolland*, Editions Volk und Wissen, Berlin and Leipzig. Series, Volk und Wissen Kurzbiographien. A popular biography, which is not very reliable; some old errors and mistakes are repeated.

967. Connes, Georges, "The Tragedy of Romain Rolland," *The University of Buffalo Studies*, XVIII, no. 3 (January), 135–150. This interesting article, which is a lecture delivered by M. Connes, leans heavily on A. R. Levy, *L'Idéalisme de Romain Rolland*, and repeats essentially the same judgments about Rolland: Rolland, beginning with a highly idealistic faith, looking to the mind, the spirit, and the heart to help mankind to attain its true goal of universal harmony and unity, towards the latter part of his life forgot his ideals and faith insofar as he not only admitted, but even advocated, resort to violence to fight against fascism, against the occupying forces. The three tragedies of Rolland, according to M. Connes, are: the first World War; Russia; the German occupation of France. As in Levy there is much material that is provocative of thought. But a deeper study of the subject, taking into account many lesser known writings of Rolland, which neither Levy nor Connes knew, would undoubtedly modify their conclusions.

968. Schierer, M., «Romain Rolland—Jean-Christophe et l'Allemagne dans la crise de la *Révolte*,» *Revue de littérature comparée*, XXII (juillet–septembre), 340–362. Written on the basis of Rolland's correspondence and of documents supplied by Mme Romain Rolland, this article is probably the best on the subject. The theme of *La Révolte* is the struggle between the two Germanies: Weimar and Potsdam. The latter triumphed. This is the fraud discovered by Christophe. Schierer discusses in some detail Rolland's contacts with Germany; his judgments about Germany, German music, etc., his acquaintances with leading Germans of the day, quotations from various of Rolland's works which seem to show direct German influence.

1949

969. Claudel, P., «La pensée religieuse de Romain Rolland,» *Revue de deux mondes*, No. 2 (15 janvier), pp. 193–211. Claudel's article, written from the point of view of a devout Catholic, seems to be another in the series of attempts to annex Rolland to the Catholic Church, after his death. Claudel's article, which is interesting and informative about his relations with Rolland, is inadequate in its account of Rolland and religion. He neglects pertinent material available, especially Rolland's many "anti-clerical" remarks concerning organized religion and the Church as a lay power. This appeared also in Claudel, *Accompagnements*, N.R.F. Gallimard, 1949, pp. 62–88.

APPENDIX

The following are some of the more important and interesting passages from *Jean-Christophe* that appeared only in the *Cahiers de la Quinzaine* edition.

One complete chapter of *La Révolte, Cahiers de la Quinzaine*, 8e série, 4e cahier (13 novembre 1906), pp. 140–148, was omitted in all later editions.

". . . Christophe . . . apprenait aussi, par ses amis d'un jour, à connaître un peu la littérature contemporaine en Allemagne. . . .

"Il avait vécu jusque-là tout à fait en dehors du mouvement littéraire. Son éducation était restée fort incomplète: il n'y avait point de livres à la maison, . . . Il avait économisé sou par sou pour acheter une belle édition de Shakespeare—l'homme du monde qu'il aimait le mieux. Quelques pièces de Kleist et de Hebbel, qu'il avait eu occasion de voir jouer, avaient exercé sur lui une fascination, dont il se défendait. En somme, il en était resté aux grands classiques allemands,—à quelques exceptions près, comme Keller. . . . D'ailleurs, il avait peu de temps pour lire. Il ne sortait guère de sa musique; et la musique est presque toujours en retard sur les autres arts: car son domaine est dans les profondeurs de l'âme, où, comme au fond des mers, se propage tardivement l'ébranlement des tempêtes qui passent à la surface.

"Aussi, lui, qui se croyait d'esprit assez avancé parmi les musiciens, fut-il fort surpris de voir que ses idées étaient depuis longtemps monnaie courante, et même un peu usé, dans la littérature,—particulièrement au théâtre. . . . Le réalisme n'avait pas seulement été atteint, il était dépassé. —On était alors dans cette période de lassitude intellectuelle, qui suivit le bref et ardent élan de la *Freie Bühne* de Berlin. Toutes les sympathies de Christophe, aussitôt qu'il le connut, allèrent à ce mouvement, qui s'accordait avec sa foi dans la nature et sa soif de vérité, avec ses sentiments actuels de révolte contre l'idéalisme mensonger, contre le succès d'un Wildenbruch, Schiller domestiqué, idéaliste mené en laisse, Shakespeare patenté de la *Sieges Allée*. Il se jeta avidement sur les livres que lui prêta Mannheim; et il fut d'abord saisi par l'accent de vérité, si nouveau pour lui, qui retentissait dans les pièces de Halbe, de Schlaf, de Hirschfeld, surtout de Hauptmann. Certaines scènes de ce dernier, certains dialogues, certains silences, et l'atmosphère crépusculaire où baignaient les âmes et les choses, lui causaient une émotion inexprimable.

"Mais à mesure qu'il avançait dans ses lectures, il sentait un malaise, une gêne, une irritation croissante. Calme et morne, l'atmosphère décolorée s'amassait autour de lui, comme un brouillard opaque. Silencieuse, subtile, tenace, elle s'incrustait en lui; elle pénétrait par tous ses pores. . . . Une hantise perpétuelle pesait sur tous ces êtres,—une sorte d'envoûtement. Tous succombaient sous le faix d'une hérédité de malheur ou de vices: alcoolisme, névrose, lypémanie, sadisme; tous avaient l'obsession de cette hérédité, et nul n'osait résister. . . .

"Le manque de volonté: la maladie héréditaire en Allemagne! Les plus grands n'y avaient point échappé,—le plus grand de tous, le divin Goethe lui-même, le clair génie de l'incertitude, qui tira un merveilleux parti de son indécision universelle: ce fleuve immense, qui roulait toutes les eaux de la terre, et où le monde entier se reflétait, avait fini par se perdre dans le sable,—comme le Rhin.

"Ce mal de la volonté, que la Prusse, au cours du siècle, avait traité victorieusement par le fer, reparaissait maintenant plus aigu que jamais. On eût dit que toute la force de la nation s'était dépensée en deux ou trois êtres prodigieux, un Bismarck, un Wagner, et qu'après . . . il ne restât plus assez de feu sous l'écorce distendue et refroidie de l'Allemagne. Dans cette Allemagne—Hamlet, combien de fois la tension gigantesque des énergies ne cache-t-elle pas des âmes vagues, des volontés sans racines profondes, des intelligences mal accoutumées à l'action. . . . La littérature nouvelle dévoilait sans pudeur ce mal profond de l'âme. Tous les héros de ces poètes étaient comme celui de Jean-Paul, l'homme qui avait trois âmes et pas une volonté. . . .

". . . Quoi! Tous, des vaincus d'avance? Pas un qui osât engager la lutte avec cette «Nature». . . . Comme si une puissante volonté n'était pas, elle aussi, la «Nature». . . .

Hérédité! Hérédité! Ils n'avaient que ce mot à la bouche. Ils répétaient avec pédantisme cette science de pacotille, qu'ils avaient apprise de Zola et d'Ibsen. . . . Semblables à ces ignorants, qui, lorsqu'ils feuillettent un dictionnaire de médecine, se découvrent toutes les maladies, ils étaient devenus des maniaques de l'hérédité. . . .Cette obsession les minait: ils voyaient des *Revenants* partout; ils étaient des *Revenants*; ils avaient peur de se marier, de vivre. Ces lâches en arrivaient parfois, dans leur honteuse panique, à perdre tout sentiment humain: comme le triste heros de Hauptmann, Alfred Loth, quand ils voyaient souffrir les êtres qui leur étaient le plus chers, . . . ils les abandonnaient ainsi que des pestiférés. . . . —Christophe qui, lui aussi, était un *Revenant*, s'indignait contre ces gredins, qui, non contents d'être vils et de fuir la bataille, faisaient tout pour accabler ceux qui luttent bravement contre leur hérédité. Lui qui sentait gronder au fond de lui l'alcoolisme paternel et les obscures folies, les hallucinations et les brutalités de ses ancêtres flamands, il connaissait, lui aussi, les bêtes de proie héréditaires: elles le guettaient. . . . Et le sentiment du danger, au lieu de l'accabler, dilatait ses forces, et lui causait une exaltation héroïque. . .

"D'ailleurs même chez cette «plus jeune Allemagne» (*Jüngst deutschland*), éprise d'un idéal de vérité nouveau, comme le vieux fond de la race reparaissait toujours sous le badigeon! Brusquement, on retrouvait, en dépit d'eux, la sentimentalité germanique . . . des allures énigmatiques et mélodramatiques, les enfantillages romantiques et mystiques . . . une manie de confession sentimentale. Toujours des âmes nostalgiques, languissantes, solitaires. . . . Et naturellement, la belle cause de la vérité en art avait été aussitôt compromise par ses défenseurs débiles. Combien peu d'âmes avaient été capables de la supporter longtemps! . . . Et c'était maintenant une réaction de l'idéalisme le plus faux, un néo-idéalisme de littérateurs blasés, qui n'avaient même plus l'excuse de puiser aux sources vives de la nation, qui trouvaient plus de saveur aux boissons étrangères ou rares, et mêlaient bizarrement, pour réveiller leur soif, Maeterlinck et Nietzsche, Ibsen et d'Annunzio, Verlaine et Oscar Wilde. Ils se disaient des Dionysiens, émancipés des apparences. Cela leur donnait beau jeu pour tourner le dos à la vie et divaguer à leur aise. Afin que rien ne vînt troubler leur vision de somnambules, ils décrivaient le monde, les yeux fermés. . . . Le grand public assistait à ces volte-face du goût, avec une quiétude parfaite: rien ne parvenait à l'étonner. . . .

"Et parmi ceux qui avaient prophétisé un réveil de la nation, plus d'un déclarait amèrement qu'ils s'étaient trompés, que la bataille était perdue, perdue sans restriction, que le mensonge, la bêtise, la routine, avaient vaincu. Le soir était retombé, et il n'y avait pas eu de jour. . . . Comme une torche tordue par le vent, le fantôme dément du grand Nietzsche s'agitait dans le souterrain sans air et sans lumière, creusant, fouillant sa mine, criant que le jour était proche, que l'aurore commençait à luire, et s'enfonçant, pour la chercher, avec des éclats de rire frénétiques, dans les entrailles de la nuit. Toute la caverne était illuminée. . . . Et puis un vent glacial avait soufflé la torche. . . ."

The following interesting German poem and its French translation were omitted from *La Révolte, Cahiers de la Quinzaine*, 8e série, 6e cahier (11 décembre 1906) (*L'enlisement*), pp. 235–236.

Sei dennoch unverzagt. Gieb dennoch nichts verloren,
Weich deinem Schicksal nicht. Steh höher, als der Neid,
Vergnüge dich an dir und acht es für kein Leid
Hat sich gleich wieder dich Glück, Ort und Zeit verschworen.
Was dich betrübt und labt, halt alles für erkoren,
Nimm dein Verhängnis an. Lass alles unbereut.
Thu, was gethan muss sein, und eh' man dir's gebeut.
Was du noch hoffen kannst, das wird noch stets geboren.
Was klagt, was lobt man doch? Sein Unglück und sein Glücke
Ist sich ein jeder selbst. Schau alle Sachen an;
Dies alles ist in dir, lass deinen eitlen Wahn.
Und eh' du weiter gehst, so geh' in dich zurücke.

Wer sein selbst Meister ist and sich beherrschen kann,
Dem ist die weite Welt und alles unterthan. . . .
(There follows the French translation of the poem.)

The following interesting comment on Parliamentary manners was also omitted in later editions. *Cahiers*, 9e série, 14e cahier (1908), pp. 186–187; *La Foire sur la place*, 17th ed., pp. 207–208, éd. déf., pp. 162–163.

"Roussin s'égayait des étonnements de Christophe . . . il était un autre homme.

"Christophe l'entendit à la Chambre, dans une de ces séances, où cinq ou six cents bourgeois mal élevés causent tous à la fois, au-dessous de la sereine *Ecole d'Athènes*. . . . [Rolland continues to criticize the French parliament,] which he compares to the theater, likening the deputies and senators to the audience at one of the old Italian operas, where one comes to hear the famous arias.]—"Roussin était un des chanteurs les plus en vogue au Théâtre Bourbon. Il prenait une voix de tête, des tons aigus. . . ."

Of a certain type of man of letters, Rolland wrote in the *Cahiers*, 9e série, 14e cahier (24 mars 1908), pp. 201–203; *La Foire sur la place*, 17th ed., p. 226; éd. déf., p. 174:

"Je ne veux point qu'ils le fassent.

"Qui n'a connu des types de ces misérables hommes de trente à cinquante ans, qui ont toujours vécu d'une vie uniquement littéraire, enfermés dans l'horizon des cafés, des cénacles, des coulisses, des bureaux de rédaction, et qui ont brûlé tout leur feu dans des discussions d'esthètes et les amours faciles! [Rolland describes at some length the miseries and foibles of these "literary men", who know so little of real life.] . . . Combien d'Hedda Gabler parmi les hommes! . . . et par quelque séduction perfide, au bon moment! Ils souffrent, ils souffrent tant!—Sans doute. Mais ce n'est pourtant pas une raison pour faire souffrir les autres,—et les plus innocents de tous. C'est ce raisonnement hideux:

"—Je suis malheureux. Il faut que tu le sois autant que moi. . . .

"Le type est de tous les pays."

The following short remarks about love and the artist who feels himself one with the universe point the way to his later studies on India, Gandhi, Ramarkrishna, and Vivekananda; *Cahiers*, 9e série, 14e cahier (24 mars 1908), p. 231; *La Foire sur la place*, 17th ed., p. 261; éd. déf., p. 198:

". . . les êtres qu'il rêvait. Pour un coeur un peu riche, toute minute est grosse de la vie des siècles. Des millions d'êtres ont goûté et goûteront après nous les jours, qui nous caressent avec la même fraîcheur. Il suffit d'un peu d'amour pour retrouver au travers de l'heure qui passe les millions de ceux qui ne sont plus et de ceux qui seront.—Christophe était heureux."

The comments on Italy, which were omitted from later editions, are very interesting: *Cahiers*, 10e série, 9e and 10e cahiers (16, 23 février 1909), pp. iii-v, at the end of the volume; *Dans la maison*.

La Voce

"Vox Italiae

"La lutte que soutient Christophe, n'est pas limitée à la France. Partout se livre le même combat contre les pourrisseurs de la pensée européenne. Dans toute l'Europe, nous avons des frères d'armes. C'est notre devoir et notre joie de leur donner la main.

"A ceux qui aiment l'Italie en France,—(et combien leur amour est douloureusement ravivé par l'affreuse blessure, dont elle souffre aujourd'hui!)—je signale le groupement des jeunes écrivains et artistes florentins, qui viennent de fonder un nouveau journal hebdomadaire: *la Voce*. A leur tête sont deux jeunes gens d'un grand courage et d'une libre et riche intelligence: Giuseppe Prezzolini et Giovanni Papini. [Rolland then calls on the friends of Jean-Christophe to learn Italian if necessary and to read the new publication. It is necessary, he says, to remain in perpetual communion with the Latin genius.] . . . La civilisation latine, c'est notre âme même que nous redécouvrons, notre âme perdue, cette grande âme méditerranéenne, riche de trente siècles de civilisation, et brûlante de lumière.

"Notre chère Italie fut—(redeviendra, j'espère)—l'avant-garde de l'Europe dans les combats de l'esprit, comme elle l'est, hélas! dans les combats de la terre contre la destruction et le feu qui la minent,—ce même feu qui dévore des villes, et qui fait se lever superbement les fruits de la terre et les génies. . . . [Although the French, he says, know the value of Italian light, the beauty of their painting and sculpture, they largely ignore the beauties of Italian poetry and music.] Retournons-y. Allons-y boire. Elle est nôtre. En reprenant possession d'elle, nous ne ferons que reprendre conscience de notre grandeur latine et de notre devoir magnifique dans le monde. . . . [There follows the translation of some extracts from an article by Papini, from *La Voce*, December 20, 1908.]

SUPPLEMENT

1A «Printemps romain» (Fragment tiré des *Souvenirs de jeunesse*, qui vient de sortir de presse à la Guilde en édition originale.) *La Guilde du Livre*, Lausanne, Bulletin mensuel, 12e année, No. 4 (avril 1947), 98–101.

2A *Souvenirs de Jeunesse*, Introduction by André Bonnard. Lausanne: La Guilde du Livre, 1947.

1888

3A «Pages de Journal,» *Les Etoiles* (30 octobre 1945). Fragments dated January 3, December 2. Judgments about the Goncourt brothers, whose *Journal* he dislikes. Rolland and Suarès had organized their own little claque against the great cabal which had been organized against the drama *Germinie Lacerteux* (third representation).

1897

4A «L'Avenir du Socialisme» (Pages de Journal), *Terre des hommes*, I, No. 11 (8 décembre 1945). Extracts dated June 1897. Socialism is the sole source of future life, society, art. Vestiges of monarchy must be done away with. Judgments on Millerand and Jaurès.

1914

5A «Fragments inedits du Journal de Romain Rolland. Les Jours noirs de 1914,» *Les Lettres françaises*, (17 février 1949).

1915

6A «1915 . . . Le Problème allemand vu par Einstein» (Pages de Journal), *Quadrige*, No. 9 (juillet-août 1946), 35–38. Dated September, 1915. An interesting description of Einstein, and an account of his opinions about Germany.

7A. Letter to Víctor R. Haya de la Torre, published by Haya de la Torre, *Por la Emancipación de América Latina*. Buenos Aires: M. Gleizer, Editor, 1927; pp. 15–16. Letter dated March 15, 1926.

8A. «Par dela,» *Quadrige*, No. 2 (août-septembre 1945), 7–10. This text was to have constituted a chapter in *Le Voyage intérieur*, entitled «L'Oeil». "Au-dessus de la mélée," he says, is the expression of the action of his whole life, but this chance title betrayed him; one sees the man suspended high in the rigging above the vessel, but does not see what he is seeking: the vessel's route. His very nature, he says, was from childhood to see. And early in adolescence he saw the present-day renewal of the end of the ancient world, the approaching fifth act of the tragedy of the Occident. Since 1914 Europe has dropped the reins of human destiny. «Le sommeil de l'Asie a pris fin». His action is not in the present struggle, but in the future, when bruised humanity will have to conclude another pact with life, and will resume its march towards the summits, from whence it has fallen. No one can know whether that will be in one or in ten centuries. It is even doubtful if humanity will be repeated. He warns against belief in the "eternal return." Civilisations and their knowledge have disappeared, and this makes one realise the uncertainty of repetition. He concludes that it is his duty to help to preserve science, not so much the techniques as its methods, its faith, its virtue, its intuitive spirit.

1927

9A Extracts from his Journal. *La Marseillaise*, 6 décembre 1945. Dated December 27, 1927. Recounts a visit from Scott Nearing and Laurence M. Sears. Sears had just passed nine years in North China, and says that *Jean-Christophe* has had a great influence there.

1932

10A Introduction to Hyakuzo Kurata, *Le Prêtre et ses disciples*. Translated from the Japanese by Kuni Matsuo and Steinsilber-Oberlin. Rieder. Introduction pp. 9–18. The poets of this school have felt the influence of Tolstoy and the great religious currents of the Orient and the Occident. Rolland discusses briefly the principal characteristics of this school. He says that he has been in contact with them and with other artists of the younger generation for the past ten or fifteen years.

"En téte de ce beau groupe de libres et purs idéalistes, Hyakuzo Kurato, qui est leur frère aîné, marche, «*faisant flotter*, comme il me l'écrit, *la rouge bannière de l'âme, –plus rouge . . . que celle des révolutions*», –fleur du feu de l'amour et de la connaissance,—qui sera aussi, je le crains—(et pourquoi le craindrais-je? C'est la loi héroïque)—qui sera aussi la fleur de leur sang, dont ils devront semer la route qui les mène à l'Unité humaine . . ."
Rolland insists on the religious nature of their art, on the formula at the heart of it: "Le salut est et sera par l'amour du Bouddha . . . l'amour pour tous les êtres. . . ." In these works the two currents of art and religion are united in even a better equilibrium than in the most beautiful dramas of Claudel—where the equilibrium is frequently broken for the sake of art.

1933

11A «La Paix est mortelle pour l'hitlérisme,» *Monde*, (24 mars 1933). Dated March 23. War is the last resort of bankrupt states; it can only serve Hitler's dictatorship. Peace alone is mortal for dictatorship. This is one of the first hints of his later demand for an alliance between the U.S. S.R., Great Britain, and France against Nazi Germany.

1936

12A «Ernest Renan vu par Romain Rolland» (Letter to Serge Radine), *Journal de Geneve*, 25–26 janvier 1947. Supplément littéraire. Dated from Villeneuve, January 11, 1936. He calls Renan's sister "cette «Antoinette»." There are some interesting remarks about Renan, and an interesting suggestion concerning the camparison of the various editions of the *Vie de Jésus* for a study of Renan's thought.

1937

13A «Le Duel,» REGARDS, (14 juillet 1937). Dated June 25. The Spanish Civil War has solidified the internationalism of all the parties: internationalism of the peoples of the world; internationalism of the financiers; internationalism of nationalisms themselves. When the field will be cleared of its ruins, there will be only two armies opposite one another: revolution and reaction. «Et ce sera vraiment le duel des classes. . . . L'immense bloc des peuples de tous les pays—ouvriers, paysans, libres intellectuels, classes moyennes prolétarisées—prenant conscience de leur union et de leur force, se rendront maîtres de leur maison,—qui est le monde.»

1944

14A «Un message de Romain Rolland aux *Lettres françaises,*» *Les Lettres françaises* (16 septembre 1944). Rolland signs the appeal of the *Comité National des Ecrivains*. The value of France is felt since her very existence has been jeopardized. Whoever says France, says—must say—liberty and humanity. These values must be defended. They are the mission of the true France.

15A Letters to Maurice Mignon. Published by Mignon in *Etudes de Littérature nivernaise*. Dated August 18, and November 11.

16A «Romain Rolland: Lettres inédites,» *L'Age nouveau*, No. 35 (mars 1949).

17A *Correspondance entre Louis Gillet et Romain Rolland*. Choix de lettres. Preface by Paul Claudel. A. Michel, 1949, 376 pp. Cahiers Romain Rolland, 2.

TITLE AND SUBJECT INDEX

(Entries referred to by numbers 1–618 are by Rolland; those referred to by numbers 619–969 are about Rolland and his works.)

AUTHOR INDEX

NORTHWESTERN UNIVERSITY
The Graduate School
1950

From time to time, The Graduate School of Northwestern University authorizes through the Editorial Board of *Northwestern University Studies* the publication of monographs in various fields of learning. A list of these publications appears below. Orders and inquiries are to be addressed to The Graduate School, Northwestern University, Evanston, Illinois.

Northwestern University Studies in the Humanities

No. 1. *Tales from the French Folk Lore of Missouri* by Joseph Médard Carrière $4.00

No. 2. *Kant's Pre-Critical Ethics* by Paul Arthur Schilpp $2.50

No. 3. *Luise Hensel als Dichterin* by Frank Spiecker $1.50

No. 4. *The Labors of the Months in Antique and Mediaeval Art* by James Carson Webster $10.00

No. 5. *Forgotten Danteiana* by J. G. Fucilla $1.00

No. 6. *Speech Development of a Bilingual Child* by Werner F. Leopold $2.25

No. 7. *L'Histoire de Gille de Chyn* edited by Edwin B. Place $2.50

No. 8. *The Aesthetic Process* by Bertram Morris $2.25

No. 9. *The Classical Republicans* by Zera S. Fink $4.00

No. 10. *An Historical and Analytical Bibliography of the Literature of Cryptology* by Joseph S. Galland $5.00

No. 11. *Speech Development of a Bilingual Child, Volume II* by Werner F. Leopold $5.50

No. 12. *Bibliography of the Published Writings of John Mill* by Ney MacMinn and others $2.50

No. 13. *Political Forgiveness in Old Athens* by Alfred P. Dorjahn $2.50

No. 14. *Education for Journalism in the United States from Its Beginning to 1940* by Albert Alton Sutton $2.00

No. 15. *Analytical Syllogistics: A Pragmatic Interpretation of the Aristotelian Logic* by Delton Thomas Howard $4.00

No. 16. *Fair Rosamond: A Study of the Development of a Literary Theme* by Virgil B. Heltzel $3.00

No. 17. *The Nonsense of Common Sense 1737–1738* by Lady Mary Wortley Montagu. Ed. by Robert Halsband $3.00

No. 18. *Speech Development of a Bilingual Child, Volume III* by Werner F. Leopold $5.00

No. 19. *Speech Development of a Bilingual Child, Volume IV* by Werner F. Leopold $5.00

No. 20. *Critical Prefaces of the French Renaissance* by Bernard Weinberg $5.00

No. 21. *Le Panorama Littéraire de l'Europe (1833–1834)* by Thomas R. Palfrey $3.00

No. 22. *A Critical Bibliography of the Published Writings of Romain Rolland* by William Thomas Starr $3.50

No. 23 *Juan de Segura: Processo de cartas de amores*, edited with translation and commentary by Edwin B. Place (in press)

Northwestern University Studies in the Social Sciences

No. 1. *Predicting Criminality* by Feris F. Laune $1.50

No. 2. *Shamanism in Western North America* by Willard Z. Park $2.25

No. 3. *Seventy Years of Real Estate Subdividing in the Region of Chicago* by Helen Corbin Monchow $2.25

No. 4. *The First Scientific Exploration of Russian America and the Purchase of Alaska* by James Alton James $2.00

No. 5. *Compulsory Health Insurance in the United States* by Herbert D. Simpson $ .75

No. 6. *The Neapolitan Revolution* by George T. Romani $4.00

Northwestern University Studies in Mathematics and the Physical Sciences

No. 1. *Mathematical Monographs* by D. R. Curtiss, H. T. Davis, H. L. Garabedian, H. S. Wall, E. D. Hellinger $2.25

No. 2. *A Catalog of Illinois Algae* by Max E. Britton $3.00

Northwestern University Studies in the Biological Sciences and Medicine

No. 1. *A Study in Neotropical Pselaphidae* by Orlando Park $7.50

Not in series
Galileo: Two New Sciences translated by Henry Crew and Alfonso de Salvio $3.50

Remittances should be made payable to Northwestern University, and should be sent with orders to The Graduate School, Northwestern University, Evanston, Illinois

Prices include postage